Aging in Community

Aging in Community

Janice M. Blanchard, MSPH

Editor

Revised Edition

Second Journey Publications
Chapel Hill, North Carolina

Bolton Anthony, General Editor

Manufactured in the United States of America.

Second Journey Publications
4 Wellesley Place
Chapel Hill, NC 27517

(919) 403-0432
www.SecondJourney.org

ISBN 978-1482302653

Cover design by Michael Brady Design

Front cover: Dene Peterson shares a moment with a friend on the commons between homes at Elderspirit Community, Abingdon, VA, one of the first elder cohousing communities in the nation. For more information, see elderspirit.org or elderspirit.net.

Back cover: Photos courtesy of Jim Leach. Scenes from Silver Sage Village, an elder cohousing community in Boulder, CO. For more information, see silversagevillage.com and whdc.com.

CONTENTS

Table of Contents v

Introduction
    by Janice M. Blanchard 1

PART 1
A Third Way 5

Moving Beyond Place: Aging in Community
    by William H. Thomas and Janice M. Blanchard 7

        "Friends" (Poem) by Craig DeBussey 18

Creating Community in Later Life
    by Bolton Anthony 19

Reweaving the Social Fabric of Our Communities
    by Janice M. Blanchard 27

Not So Big Communities: A Promising Vision for All Ages
    by Sarah Susanka 35

        "My Garden" (Painting) by Teddi Shattuck 42

We All Share the Same Sky
    By Teddi Shattuck 43

PART 2
Creating the Physical Container 47

Pocket Neighborhoods: Mending the Web of Belonging
    by Ross Chapin 49

An Artist Colony Where You Never Have To Go Home
by Tim Carpenter 57

"What if?" (Poem) 62

The Shared Housing Option
by Marianne Kilkenny 63

Senior Cohousing: Taking Charge of The Rest of Your Life
by Charles Durrett 69

"How to Build Community" (Poster) 78

Lessons of an Accidental Developer
by Dene Peterson 79

From the "Grain Elevator Series" by Walter Hurlburt 86

Aging in Community: It Takes a Village
by Ben Brown 87

Life in Takoma Village Cohousing
by Ann Zabaldo 95

PART 3
Creating the Social Architecture 99

A Little Help from Our Friends
by C. Baldwin, J. Willett, R. Kostiuk, and N. Galucia 101

"turn your ears on" (Poem) by Kit Harper 114

The Circle of Care: Mobilizing Assets in the Community
by Joan Raderman 115

Intergenerational Community Building
by Kristin Bodiford 123

"The Room" (Painting) by Suzanne Knode 138

The Sharing Solution
by Gaya Erlandson and Janelle Orsi 139

Continuing Care Options: The Next Generation of Care
by Carol A. Barbour.................................. 153

"Sleepless" (Poem) by Dolly Brittan 164

Life at Beacon Hill Village
by Susan McWhinney-Morse........................... 165

PART 4
Research and Policy Considerations 169

The Aging Middle Class and Public Policy
by William F. Benson and Nancy Aldrich 171

Connected to Community: Current Aging-in-Place Choices
by Susan Poor 183

"Who are you?" (Poem) by Karolyn Merson. 196

Online Surveys Engage Older Adults in Community Planning
by Mia Oberlink..................................... 197

Aging Better Together
by Anne P. Glass 203

The Ties That Bind
by Tobi A. Abramson................................. 211

Getting Older Then and Now
by Richard I. Bergman 217

PART 5
Reflections .... .223

Isn't This Where We Started? Irony and Remembering in Late Life
by Philip B. Stafford 225

"Friends — In and Out of Aging" (Poem) by John Clarke . . .233

Back to the Garden: Woodstock Nation Values Re-emerge
by Janet Stambolian and Janice M. Blanchard 235

About the Editor 246

Acknowledgments 247

Betty Friedan's 1963 watershed book,

The Feminine Mystique, defined — to the great relief of many American women — "the problem that has no name." By every societal measure, women living the mid-century, middle-class American Dream should have been thrilled with their roles as suburban housewives and mothers. The problem was, Friedan revealed, that many felt dissatisfied with their lives and longed for something more meaningful than maintaining homes and caring for their families.

As a family caregiver and, then, later as a gerontologist, I experienced similar nagging feelings about "aging in place." Was this truly a panacea for everything that was wrong with the institutional alternative? And given that the institutional alternative — and the steep cost of life in a nursing home — wasn't really an alternative for most of us, why quibble with the alternative? Didn't research confirm overwhelmingly that most Americans wanted to age in place? Like Friedan, however, I could not reconcile the discrepancies between people's ideals and what is real for so many elders.

Introduction
by Janice M. Blanchard

The reality is that millions of older Americans struggle physically, financially, and emotionally to stay in homes and communities that are not designed to accommodate their changing needs. Without meaningful social connection and support, many suffer the same three plagues that afflict residents in nursing homes — loneliness, boredom, and helplessness. The aftermath of 9/11 and Hurricane Katrina — and most recently, Hurricane Sandy — disproportionately put elders aging in place at risk; and they died in these disasters in significantly greater numbers than any other segment of the population. The question is inescapable: Isn't

1

there a better way to care for our elders than committing them to long-term-care facilities or leaving them to age in place, at home, often alone?

How did we end up with at these two diametrically opposed options for living out our later years?

Throughout most of human history, people have in fact aged *a third way*, what we are calling *aging in community*. Up until the turn of the last century, most people lived out their lives in the family home, relying almost solely on a tightly knit social web of family, friends, neighbors, and other community support. Of course, old age was uncommon; for hundreds of years, the average life expectancy was only 40 years, and very few made it past the age of 65.

In the Middle Ages, the Church provided alms or maintained poorhouses for those who needed care. Great shame, dread, and fear were attached to being banished to the poorhouse — the predecessor of the modern day nursing home. For centuries, in the often over-crowded and decrepit buildings, little distinction existed among the "inmates" — the old, young, poor, physically infirm, mentally ill, and even petty criminals. Often located on a farm on the outskirts of town, these institutions were overseen by a warden. The inmates lived together in the same rooms, wore uniforms, were confined to the property, and scorned by the community. Conditions were such that many considered life at the poorhouse a fate worse than death.

Although modern day nursing homes have evolved and improved dramatically from these dreary beginnings, there remains a deep-seated fear of institutional long-term care in our collective consciousness. Indeed, to this day, people still fear moving into a nursing home and losing their independence more than death. Notably, what people dread most about nursing homes tends to be the opposite of what they *perceive* as being attainable at home. Thus, in the American psyche, aging in place has become the reverse negative of institutional long-term care: Everything we fear most about institutional living — loss of control, independence, and dignity; being cared for by strangers in an unfamiliar and sterile environment; helplessness, loneliness, and boredom; and separation from loved ones — we believe can be avoided if we can find the means to stay in our own homes. As a result, many people are willing to do *whatever it takes* to avoid institutional care. Ironically, in so doing, many elders create the same circumstances and feelings that they so desperately want to avoid.

Today, with advances in medicine and technology, people live longer than ever before — since 1900 we have almost doubled life expectancy at birth. If we successfully make it to age 65, we can expect on average to live another 20 years. And those are just averages; chances are 1 in 5 we will live to age 90, and 1 in 10 to age 95. The fastest growing segment of the population is age 85 and older. In five short years, there will be more people aged 65 and older in the world than children under the age of 5, turning the human population pyramid on its head!

Never before in human history have we had this many older people, in sheer numbers or as a proportion of the population. Our homes, communities, and our society, however, have been slow to catch up to the demographic shift underway. We still live in a world dominated by values, institutions, and infrastructure devoted to young adults, families, and children. It is a difficult world to navigate when we become old. Even with great medical care, good genes, and a life devoted to healthy living, it is highly likely that at age 85 or older, we are going to need some assistance, whether it is getting to doctors' appointments, paying bills, or getting up and down the stairs to do the laundry. With thoughtful planning, many of these types of challenges can be met with minimal costs… which leads us back to the question we originally posed: Isn't there a better way and a better place for our elders — and for ourselves — to age, than in a long-term-care facility or home alone?

The good news is, yes! In this collection of essays, you will find an informative and diverse sampling of an ever-expanding menu of options that are proliferating around the country. A grassroots movement is abroad in the land, gathering momentum to reconceive "old age" and redesign the places in which we grow old and the relationships that sustain us as we age. One of the unique features of this collection of writings is that it reflects the eclectic backgrounds and inspirational personalities who are drawn to design, create, document, and celebrate aging in community.

These include internationally acclaimed architects who challenge us to rethink how we inhabit our homes and connect with our neighbors, leaders in academic and policy circles who illuminate the connections between aging in community and the big picture of aging, and practitioners and cultural creatives who work tirelessly to create new options that help elders remain in their home of choice, meaningfully engaged with their community. And finally, there are our elders themselves who, by "living the change," are helping us grasp the new possibilities. Their vision and voices are integral to aging-in-community values. We are pleased to feature in this issue four "profiles" by elders who are helping lead change in diverse ways.

It is exciting to see how far we have come in the few short years since my colleagues and I coined the phrase, "aging in community." If you Google the phrase now, you will find 57,800 references to articles, initiatives, and research in this area. The book you hold in your hands is culled from the wisdom and experiences of colleagues and friends who are blazing this trail together. From essays that describe the vision of aging in community, to specific programs you can adapt to your neighborhood, we hope these writings will inspire you to create ways to age at home while nurturing and deepening a meaningful connection to community.

Aging in Community has emerged

as a broad new category of options that offers *a third way*. We are not limited in our choices to, on the one hand, nursing homes and other forms of institutional care and, on the other, aging in place, which often becomes *aging alone*. In this section we introduce and explore the concepts of aging in community and show how reframing *where we age* and with whom redefines *how we age*.

In the opening essay, "Moving Beyond Place" (page 7), visionary author and physician **William Thomas** and I deconstruct the *false choice* between institu-

Part I

A Third Way

tionalization and an idealized vision of "home." Finding a third way to a more supportive — and more personally *meaningful* — aging will require that we move beyond the old frontier values of independence, self-reliance, and individualism and embrace interdependence, mutual support, and collaboration.

Second Journey founder **Bolton Anthony** explores the dual meaning of community as both the *concrete places where we live* (whose design can either encourage or discourage our interaction with others) and the *intangible network of relationships*, which supports and sustains our personal growth and spiritual deepening in his essay, "Creating Community in Later Life" (page 19).

In "Reweaving the Social Fabric of Our Communities" (page 27), I delineate the converging factors that negatively impact our relationships with each other, then address how we can reknit our communities with caring relationships imbued by the beliefs, values, and assumptions that foster aging in community.

5

In "Not So Big Communities: A Promising Vision for All Ages" (page 35), author and architect **Sarah Susanka** envisions a type of community informed by the same "Not So Big" sensibility as the pioneering work she has been doing in home and life design over the past few decades.

We conclude the section with a profile by artist **Teddi Shattuck**, a resident at the Burbank Senior Artists Colony, who shares her experiences living in this innovative elder community of artists in "We All Share the Same Sky" (page 43).

Moving Beyond Place: Aging in Community

by William H. Thomas and Janice M. Blanchard

IN 1519, THE VENETIAN SCHOLAR Antonio Pigafetta WAS AMONG those who accompanied Captain Ferdinand Magellan on the three-year voyage that became the first known circumnavigation of the earth. During his travels, Pigafetta kept a detailed diary in which he noted that the lifespan of the average Brazilian Indian was between 124 and 140 years (a longevity he attributed to the Indians' retention of what he called a primitive innocence similar to that of the Biblical patriarchs).[1]

The standard for exaggerated claims had been set by Christopher Columbus 30 years earlier. In one of the explorer's early letters he gushed over the seemingly limitless supply of food available in the New World, calling it "a veritable Cockaigne" or land of plenty.

Such observations were welcomed by rich and poor alike because they offered hope at a time when few people lived past the age of 40 and

Cockaigne, the medieval mythical land of plenty, as portrayed by Pieter Bruegel the Elder (1567).

devastating famines were a common occurrence. Pervasive scarcity, back-breaking labor, and the prospect of early death led people to imagine a land where food and good health came effortlessly — to everyone. They dreamed of a utopia called Cockaigne in which there was no need to work, the streams ran with water that restored the full bloom of youth, and the houses were roofed with meat pies.

Today, of course, the fanciful legends of Cockaigne can seem juvenile, encouraging us to believe that we have outgrown the need to console ourselves with imagined utopias. But such is not the case, certainly for many people growing old now.

TODAY'S FEAR: OLD AGE IN AN INSTITUTION

THE PARADOX OF MODERN SOCIETIES is that they provide the stability and affluence that enable many people to grow old, while at the same time denying older people a suitable role within the social order. Old age does not occur in a vacuum. How we define, experience, and perceive old age is influenced by a number of complex and interrelated factors, including social policies, politics, demographics, economics, and cultural values, as well as class, gender, and races/ethnicity. While theories of aging evolve over time within gerontology, it is apparent that social policy and public opinion are often slow to catch up. In public discourse and policy, aging is still largely defined by a biomedical perspective that emphasizes dependency, loss, and decline. Not surprisingly, the proposed solutions are rooted in the same soil. As a consequence, more than 70 percent of long-term-care dollars are spent on skilled nursing facilities, or nursing homes, that conform to the medical model.[2]

At the beginning of the past century, an American could reasonably expect to die at home, surrounded by loved ones and consoled by the most familiar of surroundings. Today, most older adults die in unfamiliar and impersonal hospital and nursing home environments. While a relatively small percentage of older adults find themselves living in nursing homes on any given day (5 percent of the population over age 65), the risk for a 65-year-old of entering a nursing home for some period of time is 46 percent and increases with age. With the survival rate increased to age 65, it is estimated that the number of 65-year-olds who will spend some time in a nursing home will double by 2020.[3]

People fear nursing homes. Indeed, when asked what they fear most, older people ranked loss of independence and placement in a nursing home above the fear of death.[4]

Aging in Place: Still "Dreaming of Cockaigne"

This brew of fear and loathing inspires millions of older Americans to dream of growing old in their longtime homes, or "aging in place." Indeed, the ideal of growing old in one's own home has developed into a powerful idealized counternarrative, the opposite of a dreadful old age cursed with indignity, a loss of autonomy, and the looming terror of institutionalization. The power that animates "aging in place" as a concept is its implied promise of freedom from that which we fear most. Rather than experience a loss of independence, we remain masters of our own domain. Instead of being cared for by strangers, we are sheltered within the bosom of our families or at least come to rely on a trusted homecare aide. Instead of being placed in an institution, we stay safe, secure, and comfortable within the walls of our own homes. This is the most consoling of all the ideas that we associate with old age. We have come to believe that in all times and in all ways, "home is best." Indeed, some 92 percent of Americans age 65 and older who participated in 2000 in an AARP survey said they wanted to live out their lives in their current homes; even if they should need help caring for themselves, 82 percent said they would prefer not to move from their current homes.[5] With this idealized notion of the old age that awaits us, we are still "dreaming of Cockaigne."

The bitter truth is that an older person can succeed at remaining in her or his own home and still live a life as empty and difficult as that experienced by nursing home residents. Feeling compelled to stay in one's home, no matter what, can result in dwindling choices and mounting levels of loneliness, helplessness, and boredom.[6] This difficulty is often compounded by the fear that someone (a state official or even a friend or family member) will discover the true state of affairs and enforce the ultimate sanction. Because it is fixated on a location (the private home) and pays little heed to the factors that make up actual quality of life, commitment to aging in place can turn out to yield benefits that are as mythical as those of Cockaigne, and may actually do harm.

Aging in Community: A Third Way

Our culture has constructed a continuum that positions institutional long-term care at one end of a spectrum, and an idealized vision of aging in place at the other. The challenge is to escape this false choice. An increasing number of Americans are searching for, and finding, a third way.

Historically, American cultural values of independence, self-reliance, and individual responsibility have supported the notion that elders can and should age in place. The *New York Times* columnist David Brooks recently challenged this ideal:

> This individualist description of human nature seems to be wrong. Over the past thirty years, there has been a tide of research in many fields, all underlining one old truth — that we are intensely social creatures, deeply interconnected with one another, and the idea of the lone individual rationally and willfully steering his own life course is often an illusion.[7]

The United States faces a range of issues that must be addressed cooperatively. Global warming, a faltering economy, a troubled healthcare system compound the challenges that come with an aging population. New responses to these challenges, from senior cohousing to shared households to cooperative urban "villages," point to the emergence of a new doctrine: People working together can create mutually supportive neighborhoods to enhance well-being and quality of life for older people at home and as integral members of the community. This is the essence of "aging in community."

We use the word *community* to refer to a small group of people who voluntarily choose to rely on each other and to be relied upon over an extended period of time. Aging in community presumes that those who embrace it have a high degree of interest in a way of life that offers daily opportunities for social connection in the context of smaller, clustered, village-like settings, whether urban or rural. The qualities of aging in community are highlighted below.

THE QUALITIES OF AGING IN COMMUNITY

- **INCLUSIVE** — People of all ages, race/ethnicities, and abilities, especially elders, are welcome.
- **SUSTAINABLE** — Residents are committed to a lifestyle that is sustainable environmentally, economically, and socially. Size matters. People need to know each other, and scale determines the nature of human interaction. Small is better.
- **HEALTHY** — The community encourages and supports wellness of the mind, body, and spirit and, to the same degree, plans and prepares programs and systems that support those dealing with disease, disability, and death.

- **ACCESSIBLE** — The setting provides easy access to the home and community. For example, all homes, businesses, and public spaces are wheelchair-friendly and incorporate Universal Design features. Multiple modes of transportation are encouraged.
- **INTERDEPENDENT** — The community fosters reciprocity and mutual support among family, friends, and neighbors and across generations.
- **ENGAGED** — The community promotes opportunities for community participation, social engagement, education, and creative expression.

The concept is focused on building vital communities that engage people of all ages and abilities in a shared, ongoing effort to advance the common good. A useful analogy envisions the people who populate an "aging in community" setting as bricks, and the relationships that develop between them as the mortar. Together, the bricks and mortar create "social capital." In this society, the value (rising and declining) of financial capital is measured obsessively, while our stock of social capital earns surprisingly little attention. It is the web of informal, voluntary, reciprocal relationships found within the mundane routines of daily life that forms the core of any society's social capital. Aging in community embraces strategies that help people intentionally create and deploy the resources of social capital alongside financial capital resources.

The current practice of institutionalizing elders in need of care is undesirable because it consumes large quantities of financial capital while it also destroys reservoirs of social capital. Aging in place, with its dwelling-centric approach, relies heavily on dollar-denominated professional and paraprofessional services while offering older people little or no opportunity to create or deploy reserves of social capital. Aging in community presents a viable and appealing alternative to both approaches.

TYPES OF COMMUNITIES

TODAY, AS 78 MILLION BOOMERS TURN 60 and beyond, we stand at a crossroad that will redefine the second half of life. The vanguard of this generation is already at work redefining core elements of the experience of aging. One facet of this cultural revolution in aging is the emergence of so-called intentional communities that address a constellation of desires — for a sense of place, sustainability, shared values and goals, diversity, and respect and support for elderhood as its own distinct life phase — a phase of life that lies beyond adulthood.

As work and family responsibilities shift and retirement looms in the future, some boomers are reflecting back on the peak experiences of their youth. They lived together in a variety of household settings with friends who shared the daily rhythms of life and who really cared for one another. Boomers bonded in ways unheard of by their parents with unrelated people outside their families.

A growing number seek to rekindle this vision of building custom communities with select friends and kindred spirits. Recent research found that about a quarter of boomers interviewed are interested in shared housing ("private living units with communal living areas"), and a third indicated interest in a "clustered living community" with a campus-like setting, private space for residents, and such shared amenities as a dining room, library, and laundry (this form of living is also referred to as cohousing). Some yearn for an urban, intergenerational, and diverse community, while others seek rural, back-to-the-land places.[8] The boomer generation is likely to do for aging services what they did for the ice cream industry 40 years ago. Three flavors will no longer be enough.

INTENTIONAL COMMUNITIES

"Intentional communities" are planned residential groupings, usually founded on similar spiritual, social, or political beliefs or other shared values or goals. Resources and responsibilities are often shared, although the degree varies significantly among different community models. Intentional communities include cohousing, communes, ecovillages, ashrams, kibbutzim, and cooperative housing. The fastest growing type of intentional community is cohousing, an arrangement of resident-designed-and-managed housing, usually in developments of about 30 homes that include shared facilities, require residents to share responsibilities and resources (but not incomes), and are not necessarily devoted to any particular age group. The concept was imported from Denmark in the early 1990s. From about 16 communities in 1995, the number of cohousing communities in the U.S. had grown to about 113 in 2008, with 111 currently in the planning stages, including several senior cohousing communities designed by and for adults 50 and older.[9]

Elderspirit is one of the first senior cohousing communities, founded by former nuns who left their order in the 1960s over philosophical differences. Dissatisfied with the current options for retirement living, they decided to build a new type of community dedicated to personal growth, mutual support, and spiritual depending in later life as a meaningful way for aging. Elderspirit has 29 units. Residents are of mixed income levels and must be at least 55 years of age. The development is built along the scenic Virginia Creeper Trail, within easy walking distance of shops and downtown Abingdon, Virginia.

Hope Meadows is a mixed-income, intergenerational community in Rantoul, Illinois, founded in 1994 and dedicated to addressing the challenge of children living for years in foster care without permanent families. Hope Meadows illustrates that ordinary people are capable of extraordinary compassion, caring, and love, regardless of their age, class, or ability. The resident seniors serve as honorary grandparents and agree to volunteer at least six hours per week in exchange for reduced rental housing. Even more than their volunteer work, it is the caring relationships they develop with the children and other adults that has been identified as a key factor in healing the children and providing stability to the community, while also enhancing the lives of the elders. As the older residents age, the community is helping them to continue to live in their homes and stay connected.

SPONTANEOUS COMMUNITIES

Notably, the U.S. is home to many successful communities that developed spontaneously in already established places. Within small towns and suburban and urban areas in every state, one can find a community in which traditional ideas about caring for one's neighbors still prevail. Often, however, as people age they may require more specialized support than other residents are able to offer on a regular basis. Established communities are developing new capacities to deal with this challenge.

The Beacon Hill neighborhood in downtown Boston is such a community. In 2001, several friends and neighbors came together to create a plan, the Beacon Hill Village, to help each other stay in their homes and remain meaningfully connected to the community. The Village model uses a nonprofit organization to vet and organize programs and services for older adult residents. To help defray costs, the organization charges residents a yearly membership fee, with discounts for those in financial need. Beacon Hill Village has received considerable media attention in recent years, resulting in thousands of inquiries about replicating the model. There are currently fifteen other communities officially affiliated with Beacon Hill Village, with many others underway. [10]

THE TRILLION DOLLAR QUESTION

While our culture seems to revere the notion of aging in place, our public policy continues to favor institutionalization for those requiring long-term-care services. The conflict between what people say they want (to receive services in their own homes) and the way their tax dollars are spent has become especially acute. This situation exists despite studies showing that, on average, it costs about half as much to maintain an elder at home as compared to placement in a nursing home.[11] Given that three-fourths of the nation's long-term-care budget is spent on nursing homes, and Medicaid is the largest source of payment for that care (about half), the need for a rebalancing of the public funds committed to meeting the needs of frail elders becomes clear.

Because of its intense focus on independence, the concept of aging in place leads, rather directly, to an emphasis on the dollar; paid professional services are required to provide care that will allow individuals to remain in their own homes. The combination of an aging society with the enshrinement of the private home as the only acceptable locus for aging yields cost projections that boggle the mind. Consider the following: The post–World War II generation that is now approaching old age has about 70 million members. If we imagine making a trillion dollar investment in the care of that generation, simple arithmetic tells us that that provides a per capita amount of just under $15,000 dollars. That is not $15,000 a year but rather for the entire period that members of this generation will need care, barely enough to cover two years of in-home supportive services in 2005.

The cost of an independence-based public policy, centered on the concept of aging in place, lies far beyond what our society can afford. At the same time, the use of mass institutionalization to cope with the needs of frail older people is gradually being seen as morally unacceptable. It is in this context that a third way becomes increasingly attractive. We need a public policy that facilitates the blending of financial resources (such as personal savings, pensions, and money from government programs like Medicare and Social Security) with social capital (which is created and maintained by healthy families and communities). For this blend to occur, we will have to confront and overcome deeply held and highly negative preconceptions about age and aging.

Conventional wisdom holds that the aging of America is, by necessity, a bad thing. The inventory of losses and unwelcome burdens is long and has been detailed in scholarly journals and the mainstream media. Omitted from these calculations, however, is an accounting of what age and aging contribute to everyone. The virtues of aging remain invisible.

Occurring parallel to this phenomenon of a rapidly aging society are shifts in family patterns (particularly the trend toward smaller family size, childlessness, alternative families, and divorce); increased mobility of families; the growing number of women in the workforce; increased life expectancy past the age of 85; spiraling healthcare and long-term-care costs. Another factor is the increased social acceptance of age-segregated communities.

Still, new opportunities and hopeful paradigms are emerging: an increased interest in civic engagement in older adults; a conscious-aging movement that promotes a new vision of elderhood; and examples like Hope Meadows that show intergenerational community as a tool that can be used to address social challenges that young and old face.

At its most fundamental level, human longevity creates the possibility of multigenerational families and communities that contain three and sometimes even four or more generations. Because it is the multigenerational transmission of culture, values, and wisdom that is most essential to our humanity, strategies that strengthen interaction and ties between generations contribute enormously to our stock of social capital.

The concept of aging in community is presented here as a useful successor to the concept of aging in place because the former shifts the emphasis away from dwellings and toward relationships. As the models described above demonstrate, the aging-in-community idea will be replicable across the spectrum, from rural to urban. With a high value placed on economic sustainability, it is critical to explore ways to extend the opportunity to age in community to the broadest possible segments of the population.

United by the intention to create innovative alternatives to current housing choices, the new movement for aging in community promises to inspire the entire national conversation about aging and to engage the skills, spirit, and imagination of architects, planners, builders, and community activists of all ages.

Coauthor **William H. Thomas**, MD, is an international authority on geriatric medicine and eldercare from upstate New York. He is the founder of the Eden Alternative, a philosophy and program that has helped deinstitutionalize nursing homes in all 50 states and worldwide over the past 20 years. A self-described "Nursing Home Abolitionist," he is also creator of the Green House®, a radically new approach to long-term care where nursing homes are torn down and replaced with small, home-like environments where people can live a full and interactive life. He is the author of *What Are Old People For? How Elders Will Save the World* and Professor of Aging Studies and Distinguished Fellow, Erickson School, University of Maryland, Baltimore County, Baltimore, MD. Access the video, "Elderhood Rising: The Dawn of a New Age," at http://www.youtube.com/watch?v=ijbgcX3vIWs.

Janice M. Blanchard, MSPH, is a gerontologist and nationally recognized writer, speaker, and consultant on aging issues. See her full biography on page 246.

Notes

[1]   This essay is adapted with permission from an essay of the same title published in *Generations* 33:2, Summer, 2009. Copyright @ 2009. American Society on Aging, San Francisco, California. http://www.asaging.org/.

[2]   Carroll Estes and Associates, *Social Policy and Aging: A Critical Perspective* (Thousand Oaks, CA: Sage, 2001).

[3]   B.C. Spillman and J. Lubitz, "New estimates of lifetime nursing home use: Have patterns of use changed?" *Medical Care* 40(10) (2002):965–75.

[4]   *Clarity*, "Seniors fear loss of independence, nursing homes more than death." November 12, 2007. marketingcharts.com/direct/seniors-fear-loss-of-independence-nursing-homes-more-than-death-2343/ (accessed August 31, 2012).

[5]   AARP, "Fixing to stay: A national survey of housing and home modification issues" (Washington, DC: AARP, 2000). http://assets.aarp.org/rgcenter/il/home_mod.pdf (accessed August 31, 2012).

[6] W.H. Thomas, *Life Worth Living: How Someone You Love Can Still Enjoy Life in a Nursing Home — The Eden Alternative in Action* (Acton, MA: Vanderwyk and Burnham, 1996).

[7] David Brooks, "The Social Animal," *New York Times*, September 11, 2008. nytimes.com/2008/09/12/opinion/12brooks.html (accessed August 31, 2012).

[8] Metlife Mature Market Institute, AARP Health Care Options, and Mathew Greenwald and Associates, *The Future of Retirement Living* (Westport, CT: Metlife Mature Market Institute, 2004).

[9] Donna Freiermuth, "A 2008 map of where cohousing communities exist." cohousing.org/cm/article/map08 (accessed August 31, 2012).

[10] As of August 2012, there are (according to the Village to Village Network,) 90 affiliated villages "open", with another 130 in development, located in 38 states and the District of Columbia.

[11] *Social Policy and Aging.*

Friends

A Poem by Craig DeBussey

… They come into our lives as gifts; a timepiece, a photograph.
Valuable things, but ones we are meant to live with, to enjoy.
The meal you prepare without looking at a recipe.
One you have made for years, not easy, but forgiving.

They are the walking stick you take on your walks,
 Not because you need it, but because it feels good in your hands.
The stone in your pocket, carried for the company of something
    familiar.

They are something unplanned, the painting you bought for yourself
    on vacation.
The one that lets you see and hear and hold the blessings
 That come as rewards for the effort of any journey.

They are the laughter you need in the middle of a week or a month
    that is relentless.
Let your guard down – let the dogs out – leave the dishes in the sink,
Come over here, listen to this, and laugh 'til the tears come.

They are the gifts you will have to give up, before you are ready to
    turn them loose.
When they are gone, they leave a hole, achingly deep and wide. It
    cannot be filled.
They are the places you go back to visit, when you have time,
 And sometimes when you don't, because you want to see them
    again.
The places you want to be, because they are where you feel most like
    yourself.

Craig DeBussey is a physical therapist in Chapel Hill, NC (for 25 years)
and enjoys poetry and woodworking in his leisure time.

CREATING COMMUNITY IN LATER LIFE

by Bolton Anthony

THE AD BELOW IS A KNOCKOFF of one that appeared in a trade publication marketing East Coast retirement properties to baby boomers. Though the promise it makes is as empty as the hype of a Bourbon Street barker, the ad's images and evocative language tap into enormously powerful human desires. As we enter later life — and every 8 seconds for the next 16 years, someone from the boomer generation will turn 65[1] — we feel a need to heal our dual *estrangement* from our own selves and from the natural world.

✚ You long to "rediscover yourself" and live more *authentically.* Midlife forces us to confront "the lost and counterfeit places within us." It challenges us to release "our deeper, innermost self — our true self." It challenges us "to come home to ourselves [and] become who we really are."[2] An age-old question resurfaces. Though we thought we resolved it in our youth, it returns with new urgency born of our sense that time is running out: Who am I? In the tumult of raising a family and making a career we had somehow lost track of ourselves. Who am I *now* — now that the nest is empty and the ca-

Last Chance Mountain

A *village* THAT LIVES UP TO THE MOUNTAIN

{*relax* HERE}

{*play* HERE}   {*indulge* HERE}

Nestled at ease among the near-limitless expanses of one of the East's last surviving wilderness areas, Last Chance Mountain is synonymous with luxurious adventure. The rustic elegance of its mountaintop Village welcomes your mind, body and spirit to reconnect with nature and rediscover yourself. This is where your family comes to play. This is where you come to relax. This is where you revel in luxury. This is your mountain. This is your home.

reer winding down? Once the frenetic activity of midlife starts to wane and things quiet a bit, we can hear the "still, small voice"[3] calling us to "come home" to ourselves.

✚ **You long to live *more simply*.** We feel an urge to slim down and disencumber ourselves: lose those extra pounds, clear out the attic and our storage unit (assuming we've kept ourselves to one!), and rid ourselves of useless regrets and poisonous resentments. The Hindus call this time of life our Forest Dwelling period, when it is appropriate to leave behind our previous things, roles, and duties — a letting go we in the West often find very threatening. But as Drew Leder writes in *Spiritual Passages*: "To the Hindu, aging is more than a series of meaningless losses. There are modes of liberation contributing to spiritual growth. If age strips away pride, pleasures, and profit, all the better… If our responsibilities are diminished, the time available to explore the sacred expands."[4]

✚ **You long to "reconnect with nature."** We have vague memories of a natural world rife with magic and mystery. As adults, weren't we supposed to put aside such "childish" views? And yet, our intimation — shared with Native Americans — that "*the Earth is alive*," is a stubborn one. We dwell among "other beings, other forms of awareness, our voices interweave among others more-than-human,"[5] Anthony Weston assures us. Step outside at dawn and catch the mere snippet of a bird's song, and you are instantly transported back into this primal oneness with the world. It is only a matter of letting "the soft animal of your body love what it loves."[6]

✚ **And finally, we long for *community*.** We long for companions who will share our excitement for this "second journey" in life — companions who will help sustain our own efforts to live more simply and authentically. For the paradoxical truth is, "We never get to the bottom of our selves on our own." Indeed, we only "discover who we are face to face and side by side with others in work, love and learning." Remember those three words: work, love, and learning.[7]

Community is what the developers of Last Chance Mountain are hawking — community served up with a heavy dollop of nostalgia. "The rustic elegance of its mountaintop Village" evokes images of a simpler time. "This is where your family comes to play" — as if all families were still like the Waltons. "This is *your* mountain": not *our* mountain — strange community, that. (Never mind the presumption that one could actually *own* a mountain — that all this bounteous world, including this body I walk around in, was ever anything other than on temporary loan.) "Relax HERE. Play HERE. Indulge HERE," the ad whispers. But who are the guests at this feast? The short answer is those who share our "lifestyle."

That leads us to a useful label for Last Chance Mountain, coined by the authors of *Habits of the Heart*: a "life-style enclave." Unlike genuine community, which celebrates diversity and "the different callings of all," life-style enclaves celebrate "the narcissism of similarity."[8] Those similarities usually include *age*: Sun City developments, for example, enforce a 55+ age restriction. And they *always* include *income level*: Only those who, like us, can afford to "revel in luxury" are welcome; and, in case of doubt, the guard at the gatehouse can pull your credit report. More importantly, community at Last Chance Mountain embraces only *private* life, and its rituals revolve around leisure and consumption.

"We never get to the bottom of ourselves on our own. We discover who we are face to face and side by side with others in work, love and learning."
— Habits of the Heart

Poking fun at Last Chance Mountain is a bit like hunting game with a Kalashnikov (though, trust me, it *is* a real place, and my only change to the advertisement copy was to rechristen the mountain). But it is important to locate developments like Last Chance Mountain within their sociohistorical context: They are outgrowths of a view of retirement as "a time to take it easy, enjoy leisure activities and a much-deserved rest from work." This view, according to Marc Freedman, author of *Prime Time*, is largely the invention of one man, Del Webb, the Arizona developer/promoter whose Sun City launched the retirement community industry. It is a view that Freedman believes has lost its hold on the American imagination. When asked to choose, Americans between the ages of 50–75, by a margin of three to one, preferred to think of retirement as "a time to begin a new chapter in life by being active and involved, starting new activities, and setting new goals." The numbers are even more dramatic among the boomer and pre-boomer cohorts.[9]

The subtitle of Freedman's book contends that "Baby Boomers Will Revolutionize Retirement and Transform America." The obvious next question is, "How?" And, specifically, how in relation to the issue of community?

First — though it's a bit late in the game — let's make an important clarification. "Community" has *two* aspects. When we speak of "new model communities," we mean the *physical* container. When we speak of "new models **of** community," we mean the *spiritual* (for want of a better word) container — the social architecture. So let me conclude with a potpourri of unsystematic ideas about where our dual search might be leading.

First, it takes only a cursory investigation to discover a vanguard of new communities, whose hallmarks are sustainability and Traditional Neighborhood Design. The more compact design of these communities encourages bicycling and walking for short trips by providing destinations close to home and work. The "sense of place" they create invites community and connects people to each other and the natural world in mutual respect. Simultaneously, interest in cohousing and other intentional community models is intense, though it is still a ways from becoming mainstream. And the ranks of architects committed to sustainable design in harmony with the environment are swelling.

This said, you may rightly point out, "Our suburbs are filled with houses that are bigger than ever." The square footage of new homes continues to soar in inverse relation to the dwindling size of the American family. Those are not cabins they're building on Last Chance Mountain. Where's the evidence of a desire to live more simply? Architect Sarah Susanka, author of *The Not So Big House* (the brisk sales of which are at least anecdotal evidence that change may be in the wind), laments: "So many houses, so big with so little soul." Then she asks, "Are the dreams that build them bigger? Or is it simply that there seems to be no alternative?"[10] I agree with Susanka that it is the latter. Developers are conservative by necessity; the stakes are high, and deviating from a tried and true formula is fraught with risk. Change will come as successful innovations become more visible and the aging boomers come to understand with greater clarity their hearts' desires.

The places we live are the *physical containers* which — by virtue of their wise or careless design — encourage or discourage our interaction with others and with the more-than-human world. But our deepest sense of community is rooted in the intangible, in that *network of relationships* which supports and sustains our personal growth and spiritual deepening and expands our opportunities for service and engagement in the world. In the past, these networks grew in the soil of small-town life, extended family, and church affiliation. Such primary communities for many — for most? — have lost their relevance. The task we have set ourselves, then, is the monumental one of creating surrogates for the extended family and church community and the various roles they have played through the many seasons of our lives.

Reflecting on the deep friendships we form in our teens and twenties may give us clues about how to go about creating community in later life. Those early friendships grew in the soil of shared, usually intense experiences. Later life is less about experience and more about meaning. Later life calls us to reflect on and understand our cumulative experiences — a radically "unshareable" activity. If we are to create new friendships in later life, we must consciously create new shareable experiences. If they are to be deep friendships, they must be around experiences that engage our deepest, emergent self. That's probably not golf — or, more generally, leisure and consumption, the stock and trade of lifestyle enclaves. It *may* be those things which have to do with "work, love and learning" (remember those): it may be social action, or the "Great Work"[11] of caring for Earth, or a

---

"Human conversation is the most ancient and easiest way to cultivate the conditions for change — personal change, community and organizational change, planetary change."
— Margaret Wheatley

---

deep engagement in teaching and learning. At the same time — though it would seem to be an example of exactly what I am arguing for — I have misgivings about the intense negotiations that, at least from the outside looking in, seem characteristic of most cohousing developments. A certain *indirection* seems called for. Couples who spend a lot of time "working on their relationship" rarely succeed as well as couples who simply "do things together."

Finally, I have been for a very long time interested in what I called Communities for Imagining the Future, a *network* of centers around which sustainable residential developments might emerge. Each center — and these might include colleges, retreat centers, organic farms, earth literacy centers, holistic healing centers — would be a kind of *magnet* that serves as the "strong attractor" not only for the residential community, but also for a certain kind of *conversation* within the culture. I firmly believe, with Margaret Wheatley, that significant change — "personal change, community and organizational change, planetary change" — begins with conversations about things that matter.

How can I live more simply and authentically? When do I feel most alive and creative? What is the work I am called to? What is the Earth asking of me? What is my gift to the family of Earth? These questions speak to all of us in every season of our lives, but they have special urgency for elders whose personal work is focused on the legacy they will leave and whose societal role is to speak for the unborn generations and for the Earth. My vision for Communities for Imagining the Future is not one I've succeeded in moving forward.

Several years ago, in connection with a class I was teaching, I re-read *Watership Down*,[12] Richard Adams' novel about an intrepid band of rabbits on an epic journey in search of "home." One could learn all one needs to know about community from this "children's" classic: that community is born in our shared experiences, that it is the stories we tell which hold our sense of community, that our very survival depends on our trust in the rich diversity of gifts each brings to the group. And finally, that what we want most from life is the sense of participating in an *adventure*. Not Last Chance Mountain's "luxurious adventure" (which is a contradiction in terms), but an adventure where the outcome is in doubt, and courage and hope are called for. The outcome will be in doubt if the challenge we have set ourselves to is bold enough. The hope we will need is not an excessive confidence that we will win through to the end, but the simple willingness to take the next step. As Tennyson's Ulysses says to his aging companions, "Come, my friends. 'Tis not too late to seek a newer world." Adventure, yes, that's what we want — even in later life.

Bolton Anthony, who founded Second Journey in 1999, has worked as a teacher of English and creative writing to undergraduates, a public librarian, a university administrator, and a social change activist. He lives in Chapel Hill, North Carolina.

Notes

[1] Maria Polletta." Rate at which Baby Boomers will turn 65." May 27, 2011. azcentral.com/news/election/azelections/azfactcheck/fact-story.php?id=242.

² Sue Monk Kidd, *When the Heart Waits: Spiritual Direction for Life's Sacred Questions,* p. 4. New York: Harper, Collins, 1990.

³ Harry R. Moody and David Carroll. *The Five Stages of the Soul, Charting the Spiritual Passages That Shape Our Lives,* pp. 3–5. New York: Anchor Books, 1997.

⁴ Drew S. Leder. *Spiritual Passages: Embracing Life's Sacred Journey,* p. 21. New York: Tarcher/Putnam, 1997.

⁵ Anthony Weston. *Back to Earth: Tomorrow's Environmentalism,* p. 79. Philadelphia: Temple University Press, 1994.

⁶ Mary Oliver. "Wild Geese" in *New and Selected Poems,* p. 110. Boston: Beacon Press, 1992.

⁷ Robert N. Bellah, et. al. *Habits of the Heart: Individualism and Commitment in American Life,* p. 84. New York: Harper and Row, 1985. Few books have provided such a penetrating analysis of the historic tension in American culture between individualism and communitarianism. As this tension again plays itself out in the strident rhetoric of the current election campaign, it is fitting to include the full quote: "There are truths we do not see when we adopt the language of radical individualism. We find ourselves not independently of other people and institutions but through them. We never get to the bottom of ourselves on our own. We discover who we are face to face and side by side with others in work, love and learning. All of our activity goes on in relationships, groups, associations, and communities ordered by institutional structures and interpreted by cultural patterns of meaning. Our individualism is itself one such pattern. And the positive side of our individualism, our sense of the dignity, worth, and moral autonomy of the individual, is dependent in a thousand ways on a social, cultural, and institutional context that keeps us afloat even when we cannot very well describe it. There is much in our life that we do not control, that we are not even 'responsible' for, that we receive either as grace or face as tragedy; things Americans habitually prefer not to think about. Finally, we are not simply ends in ourselves, either as individuals or as a society. We are parts of a larger whole that we can neither forget nor imagine in our own image without paying a high price. If we are not to have a self that hangs in a void, slowly twisting in the wind, these are issues we cannot ignore."

⁸ *Habits of the Heart.,* p. 72.

⁹ Marc Freedman. *Prime Time: How Baby Boomers Will Revolutionize Retirement and Transform America,* p. 224. New York: Public Affairs, 1999.

Freedman's history of how modern retirement was "invented" is a spellbinding one.

[10] Sarah Susanka. *The Not So Big House: A Blueprint for the Way We Really Live.* Newtown, CT: Taunton Press, 2001, p. 7. Susanka's book bears the appropriate dedication: "For our grandchildren."

[11] Thomas Berry. *The Great Work: Our Way into the Future.* New York: Bell Tower, 1999.

[12] Richard Adams. *Watership Down.* New York: Avon Books, 1972.

Reweaving the Social Fabric of Our Communities

by Janice M. Blanchard

We are all longing to go home to some place we have never been — a place half-remembered and half-envisioned we can only catch glimpses of from time to time... Community means strength that joins our strength to do the work that needs to be done. Arms to hold us when we falter. A circle of healing. A circle of friends. Someplace where we can be free.
> — Starhawk

AGING IN COMMUNITY IS NOT NEW. Throughout most of human history, elders have aged in community — at home and as integral members of their communities. Humans, as social animals, have depended on cooperation and caring for one another for survival. The sharing of basic resources such as food and shelter and the commitment to help each other, often to include nurturing and caring for our young, elders, sick, and disabled, has contributed significantly to our evolution as a species.[1] In turn, elders have played essential roles as teachers, spiritual advisors, healers, and as the bridge between the past, present, and future.

THE FRAYING OF OUR SOCIAL TAPESTRY

OVER THE PAST CENTURY OR SO, numerous factors and trends have converged that have negatively impacted our relationships with our family and friends, our neighbors and community ties, with our work and "free" time, and with our elders. Consequently, the social fabric of society has become worn and frayed. As our relationships have unraveled, our nation has become increasingly polarized and radicalized in political and religious viewpoints, particularly with regard to moral issues, including our obligation to elders.[2] Income has surpassed race in segregating communities,[3] and

27

while the income of the middle class has shrunk to an all-time low, the gap between rich and poor has become staggering.[4]

Close personal friendships and social networks — key to psychological well-being, community health, and social capital — are likewise shrinking. Americans report one-third fewer friends than two decades ago, with 25 percent having no one to confide in,[5] and with well over half reporting that they know only some (29 percent) or none (28 percent) of their nearby neighbors.[6] The disintegration of intimate social connections is particularly poignant among older adults, as divorce[7] and suicide[8] rates soar to the highest of any age group. America is only a few percentage points away from being predominately a nation of singles — only 51 percent of adults are currently married according to 2010 census data, compared to 72 percent in 1960.[9] Single-person households are skyrocketing, with about 28 percent of all households now consisting of one person, and a startling 40–50 percent of all households occupied by singles in cities like Atlanta and Washington, DC.[10] This is not just a result of young people delaying marriage and children; one-third of single households are persons aged 65 and older.[11]

The decline in American civic engagement, social interaction, and social capital has been well documented over the past several decades.[12] Our social compact — the implicit agreement with our government, strengthened through Congressional laws, to provide economic, health, and social security for our children, elders, disabled, and others in need — has become a topic of current political debate. Ageism, in the workplace and on the street, is on the rise.[13] For elders today and boomers turning 66 years old at a clip of 10,000 a day, the golden age of retirement has become a tarnished future at best.

Rebuilding our Communities through Caring Relationships

Despite this bleak picture of social cohesion and interpersonal relationships, there is hope. There are a growing number of movements afoot that empower individuals to take steps to mitigate these forces in their own lives and in their communities. Positive change is within our grasp — and it happens one person, one family, one neighborhood, one community at a time. It begins with caring for ourselves and expands by forging new relationships of caring for one another. Caring relationships manifest through acts of kindness, concern, empathy, nurturance, and understanding for another.

Notably, caring relationships between family, friends, and neighbors cannot be replaced by the caring of institutions or professional services. According to John McKnight:

> Service systems can never be reformed so they will "produce" care. Care is the consenting commitment of citizens to one another. Care cannot be produced, provided, managed, organized, administered or commodified. Care is the only thing a system cannot produce. Every institutional effort to replace the real thing is a counterfeit. Care is, indeed, the manifestation of community. The community is the site for the relationships of citizens. And it is at this site that the primary work of a caring society must work.[14]

Caring relationships are at the heart of aging in community — and a cornerstone for livable communities for all ages and abilities, as well as a great society. Central to the concept of aging in community is the deliberate consciousness to be "a darn good neighbor." Relationships between community members tend to be informal, voluntary, and reciprocal, and therefore, sustainable over time. Aging in community  promotes social capital — a sense of social trust and interdependence enhanced over time through positive interactions and collaboration in shared interests and pursuits.

Aging in community is philosophically rooted in the "conscious aging" movement that views elderhood as a distinct phase of the human life cycle, with its own gifts and challenges. In aging-in-community projects, the wisdom and experience of elders are honored and opportunities promoted to share these with others in the community. Key to the model is an asset-based community-building approach that taps into individual and group interests, skills, and experience to address the challenges and needs of both individuals and the community.

Aging-in-community projects tend to be made up of local individuals drawn together as a group to address an issue or simply to create a better way of living. Two major axes describe where aging in community takes place. The first axis is the "physical environment" — including new neighborhoods, retrofitted old neighborhoods, apartment or condominium buildings, cohousing communities, housing cooperatives, shared housing, affinity-based housing (e.g., Burbank Senior Artists Colony), and other physical housing and neighborhood structures that are the basis for defining the geographic parameters of the community.

The second axis is the "social architecture" — the intentional design and enhancement of social relationships, even the incorporation of programs and services — that will improve the quality of life of all residents and ultimately will contribute to the elders' ability to remain in their own homes or residences of choice and connected to their communities. Examples of social architecture include community-based health services such as Eden at Home, the Nurse Block Program and Share the Care, cultural enrichment programs like the Circle of Care Project and Elders Share the Arts, civic engagement programs such as the Experience Corp and Connecting Generations, community-building programs such as community gardens and farmers markets, and so forth.

To the degree that both the physical environment and the social architecture are brought into alignment from conception, the probability of creating the hoped-for outcome of a supportive neighborhood that enhances an individual's well-being and quality of life at home and as an integral part of the community across the age continuum exponentially increases.

Key Ingredients for Aging-in-Community Projects

While aging-in-community projects can theoretically occur in any geographic location or social grouping, such as within a church or synagogue, there are some core principles and beliefs which appear to be vital to their success, as outlined in Table 1 below. Central among them is a core group of people who are willing and able to take leadership of the project. While occasionally this leadership has come from outside sources such as nonprofit organizations, some of the most long-term success stories have been initiated by elders themselves from the communities they live in or want to live in, as in the case of cohousing, shared housing arrangements, and the Village model.

A great deal of the assistance elders need to stay in their homes and connected to the community are activities that most people are comfortable providing, such as transportation, picking up prescriptions or groceries, home visits, assistance with light housekeeping, and yard work. Likewise, there are many activities that elders can do for others in the community, such as walking younger children to and from the bus stop, editing the community newsletter, cooking a meal for a single working mother, and skills they did before retiring, such as bookkeeping or legal advising.

Thoughtful consideration and discussion should be given to the type of care individuals and the community are willing to provide, particularly around personal care, the type that often will make or break an elder's ability to remain in his or her home. Sometimes community and family members are willing to do whatever it takes; in other instances when personal care, such as bathing, dressing, and toileting, is needed, the expectation is that the elder will hire home health services. Notably, in most cases, the care that is needed does not require a professional — no more than a professional is needed to care for the personal needs of an infant. Still, the nature of personal care often makes this the most difficult conversation and topic of negotiation, and one that needs to occur preferably before the need arises.

Once the commitment and leadership have been solidified, there are numerous templates and resources that communities can adapt to identify the strengths and needs of their community. Starting with one or two goals and picking low hanging fruit can create a sense of progress and accomplishment. For example, if one of the concerns of residents is that no one will know if an elder is incapacitated and needs assistance, create a "smoke signal" program — have the elder leave the porch light on at night and turn it off in the morning. If the light is still on at 9:00 a.m., that gives the next door neighbor the signal that something might be wrong and the consent to come knock without fear of prying.

THE FUTURE OF AGING IN COMMUNITY

ACROSS AMERICA, AS BABY BOOMERS CELEBRATE their sixtieth decade birthdays and welcome grandchildren, even great-grandchildren, into the world, it finally is sinking in — we are getting old. Despite the media pondering whether 60 is the new 40, the fact is that we are entering retirement age. For many, for the first time in decades, our lives are wide open. There are no familiar roadmaps and few role models to follow into this new terrain.

Baby boomers, who have by mass and method redefined every other period of their life, are likely to redefine the third age — elderhood — including innovative housing arrangements and supportive networks to navigate the roads of later life. As work and family wind down, some boomers are beginning to reflect back on the peak experiences of youth, when often we lived together, in a variety of households with friends who shared the daily rhythms of life and who really cared for one another. Boomers bonded in ways unheard of by our parents, sharing personally, intimately, deeply with *unrelated* people outside our families. We bonded in ways that lasted, and we created — sometimes intentionally, sometimes spontaneously, but always authentically — communities of caring and love that resulted in enduring influences long after the physical disbanding of the groups themselves.

A growing number are beginning to rekindle this vision of building custom communities with select friends and kindred spirits. Research reveals that about a quarter of boomers are interested in "building a new home to share with friends that include[s] private space and communal living areas."[15] Some seek their own version of 50+ active adult living communities, with people their own age, background, and interests. Others are looking for an intergenerational, diverse community of all different walks of life. Some seek rural, back-to-the-land places, while others still yearn for the cultural richness of urban living. One thing is certain. For a substantial number, it won't be Sun City Centers. Like they did with ice cream, boomers will create a thousand flavors of housing and communities to live out the rest of their lives.

TABLE 1. AGING-IN-COMMUNITY BELIEFS , VALUES, AND ASSUMPTIONS[16]

The following beliefs are integral to creating aging-in-community projects:

1. Aging is a normal part of life; it is not a problem.
2. Most people prefer and benefit from living in intergenerational neighborhoods (senior housing can be part of the larger neighborhood).
3. Good neighbors balance independence and interdependence.
4. Being good neighbors enhances the feeling of belonging to a community.
5. Everyone in a community has something to give and benefits from receiving from others. Good neighbors value reciprocity, because giving and receiving strengthens social ties and provides meaning and purpose.

6. Informal relationships over time build trust, connectedness, and social capital which, like financial capital, can be intentionally earned, stored, and expended to meet our needs.

7. Most of the help people need can be provided by good neighbors, friends, and family.

8. Not everyone works full time away from home; therefore, help is often available when needed, especially when planned in advance.

9. The opportunity to get to know and help others can be enhanced with periodic community get-togethers where information and resources can be shared and planning can occur.

10. There is leadership and a core group who are willing to take action to support neighbors aging in their homes and staying connected to their communities.

11. Providing a broad range of care options as well as senior-friendly services (e.g., plumbing and electrical) can be enhanced by partnering with organizations within the larger community.

12. Each community (and individual) will have to address the threshold of the level of care that they are willing and able to provide to neighbors with physical, mental or cognitive impairment.

Janice M. Blanchard, MSPH, is a gerontologist and nationally recognized writer, speaker, and consultant on aging issues. See her full biography on page 246.

Notes

[1]   Sarah Blaffer Hardy. *Mothers and Others: The Evolutionary Origins of Mutual Understanding*. Cambridge: Harvard University Press, 2009.

[2]   D. Baldasssarri and A. Gelman. "Partisans without constraint: Political polarization and trends in American public opinion." *American Journal of Sociology* 114(2):408–46, 2008.

[3]   R. Fry and P. Taylor. "The rise of residential segregation by income." Washington, DC: Pew Research Center, Pew Social & Demographic Trends, 2012. http://pewsocialtrends.org/2012/08/01/the-rise-of-residential-segregation-by-income/

[4]   C. Morello. "Census: Middle class shrink to all-time low." *The Washington Post*, September 12, 2012. http://www.washingtonpost.com/busi-

ness/economy/poverty-was-flat-in-2011-percentage-without-health-insurance-fell/2012/09/12/0e04632c-fc29-11e1-8adc-499661afe377_story.html

[5] M. McPherson, L. Smith-Lovin, and M.E. Brashears. "Social isolation in America: Changes in core discussion networks over two decades." *American Sociological Review* 71: 353–375, 2006.

[6] A. Smith. "Neighbors online." Washington, DC: Pew Research Center, 2006. http://pewresearch.org/pubs/1620/neighbors-online-using-digital-tools-to-communicate-monitor-community-developments

[7] S. Brown and I. Lin. "The gray divorce revolution: Rising divorce among middle-aged and older adults, 1990–2009." Working paper. Bowling Green, OH: National Center for Family and Marriage Research, Bowling Green State University, 2012. http://ncfmr.bgsu.edu/pdf/working_papers/file108701.pdf

[8] H. O'Connell et al. "Recent developments: Suicide in older people." *British Medical Journal* 329(7471): 895–899, 2004.

[9] E. Klineberg. "Solo nation: American consumers stay single." *CNN Money*, January 25, 2012. http://finance.fortune.cnn.com/2012/01/25/eric-klinenberg-going-solo/

[10] "Solo nation."

[11] W.H. Frey. "Households and families," in *State of Metropolitan America*, pp.90–103. Washington DC: Brookings Institute, 2010.

[12] R.D. Putnam. *Bowling Alone: America's Declining Social Capital*. New York: Simon & Schuster, 2000.

[13] Associated Press. (2012). "Ageism in America." http://www.msnbc.msn.com/id/5868712/ns/health-aging/t/ageism-america/#.UFWFbH1rl3U

[14] J. McKnight. *The Careless Society. Community and Its Counterfeits*. New York: Basic Books, 1995.

[15] Metlife Mature Market Institute, AARP Health Care Options and Greenwald & Associates, *The Future of Retirement Living*. Washington, DC: AARP, 2004.

[16] Blanchard, McCarthy, Thomas, and Stambolian, 2011. Unpublished manuscript.

Not So Big Communities: A Promising Vision for All Ages

by Sarah Susanka

EVER SINCE MOVING TO THE UNITED STATES as a teenager in 1971, I've believed that there is a better way to shape our communities, towns, and cities than what is currently practiced in this country. I grew up in England, a country of small villages and historic towns built over hundreds of years, so when I moved here I found the American methods of construction, as well as the almost exclusive orientation to the convenience of the automobile, very limiting in terms of opportunities for human interaction.

In the world I'd come from, people of all ages lived in the village and interacted on a daily basis. There were also no retirement communities or senior centers. Seniors, or "pensioners" as we called them, were an integral and essential part of village life, like anyone else. Rather than being cordoned off to a separate community for those of their age, they lived amid and amongst the rest of us and could be seen sitting on park benches, walking their dogs, or chatting with one another outside the corner store. Though I'd never thought much about it as a child, these older members of

Cotswold cottages in England built from stone have lasted hundreds of years.

our village played a large part in my upbringing. They were like caretakers in a way, always watching, offering encouraging glances when we were playing, and looking on disparagingly when any kind of fighting or emotional outburst was being displayed. They were passing along signals about what constituted appropriate behavior, and I learned a lot from them over the course of my early childhood.

By contrast, I vividly remember driving through a Los Angeles suburb with my parents in the early seventies, and wondering what would happen as one aged in such a place where everything is so spread out. How did anyone ever get to know each other here, when everyone was safely ensconced within their automobile? What would you do if you couldn't drive? Where would you go? How would you get around without a car? How would you shop? What would you do all day if all you could see out your windows were your own front yard and the occasional passing car, with no way to regularly interact with the world? It seemed a pretty desolate future.

Back when my parents were in their 40s and 50s that vision was only a distant imagining, but now it's a growing concern. Like so many of my generation, I look at the options available for seniors like my parents, and for myself a few decades from now, and I know unequivocally that these are not choices that either my parents or I would willingly make. My parents like their independence. They've created a home for themselves over the past 40 years that fits them to a tee. The available options, an independent or assisted living facility, or a retirement community, would mean a complete break with the past, with all the places and people they know. It's the equivalent of extreme surgery just at the time in life when one feels the most vulnerable.

And the requirement that you then spend the rest of your days surrounded by people whose faculties and physical abilities are gradually waning seems a harsh sentence. Wouldn't it be better to give those who are themselves aging a view into the lives of those who are just beginning their lives, to weave generations together, as was so abundantly present in the village I grew up in?

Why is it that our current development practices require that once we lose our ability to drive, we must also lose hundreds of other freedoms, simply because there's no way for us to get around by foot since everything is far too spread out and inaccessible, with no public transportation system to help get us where we need to go? Why can't we create communities where all ages of humans can thrive, no matter their ability to maneuver an automobile?

That's the question that's been uppermost in my mind recently as I've been contemplating ways to improve the quality of our cities, towns, and neighborhoods here in the U.S. I'm envisioning a type of community that's informed by the same Not So Big sensibility as the work I've been doing in house and life design over the past few decades.

WHAT DOES "NOT SO BIG" MEAN?

I COINED THE TERM NOT SO BIG to describe a perspective that focuses on the qualities rather than the quantities of space and time.

In terms of house design, this means a home that's designed for the way we really live, with every square foot of space in use every day — a home that's an inspiration to live in because it is beautiful as well as functional. A house that's 5,000 square feet but sorely lacking in character and craft, for example, is nowhere near as satisfying to live in for most people as one that's half that size but beautifully tailored to accommodate its inhabitants' needs and aesthetic preferences.

And in terms of life design, this means a life that's filled with the things we love to do, and with ample opportunity for the kinds of experiences that allow us to grow and flourish. A life that's devoted to making it to the top of the corporate ladder at the expense of one's relationships, health, and well-being, for example, may look successful from the outside, but inside can be empty of meaning, filled with stress and frustration. But a life that is spent pursuing the things you love to do, that has time built in for connecting with others and for taking care of oneself, is successful in the true meaning of the word. It feeds our spirits, and not just our bank accounts.

A Not So Big House is *not* intended first and foremost to knock the socks off the neighbors, and a Not So Big Life is *not* focused upon accumulation of money, power, and stuff, although it doesn't preclude those things happening. It's just that those things are not *why* you do what you do.

THE INGREDIENTS OF NOT SO BIG COMMUNITY

SO HOW CAN WE TRANSLATE THIS SAME SENSIBILITY to the places we share and call our collective home...our community? If we look at what we love about the hill towns and villages of Italian Tuscany, for example, or the well-weathered stone cottages of the English Cotswolds, there's something timeless and at the same time deeply connected to nature that draws us in and makes us want to explore them and spend time in them. Most

American towns and cities have precious little of these same qualities. And because of this, whole neighborhoods are regularly torn down, only to be replaced by the next new development trend, the next quick fix to house the largest number of people in the shortest amount of time.

We don't have to continue this way. We can in fact build towns, neighborhoods, and homes that are every bit as lovely and inspiring as the European models we travel to on our vacations. We just have to recognize what it is that we like about them, and learn to emulate those characteristics in our new developments.

INGREDIENT #1: BEAUTY

At the root of the Not So Big sensibility is the notion that beauty matters and is in fact one of the most sustainable attributes a place or object can have. When something — be it a tool, a piece of furniture, a home, or a community — is lovely to look at, to work with, or to live in — in other words, when it's designed to inspire as well as to function well for its intended purpose — it is not only a delight for those who use it today, but its beauty transcends time and brings that same pleasure to every generation of people who inherit it. The making of a place that's beautiful, inspiring, and alive is the first step toward the realization of a new, more sustainable, and at the same time Not So Big form of community.

INGREDIENT #2: THE LESSONS OF NEW URBANISM

I've often characterized the Not So Big House movement as a perfect parallel with what the New Urbanists have promoted in terms of walkable, mixed-use communities and neighborhoods. The New Urbanism sprang up in the early 1980s to counter the trend toward urban sprawl, and is based on the characteristics and proportions of neighborhoods that were developed before the advent of the automobile. Over the past two decades, over 600 New Urban communities have been built around the United States, and the movement promises to continue to grow in decades to come. Now I believe it's time to weave the tenets of both the Not So Big House movement and the New Urbanism movement together into a new vision for integrated community design.

INGREDIENT #3: LEARNING FROM *A PATTERN LANGUAGE*

Another important addition to the mix of ingredients for this new type of community are some of the key concepts from *A Pattern Language*.[1] This weighty tome, first published in 1977, is a marvelous compendium of principles, or patterns, that govern successful building around the globe. The book begins with principles that apply to the city scale, with patterns named such things as "Lace of Country Streets," "Mosaic of Subcultures," and "Identifiable Neighborhoods"; and works its way down in relative scales, to neighborhood considerations such as "Degrees of Publicness," "Main Gateways," and "Hierarchy of Open Space"; then on down to the scale of the house, with patterns such as "Farmhouse Kitchen," "Alcoves," and "Sunny Counter."

This book was pivotal in the development of my own architectural work and has much to lend to the discussion of sustainable community design. At the time of its release it presented a paradigm shift in the approach it recommended to design and construction, and it continues to provide a compass for those who want to revitalize our approach to the built environment.

INGREDIENT #4:
AGING IN PLACE AND MULTIGENERATIONAL COMMUNITIES

As the baby boom generation moves ever closer to retirement, they're looking for ways to age in place rather than to move to a community of people all their own age. Studies show that over 80 percent of adults want to stay in their own homes until the end of their days. To address this desire there are a number of new initiatives being spearheaded by AARP. One in particular is called CAPS, or the Certified Aging in Place Specialist program. With increasing numbers of designers now trained to help people stay in their homes as they age, there's also an increased awareness about how we can make all homes and communities accessible, not only for those with age-related disabilities but for those with other types of disabilities as well.

Taking these understandings and applying them to the designs of new communities will allow people to stay in their homes for the full duration of their lives. By designing for accessibility without making those features look or feel institutional, we'll be creating truly multigenerational communities that are sustainable for all age groups and physical abilities... a truly inclusive environment.

As well as the obvious features required for ease of movement and general functionality, there are the critical ingredients of walkability and visibility. We feel most alive when we can see others fully engaged in their own activities. Being able to take a stroll on fairly level surfaces, placing benches and sitting areas throughout the community, and having views out from every home to pedestrian walkways, green spaces, and everyday activities like farming, shopping, and playing, can transform one's later years from isolated to alive and vibrant.

Although none of this is complicated to accomplish, there's an immediate need to integrate these design characteristics into the communities being designed today to allow for aging in place in the future. It's not rocket science, but if we put it off, we'll be depriving generations to come of the type of aging experience that almost everyone today longs for.

INGREDIENT #5: NOT SO BIG LIVING

This last ingredient, the principle tenet of Not So Big living that I describe in *The Not So Big Life*, is perhaps the most critical but least quantifiable aspect of community design. A big part of what makes neighborhoods that already have the magical quality of real community so special is the connection between human beings. There's an authenticity and a genuine caring for one another that comes about as a result of a quality of interaction that's almost impossible to define in words. It truly is a quality and not a quantity, with the central characteristic being one of real interest and attention, as opposed to social obligation.

A community can be so much more than we normally appreciate when the inhabitants share a common bond around the way they engage their lives, understanding that every activity and interaction is a kind of nutrient for one's sense of well-being and personal growth. On the surface, everything looks very much the same as in any other community, but inside each individual who lives there there's a depth of experience that is rare in today's world. Although it is possible to live in a "Not So Big" way by oneself, it becomes a great deal easier when a number of people share the same aspiration and vision. They can support each other as they go about living their everyday lives, and in so doing become a community of true friends.

This process of Not So Big living is not connected with any particular spiritual tradition; yet it does acknowledge that we are spiritual creatures that crave a type of engagement with each other and with ourselves that is less superficial than we presently recognize and generally allow in conventional society. It's a challenging vision to bring into being because it is so little understood or appreciated, but one I believe we are ready to entertain and live into over the coming decades.

MIXING IT ALL TOGETHER

This vision for community design will, I believe, provide a new model for the kind of place that supports its inhabitants in living fully all the phases of their lives, from infant to elder. And it will do so in much the same way that *The Not So Big House* has provided a new model for house design over the past dozen years. It will be a community designed with true sustainability at its core, where people can live in harmony with their environs, with each other, and with themselves.

So how do we begin to make such places? Not So Big Community begins with the first imaginings about its form, and it is colored and shaped by the involvement of everyone who touches it, from the planners, designers, builders, and developers, to the long-term residents, participants, and caretakers. Community is not only a place, but also — more importantly — a process; and the more people who are fully and passionately engaged in its making, the more alive, regenerative, and sustainable that community is likely to be.

Sarah Susanka, FAIA, is an inspirational cultural visionary, acclaimed author of nine books, and an architect who describes herself first and foremost as a student of life. She became a household name in the world of home design with her *Not So Big House* series, but the true  magic behind her life story is revealed in her landmark book, *The Not So Big Life*, where she unveils the process by which she lives her own life — a process she is adept at sharing with everyone interested in more fully inhabiting their own life and realizing their full potential. Visit her Web site at susanka.com/.

NOTES

[1] Christopher Alexander, Sara Ishikawa, and Murray Silverstein, *A Pattern Language: Towns, Buildings, Construction.* Berkeley, CA: Center for Environmental Structure, 1977.

"My Garden" by Teddi Shattuck © 2010. Color images of her work may
be viewed at http://www.dcaslideregistry.com/artist.cfm?id=505

*D**uring the Great Depression*

I was fortunate to grow up with six sisters on 66 acres in Rockfall, Connecticut. I often wandered all day through the woods and fields, discovering the natural beauty that surrounded me. I learned to immerse myself in the changing seasons, not only the endless patterns and colors of Mother Nature's palette, but also the natural and man-made sounds which transformed into designs in my mind. I remember, for example, the sound of the electric wires humming in the frigid, early mornings, as I waited for the school bus. Later in the day, I tried to visually interpret these sounds into colors and designs on paper. Color fascinated me with

the play of light, and to this day this interplay is a major influence in all of my work.

In spite of the economic challenges of the day and coming from a large family, we were blessed with parents who encouraged each of us in our goals. One

We All Share the Same Sky

by Teddi Shattuck

of my favorite Christmas gifts of childhood was my first small black box of water colors. It was truly Pandora's box, introducing me to the magic, mystery, and discovery of color. I kept the paint box long after the colors were gone. Color, design, and patterns became the magical ingredients that have mesmerized me for hours ever since.

After high school I was thrilled to be accepted into Rhode Island School of Design. For the next two years, an entire new world opened to me. Sadly, for financial reasons, I was unable to complete my degree. The exposure and knowledge I gained, however, have stayed with me all my life.

Marriage took me to Atlanta, and "30-too-long-years" later divorce took me to California to join my four children who migrated there. Three of my children enjoy successful careers in the arts: My son Dwayne is an accomplished artist and an award-winning producer for the hit TV series, "Mad Men." My daughter Shari is a successful actress as well as a critically acclaimed author, and my daughter Stephanie has a rewarding career teaching art. My youngest daughter, Shawna, has a fulfilling career in family counseling.

As a travel agent and an intrepid explorer, I have traveled to over 100 countries, often for extended stays. I have used a pencil or paints to document my journeys and to share them with others. Painting is my passion, but it is also a language I use to communicate my experiences and impressions of people, places, nature, and other cultures.

I believe that one of the most effective methods of diplomacy and problem-solving in the world is through one-on-one human interactions. Blessed with the ability to travel, I strive to be a goodwill ambassador, creating lasting friendships and tangible pieces of art as I go. Additionally, creating art is part of my cathartic process — it is both a way of depicting the spiritual essence of my journey, as well as a visual reminder of my travels through life. I am profoundly influenced by stimulating new environments. I revel in the scents, the dissonant sounds, the myriad faces, and fantastic happenings. In response to such intense sensory input, I feel compelled to put pen or paint to paper to capture these feelings and emotions. In this heightened state of total immersion in the creative mind I lose all sense of time, and it often evokes feelings I did not know I had. Pouring color after color onto canvas or paper, deeply lost in the work, I never know where the work will take me, nor the results; but the work itself guides me forward.

One of my favorite destinations is Egypt. Recently I was invited to return to paint a mural at a school in El Qusair on the Red Sea. This ancient town was once

Teddi Shattuck painting in Egypt.

a major port for pilgrims making the dangerous crossing to Mecca. Centuries later it became a mining town, and today it's a sleepy forgotten seaside village. The mural covers a 20-foot wall, depicting many endangered African animals, such as an elephant, zebra, rhinoceros, lion, and a variety of birds. It was designed to educate children about African animals in need of protection. I enjoyed watching the delight and wonder in their faces as the animals appeared. I do not speak Arabic, nor they English, but pictures transcend language barriers.

I often thought when I was younger that when I retired I would have plenty of time to paint and pursue all the things I wanted to do. At 76, however, I am busier and more creative than ever before! I live in California in Burbank Senior Artists Colony. One of the things I appreciate about living here is having an art studio accessible 24/7, as it allows me to work late at night in a safe place. The camaraderie and the sharing of ideas and critiques are all conducive to a productive work environment. While living here I have discovered my love of writing. In five years, I have written three plays, all of which have been performed in our in-house theater.

I mentor and work at a school for at-risk kids. They are my inspiration. Most have had horrible life experiences, and we try to help them express their feelings and anger through art. Many are very gifted, and just being with them as someone who cares and shares inspires me. Our joint projects have included a film written and filmed with our help, Claymation, and various art projects. I see this raw talent and try to nurture their efforts, giving them guidance; but I receive so much more than I give.

In between creative projects, I still travel. My next trip will be an eco-adventure tour of Dutch Guiana (Surinam). I have been blessed with a life of boundless joy, colored by every hue in the rainbow.

When it is time for me to leave this earth, I will ask God to put a paint brush in my hand so I can paint rainbows across the sky. We all share the same sky.

Teddi Shattuck studied art at Rhode Island School of Design, Georgia State, University of Georgia Studies Abroad in Cortona, Italy, Glendale College Studies Abroad in Prague, Czech Republic, and with private teachers. With an extensive background in art history and as an avid traveler, her journeys to over 100 countries profoundly influence her work. Teddi's paintings are in many corporate and private collections throughout the world. She lives at Burbank Senior Artists Colony in Burbank, CA. She can be reached at tega5@ aol.com.

By "physical container" we mean the tangible aspects of community design in all their rich variety: the site plan, the unit design, the outdoor space, the walkability of the environment in relationship to itself and the larger community. Green design, Universal Design principles, and other particular approaches to design are also included here.

In "Pocket Neighborhoods: Mending the Web of Belonging" (page 49), author and architect **Ross Chapin** describes how by marrying design elements from the past, such as large front porches, with new design approaches, such as clusters of 6 to 12 small homes, we can recreate cozy, friendly "pocket neighborhoods" that foster a sense of neighborliness and community.

Part 2
Creating the Physical Container

Artist and visionary **Tim Carpenter** shares how memories of growing up near Yaddo Artist Colony helped birth a new idea for creating an intentional permanent community. The result is the nationally recognized and award-winning mixed-income housing community, the Burbank Senior Artists Colony where "You Never Have to Go Home" (page 57).

Social entrepreneur **Marianne Kilkenny** found her inspiration for creating a custom community of like-minded people from the Golden Girls television series. She shares her story and housesharing tips in "The Shared Housing Option" (page 63).

Author, architect, and international cohousing guru **Chuck Durrett** offers an overview of the cohousing concept, along with the specific steps you can take to custom design your own aging in a community neighborhood in his retrospective essay on "Senior Cohousing" (page 69).

Dene Peterson, former nun turned "Accidental Developer," offers a companion piece to the one above. Her "lesson plan" describes the nuts and bolts of creating ElderSpirit Community in Abingdon, Virginia, one of the first senior cohousing communities in the country (page 79).

Professional writer and storyteller **Ben Brown**, in "Aging in Community: It Takes a Village" (page 87), provides an excellent overview of how boomers have impacted housing trends throughout their lives, and why local governments need to scale up efforts to meet the demand.

We conclude the section with a profile by **Ann Zabaldo**, a national leader in the cohousing movement, who writes poignantly about her experience of aging in community from the perspective of both being older and living with the challenges of multiple sclerosis (page 95).

Pocket Neighborhoods:
Mending the Web of Belonging

by Ross Chapin

Just as I was finishing writing my book on pocket neighborhoods, I was invited by a friend to a garden party. Twenty guests were invited to dine at a long table in her orchard overlooking a broad valley. It was a beautiful scene.

We all knew our host, but many of us did not know one another. At one point during the gathering, she asked that we take turns introducing ourselves and saying a few words. When my turn came, I said my name and that I was just finishing writing a book about pocket neighborhoods. Of course, the response was, "What is a pocket neighborhood?" After pausing for a moment, I suddenly noticed a connection. "This table is like a city block within a neighborhood," I said. "Look where our conversations have been happening before our introductions — one at each end, and one in the middle. These are like three pocket neighborhoods along our block." I pointed out how conversations happen spontaneously in smaller groups, while a conversation with the larger group requires organization. Then I asked them to imagine themselves as a house — each with a formal façade adorned with a bay window, two-story arched entry, and two garage doors. "Now, turn around. If we were a typical neighborhood, your stiff facades would be facing the street, while the life of your house would be oriented toward your backyard BBQ, kitchen, and family room. The street out front would be empty, except for cars. If we were at a dinner party," I continued, "there would be no conversation! We each have all the privacy in the world, yet no community." I called them back to face the table. "In a pocket neighborhood, active living spaces of houses face toward a common area shared with nearby neighbors, while quieter, more private spaces are farther back. Living in such a neighborhood, like friends around a dinner table, conversation is effortless."

THE HOME I GREW UP IN was an American classic: a shingled bungalow with a wrap-around porch, within a neighborhood of homes built at the turn of the last century in White Bear Lake, Minnesota. The street out in front seemed to have a constant stream of walkers parading by, and there was never a question that it was off limits for kids.

During warm summer evenings, I remember our porch being the scene of long, meandering conversations, typically begun with a laptop supper. Several adults, including my folks, my great aunt, and a neighbor or two stopping by, would offer up the main stories. Often us kids would add our own animated chatter to the mix. After dinner, we would head back out for another round of play in the neighborhood. When we returned after sunset, the adults would still be talking on the porch.

REVIEWING THE AMERICAN DREAM

SINCE THOSE DAYS OF MY YOUTH, the new houses being built have changed radically.

With the introduction of air conditioners, porches became a nostalgic extra, replaced with two- and three-car garages, with their wide doors and driveways flanking the street. Family life retreated indoors, taken up at first with TV and entrenched over time with ever evolving choices of electronic entertainment. Once a mecca for kids and pedestrians, the street became a kind of no-man's-land, a danger zone replete with strangers and fast cars. Today, parents chauffeur their kids to "play dates" and after-school activities, and neighbors are more likely to be seen at the grocery store than knocking at the back door.

For empty nesters, it's a different scene altogether. Without the bustle of kid's activities and the impromptu drop-by neighbor, daily life can feel lonely and isolating. Friends can be across town, and family members across the country. Who can you call in case of an emergency? Who will walk your dog or go for groceries if you break a leg or are in bed with the flu?

Ask any of the 80 million retiring baby boomers to describe their ideal home, and the answer is not likely "a large, high-maintenance house out of sight from any neighbors and tied to the world by car."

The challenge is, what other living options are there?

Exploring Another Approach

ABOUT 15 YEARS AGO I HAD AN OPPORTUNITY to explore this question. The town I live in on Whidbey Island, north of Seattle, has only 1,000 people. Yet it is only 7 miles as the crow flies to where Boeing builds their airplanes. You can imagine how the pressures of suburban sprawl seriously threaten the character of our town. In response, our town passed an innovative "cottage housing" zoning ordinance, the first of its kind in the country, to help direct new development toward neighborhood-sensitive, small-scale infill housing.

The ordinance focuses on expanding the choices for households of one and two people, such as empty nesters, singles, and single parents — a population segment today that represents more than 60 percent of American households. The carrot of the code is an incentive that allows twice the number of homes normally allowed in residential zones. The catch is that the house size is limited to 700 square feet on the ground level and no more than 1,000 square feet total, including a second floor. Such an increase in density comes from the recognition that cottage-sized homes have less impact than their plus-sized cousins. In addition to the size limitation, the ordinance stipulates that the cottages must face a usable landscaped common area, have a room-sized porch, and have parking screened from the street.

Around the time when this ordinance was passed, I met Jim Soules, a builder with a planning background and a former Peace Corps volunteer. We are both passionate about small houses and decided to test the new code as a way of demonstrating the market for smaller homes. We pooled our savings, rallied our relatives into joining us, and purchased four lots within a 5-minute walk of downtown. We came up with an approvable plan and were able to convince the local bank to lend us the capital to build eight cottages and a commons building.

A Pocket Neighborhood

The cottages we built were tucked off of a relatively busy street, like a pocket safely tucking away its possessions from the world outside. It seemed to me like a "pocket neighborhood," and the term stuck.

Our hunch that there was a market for small homes in a community setting proved true. The cottages quickly sold to working and retired single women, empty nesters, and a couple with a 3-year-old child. Within a few months, word got out about our pocket neighborhood across the country, with articles in numerous magazines, newspapers, and cable TV.

The response we received was electric. Inquiries came in from all age groups, but especially seniors, asking, "Are you building any of these in my area?" It became immediately clear that we had tapped into a deep, unmet longing for smaller, simpler  houses where neighbors actually know one another.

Design Patterns for Community

Many people respond enthusiastically to the cottage style of our pocket neighborhoods. The buildings and details are quickly familiar and easy to love. But style is not critical to what we are doing. Beneath the *skin* of the form are the *bones* that make these communities work. In the way of the "pattern languages," a structured method of describing good design practices developed by Christopher Alexander, we have identified a series of essential design patterns listed below to describe key elements of pocket neighborhoods.

Clusters of Nearby Neighbors — A larger neighborhood might contain several hundred households, but when it comes to pocket neighborhoods, I think the optimum size is around 6 to 12 households. These are your nearby neighbors, the ones you know by name and run into on a daily basis. They are the ones who "have your back" — the first to notice a need, and the first to call for assistance. Think of it as a neighborhood within a neighborhood.

Shared Commons — The shared outdoor space at the center of a cluster of homes is the key element of a pocket neighborhood. This space is neither private (home, yard) nor public (street, park), but rather a defined space between the private and public realms. Residents take part in its care and oversight, and feel a pride of ownership. A stranger walking into the commons will immediately feel they have entered private space and is likely to be greeted with a friendly, "Can I help you?"

During the daily flow of life through this commons space, nearby neighbors offer a friendly nod of greeting or stop for a chat on the porch. These casual conversations can grow to caring relationships and a meaningful sense of community — all fostered by the simple fact of shared space.

Eyes on the Commons — The first line of defense for personal and community security is a strong network of neighbors who know and care for one another. When a small cluster of houses looks onto the shared common areas, a stranger is noticed. As well, nearby neighbors can see if daily patterns are askew next door or be called upon in an emergency.

Layers of Personal Space — Community can be wonderful, but too much community can be suffocating. On the other hand, with too much privacy, a person can feel cut off from neighbors. Creating multiple "layers of personal space" will help achieve the right balance between privacy and community.

For example, a guest coming to visit might pass through an arbor into the commons. This is the first layer. From here to the front door are five more layers: a border of perennial plantings at the edge of the courtyard, a low fence with a swinging gate, the private front yard, the frame of the porch with a sittable-height railing and flower boxes, and the porch itself. Within the cottages, the layering continues with active spaces toward the commons and private spaces further back and above.

Room-sized Porches — The front porch is a particular "layer of personal space" that needs highlighting. It is essential in fostering neighborly connections. Rather than a small "key-fumbling" porch, it should be large enough for friends and family to gather, and in view of the commons, street, or sidewalk in front.

Nested Houses — Having a next-door house or apartment peering into your own can be uncomfortable and claustrophobic. In pocket neighborhoods, we design homes with an open side and a closed side so that neighboring homes can "nest" together — with no window peering into a neighbor's living space. High windows and skylights on the closed side can bring in ample light while preserving privacy.

Commons Buildings and Gardens — How many lawn mowers do you need in a close-knit neighborhood? Sharing is a central value of residents living in a pocket neighborhood. So, the answer is, one.

Some communities take it a step further with a shared multipurpose room complete with a kitchenette to host community potlucks, meetings, exercise groups, and movie nights. Larger communities may afford a community kitchen and dining hall, guest apartment, and workshop. Pocket neighborhoods of any size will enjoy the benefits of a community vegetable garden.

Beyond being amenities for residents, these common facilities cultivate relationships among neighbors and strengthen their sense of community — and they are considered by some as essential ingredients for creating community.

Plant a front yard vegetable garden

Corralling the Car — In America, nearly everyone has a car. But cars don't need to dominate our lives. Don't let garage doors be the first greeting. Shield parking areas and wide banks of garage doors from the street. In warmer climates, we locate parking areas so that residents and guests walk from their car doors to the front door. This arrangement creates an opportunity to enjoy the flowers and nod to a neighbor along the way.

Of course, there are more patterns, but these are few of the essential ones to convey the hallmark features of a pocket neighborhood.

Creating Community Where You Live Now

But let's say you do not want to move from where you live now. How can you create a stronger sense of community? Here are a few actions that most people can do with little or no money at all.

Move your picnic table to the front yard — See what happens when you eat supper out front. It's likely you'll strike up a conversation with a neighbor. Invite them to bring a dish to share. It's likely others will want to join in. Make room.

Plant a front-yard vegetable garden — Don't stop with the picnic table. Build a raised bed for veggies; plant edible landscaping and fruit trees. If you're inclined, invite your neighbors to share the garden. Along with carrots and sweet peas will come conversation and friendship — a bountiful harvest.

Build a fence bench — If you live on a street with walkers, build a bench into your front fence to offer a welcome way-stop or a foot-activated water bowl to offer their dog a cool drink on a hot day.

Make a Book Lending Cupboard — Take a book, lend a book. Collect your old reads and share them with passersby in a book-lending cupboard mounted next to the sidewalk out front. Give it a roof, a door with glass panes, and paint it to match the flowers below. Or, change the story — create a poetry cupboard with a signboard announcing, "Read a Poem, Write a Poem."

Mending the Web of Belonging, Care, and Support

For aging boomers, this seems to be the time when many of us are evaluating our living situations. Where is home? Such a fundamental question can come when our parents (or we ourselves) are facing another season with the burdens of a big house and yard, or in the wake of natural climate events that are disrupting lives within entire regions.

The sad story is that many of us lack networks of personal and social support. Family members can be spread across the country, friends live across town, and neighbors don't know one another. Too often, a listening ear or helping hand is not available when it's most needed.

Pocket neighborhoods are one answer to mending a web of belonging, care, and support among those who are physically closest to us — our neighbors. Their small scale makes it easier for neighbors to know and look after one another. The simple act of having a neighbor admire a newly planted garden or share stories about grandkids strengthens the bonds of "neighborship." This makes all the difference.

I'd like to say that pocket neighborhoods are common. The fact is, there is a lot of work to do. Neighborhood and housing advocates are speaking out. Planning officials are changing zoning and housing policy. Architects and developers around the country are creating new communities. Writers and producers are featuring stories in a range of media. One thing is for certain, though: The baby boomer generation will surely reinvent how they want to live out the rest of their lives, and for many that will be in neighborhoods that foster the same sense of community that many of us knew growing up.

Ross Chapin, FAIA, is an architect and author based on Whidbey Island, north of Seattle, WA. Over the last 15 years, Ross has designed and partnered in developing six pocket neighborhoods in the Puget Sound region — small groupings of homes around a shared commons — and has designed dozens of communities for other developers across the U.S., Canada, and the UK. Many of these pioneering developments have received international media coverage, professional peer review, and national design awards, including AIA Housing Committee Awards in 2005, 2007, and 2009. Ross's book, *Pocket Neighborhoods: Creating Small Scale Community in a Large Scale World* (Taunton Press), has received wide acclaim, including a full-page review in *USA Today*, listing on *Wall Street Journal's* Top Ten House & Home Books, and as one of *Planetizen's* Top Ten Planning & Design Books of 2012.

An Artist Colony Where You Never Have To Go Home

by Tim Carpenter

I GREW UP NEAR YADDO, AN ARTIST COLONY in Saratoga Springs in upstate New York. Saratoga Springs is known for three things — its racetrack, its mineral springs, and the arts. What a heady gumbo of neighbors — semi-connected mobsters and lowlifes, water-loving hippies, and — my favorite — artists. Small town that Saratoga Springs was, you always knew when the famous artists were there — Capote, Baldwin, Picasso, Highsmith, Puzo. It had a profound effect on me as a youngster.

Flash forward to the late '90s when I was just starting to work in senior housing and on the verge of forming a nonprofit that did outreach to that population. My epiphany came at a breakfast meeting of the Senior Housing Council in South Orange County. The guest speaker was a gentleman named Bill Thomas — a medical doctor who had created something he called the Eden Alternative. It sounded promising — and sitting there — after having gotten up at dawn and driven miles and miles across the Los Angeles sprawl — I thought, he'd better deliver.

Dr. Thomas blew my mind. He spoke about something he called *intentional community*. It was my first exposure to the concept, and my instructor was a real master. He described an assisted living community for seniors that included raised gardening beds and a shop out back for people to tinker on projects. Nothing extraordinarily radical in these suggestions. What was radical was *how* he arrived at what amenities to include. Predict who was likely to live in the facility, he urged us. Ask what are the values of the surrounding community. Create an environment that reflects them.

So I started thinking... I had logged miles to get to this breakfast. The plan for my new nonprofit was to serve communities that required similar punishing treks — miles and miles on some of the most unforgiving byways in America. Bill's idea of intentional community presented an opportunity for me to indulge two of my baser, but treasured, instincts: my inclination to "borrow" shamelessly someone else's terrific ideas and my unadulterated self-interest. I wanted to create a residential community where — based on their shared values — I could predict the type of people who would populate it. And I wanted to create it close to my office in Burbank.

Burbank — "beautiful downtown Burbank," as Carson used to quip on *The Tonight Show* — was home to an enormous population of retired professionals of a certain stripe — artists and entertainers. I'd grown up, as I said, near an artistic community that attracted artists from varying disciplines; they'd come to feed their souls, work on a project for a few months, talk with other like-minded searchers, and then go home. What, I asked myself, still sitting in the room and Bill still talking — *what if they never went home?* I wrote down "The Burbank Senior Artists Colony" in large letters on my pad below the copious notes of Dr. Thomas's ideas that I'd scribbled down. Then I drove the many frustrating miles home to pursue a dream.

After cold-calling the city of Burbank, many meetings, lots of collaboration, and the partnership of a lifetime — with the visionary John Huskey of Meta Housing Corporation — the Burbank Senior Artists Colony (BSAC) opened in May of 2005, developed by Meta like no other developer could have developed it. It boasts 141 units, residents of all artistic skills, both professional and newly acquired, and a rich variety of physical amenities that include a theater, arts studios, computer media lab, outdoor performance spaces, classrooms, and other bells and whistles intended to spark creativity. The physical amenities are more than matched by what we at EngAGE call the intellectual amenities: college-level classes provided on-site by professional artists and groups of residents who come together to create art shows, plays, films, and other forms of expressive neighborly lunacy.

It's the kind of place I'd move to grow up in, not grow old in. Trust me.

Our COO, Dr. Maureen Kellen-Taylor, a lifelong artist and influential shaper of the creativity and aging movement, designed our arts program, EngAGE in Creativity, bringing her own rich personal and professional skill set to the task. Maureen was given the California Arts Council Directors Award a few years ago for a lifetime of achievement in the field.

I tell the following story often to help listeners understand the power of BSAC — the creativity it nurtures and the beauty that emerges when a late-blooming risk taker dusts off her dreams and takes them for a test ride.

Before moving to the Burbank Senior Artists Colony, sixty-something Suzanne Knode had not had an easy time of it. She had spent years as a single parent, working hard and neglecting her own needs. More recently, she had suffered a traumatic accident that created physical struggles as well. After moving in, Suzanne attended an EngAGE writing class; she had never written much before, did not think of herself as a writer, but felt a tickle in her that she might have a story or two to tell.

She wrote a short screenplay as a class assignment. It was called *Bandida*, and it tells the story of an older woman who takes a senior bus. When the bus stops in front of a liquor store, the woman and her tennis-shoed walker are lowered down on the handicap lift. She ambles inside the store, dons a mask (à la the film *Scream*), pulls a gun, and starts to rob the place. During the course of the crime, she develops a relationship with the older Armenian shopkeeper behind the counter, and he lets her get away with the crime in the end. The screenplay is funny and touching and real — not easy to pull off for a fledgling playwright.

It was such a good piece of writing, we decided we'd try dipping our toes in the filmmaking business. We raised a little money, hired a director, recruited the cast from the residents of our communities (even the hair and makeup folks were residents), and "rented" the liquor store across the street in which to shoot it. Since EngAGE also produces a radio show called *Experience Talks*, we were already in the radio business. Darby Maloney, one of our producers, pitched the idea to Ira Glass, hoping the story would end up on *This American Life*, Ira's world-renowned show.

Well, he liked it. A lot. And the making of Suzanne's film along with her own personal story of reinvention was profiled, not on the radio show that Ira produces, but on the soon-to-be-syndicated national television show *This American Life* on Showtime. It's a beautiful piece on taking risks and living life as we get older.

Suzanne's own debut viewing of her movie was at the El Portal Theater in the NOHO Arts District of Los Angeles, and she shared it with an audience of 350 film lovers. The film had been juried into the competition at the NOHO Film Festival, and Suzanne got a standing ovation when she walked onstage for the audience talk back.

Suzanne is now working on several new film and stage projects and has also taken up painting in an EngAGE art class. She mentors at-risk teens at the school next door. Here is what she said about her changed life when profiled on the *Experience Talks* radio show: "I couldn't believe that there would be a community for me at this time in my life. I didn't think I'd be able to find something new inside of me. You know that same feeling when you got out of school and the whole world was open to you? Now, all over again, the whole world is open to me."

The moral — at least for me — to the story: *I want to be Suzanne Knode when I grow up.* She's a rock star! But I also want to be Teddi Shattuck, an amazingly talented painter (and my art teacher), who at BSAC has also discovered she's a writer and actress. (You can read her own telling of her story in this book on page 43.) And I want to be Sally Connors, a resident who has achieved dream after dream as a writer, an actor, and a singer since she moved into the community.

I want to be Walter Hurlburt who — simply because he can — spends most waking moments painting and attending almost every class of every variety. I want to be Dolly Brittan, who moved to BSAC from South Africa, after her husband died, and discovered she was an artist — a sculptor, painter, poet, and actor. She also started teaching again and mentoring children in desperate need of a guiding hand. Then she fell in love again, marrying the man who taught her sculpting class; and no one was more surprised about all this happening than she was.

What do you do when you find a model that works so well? You share it, of course. Meta Housing has scads of new initiatives at various stages: The Long Beach Senior Arts Colony will open near the end of this year — 200 units of housing for artists and artists-to-be open to discovering their till-now hidden talents. Long Beach will be the first 100 percent affordable senior arts living center. Bigger, improved, amazing.

The NOHO Senior Arts Colony opens this autumn in the North Hollywood Arts District not far from where Suzanne's film premiered. And this one has a live, open-to-the-public theater in the lobby, complete with box office and marquis, an 80-seat, state-of-the-art house operated by the award-winning troupe, The Road Theatre Company. Road Artistic Directors Taylor Gilbert and Sam Anderson will partner with EngAGE to provide high-end theatrical programs for their residents, while they stage their own annual season in their new space.

John Huskey and his team at Meta Housing have constructed thousands of units of senior (and family) housing, and John prides himself on breathing life into what could be just sticks and bricks. EngAGE now provides programming in 30 housing sites in Southern California serving nearly 6,000 seniors — and I owe it all to my mentor and partner, Mr. Huskey. Bill Thomas and I have since become friends and colleagues — Janice Blanchard, editor of this book, introduced us — so my own creative aging in community has been blessed with a splash of good fortune which has allowed me to work with and develop relationships with the people I admire and try to emulate. Not a bad way to create a community in which to grow older, with intention. Now I just need to develop a senior colony based on rock and roll — then all will be right with the world.

Tim Carpenter is the founder of EngAGE and host/producer of the *Experience Talks* radio show. EngAGE is a nonprofit that changes aging and the way people think about aging by transforming senior apartment communities into vibrant centers of learning, wellness, and creativity. *Experience Talks* is a radio magazine that shines a light on the value of experience in society, airing for 250,000 listeners on Saturdays at 8 a.m. Pacific on KPFK 90.7 FM in Los Angeles and streaming live worldwide on the Web at www.kpfk.org. The show is syndicated by the Pacifica Network to up to 100 cities nationwide. Tim serves on the board of the National Center for Creative Aging. In 2008, Tim was elected an Ashoka Fellow for being one of the top social entrepreneurs in the world, and in 2011 he received the James Irvine Foundation Leadership Award.

What if?

Love prevailed between the Syrians and their countrymen.
What if peace prevailed everywhere?
What a wonderful world it would be.
There are many "what ifs." This is only one.
But seriously, what if love prevailed?
What a glorious time that would be!

BSAC poetry group poem ©2012

This group poem is from the poetry workshop at Burbank Senior Artists Colony. Poetry Café is facilitated by educator, poet, and visual artist Hannah Menkin.

THE SHARED HOUSING OPTION

by Marianne Kilkenny

Four years ago

I come home from a long trip to the West Coast exhausted from the time change and the joys of current air travel. As I turn into my driveway, I see that the lights are on in my house and the shades are drawn. What a welcome sight for a woman living alone. I'm expected! Someone is welcoming me home.

That someone is Ginny — my "intentional" neighbor in this tiny cluster of homes — who has been taking care of the house and my two cats while I visited other states in my travels, touting the glories of living in community. In recent years it's become my purpose in life: encouraging, cajoling, and nudging those in my cohort to investigate new ways of spending our lives as we move forward into our second half of life.

NOW, FROM THE PERSPECTIVE OF 2012, it seems I've been working with the grain. Living together is back in vogue! Recent media attention to *shared housing* — by NBC-TV, ABC-TV, *The New York Times, More Magazine*, and many others — is evidence enough. Though this trend is clearly cross-generational, boomers especially want to recover vital connections with others that seem to have been the casualty of our fast-paced, Internet-based world. Too often, the rugged individualist jealously guarding his (or her) independence wakes up one morning to find himself alone in his castle, wondering what is next.

Here are some statistics that give us a baseline: According to the 2009 Census, more than 31.5 million people live alone; another 6.6 million people live with another non-related person. An AARP study found that 480,000 boomer women lived with at least one unrelated female in 2010. Women both outnumber and outlive men in American society (though the difference in average life expectancy has narrowed from 8 years in 1975 to

5.3 years in 2005). As a consequence, there is much creative ferment in the search for housing solutions that serve women.

The converging factors that are driving increased interest among boomers in shared housing include culture change, health, longevity, and demographics. Sustainability and the recent spike in home foreclosures are two other trends that tip the scale toward more housing shared with others. Rather than construct new homes, let's use and retrofit the ones that are already built, both to increase their energy efficiency and to accommodate several boomers living together under one roof. The *environmental* and *social* benefits of living with others are obvious, but sharing a home also comes with significant *financial* benefits, with sharing the rent or mortgage just the first of many ways you can reduce your living expenses.

Finding compatible housemates to live with is, of course, the obvious challenge. I've found two books you might wish to check out especially helpful: *My House, Our House*[1] and *Sharing Housing.*[2] Professional *matching services* which connect folks looking for a shared housing arrangement have begun to spring up. One example: Let's Share Housing (letssharehousing.com) is a free site that guides users through interview questions designed to match the individual lifestyles of the sharing "partners." Users can then contact one another confidentially through the site and can search nationwide for short-term or long-term housing solutions. The Golden Girls Network (goldengirlsnetwork.org/), a membership association, assists the members in setting up a Golden Girls Home.

Shared housing also has *cross-generational applications*. "Granny Flats" — or, more formally, Accessory Dwelling Units[3] (ADUs) — are making a comeback. Though by no means ubiquitous, ADUs — in the form of garage apartments, carriage houses, ancillary units — are a popular amenity and an important selling point in many new-urbanist communities. Their most attractive aspect, for

Home in a Kit
Several manufacturers deliver ADU "kits" to the building site. Some units are as small as 300 sq. ft.; the kit includes frame members, wall panels, doors, windows, siding, trim and fixtures.[4]
Photo courtesy Dale Lang/FabCab Inc.

many home owners, is the potential for extra income from renting out the unit. Other home owners, however, view the extra space as a flexible addition that can be used as a home office or provide lodging for "returning children" or elderly family members. A 2012 *New York Times* article highlighted the "granny pod" model, a teensy, prefab structure with a kitchenette, bathroom, and bedroom that can be assembled on the adult child's property. Exposure in the *Times*,[5] along with coverage by AARP,[6] is likely to ramp up the conversation about ADUs.

Make It Happen

IF SHARED HOUSING IS AN AVENUE you are interested in exploring, you might find my own experience personally helpful. My own quest to live in community kicked into gear when my parents died about eight years ago. Because I had no children, I'd spent many years talking to my friends about emulating the Golden Girls (though maybe with separate dwellings!). It was suddenly time to do something about it. No time to waste.

Since then, I have sponsored conferences, one-day events, and spoken about women wanting to live in community in our second half of life. Why women? My answer: because I am one, and I understand us better. And to state the obvious, we live longer, we have freedoms now that no women before us had — and the list goes on. To add to that, I believe in what Scott Peck said back in 1987 in *The Different Drum: Community Making and Peace*: "In and through community lies the salvation of the world."

Urgency. Yes, there is some of that, because I don't have all the time in the world now. Not like when I was 20. And maybe that is a good thing as we endeavor to bring community to a large group of aging Americans. No time to waste.

Why, What, Who?

So... what are the steps to envisioning your community? The biggest one is WHY? Why is this something you want to do or might consider doing?

Is it the connection with others? Lights on when you get home? Mutual support? Shared gardens, cooperative meals, economic advantages and resources, business opportunities, sustainability (learning, teaching, and practicing it), community support, and social networks?

Is it being with like-minded others, ease of education, health and fitness, creative expression, recreational opportunities, personal and spiritual growth, fun and laughter, and overall ease of living? The list is endless. For me, it's connection with others.

Then there is the WHAT: What will it look like, where will it be? Large or small, a shared single-family home, multiunit structures, apartments/condos? Urban, suburban, walk to town, countryside, mountainside, forest? Ecovillage, ecocity, cohousing, or a mixture of the best of these?

Also, important is the WHO — the others in your community. Who are the people you want to be living with? All artists, elders, mixed generations, couples, families, all women, like-minded or those who share your stated values and your location?

GETTING CREATIVE

I am often asked which is more important, the place or the people? Both are important.

As a spiritual person who believes we attract like people and locations to us, I know that having a written vision and/or a drawing or bullet points of what I want laid out helps. I can show it to someone, explain my thoughts, and relay my deep convictions. I also can enroll others in my vision, but only if I have one.

I often get calls, especially from women, whether married or single, who are looking for "the place to age in community." We need to cocreate them, adapting current models as needed: Cohousing, shared housing, new urbanist villages, and Naturally Occurring Retirement Communities (NORCs) all are part of the solution. Possibly a hybrid, taking the best of these, will emerge.

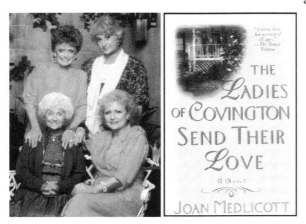

From Golden Girls to Ladies of Covington
The 1980s TV sitcom planted this concept in the popular imagination. The heady success two decades later of the Ladies of Covington series, by Asheville author Joan Medlicott, shows how deeply rooted the concept has become.

One woman wrote her WHY: "I am 55 and would love to find like-minded and like-hearted souls who want to come together for greater ease of living, companionship, looking out for one another, and a sense of continuous growth mentally and spiritually."

As of right now, I challenge you to talk, listen to others, go within, draw pictures, visit communities: clarifying your vision of your community in whatever way works for you. Maybe it's staying where you are and making it a neighborhood community, using your identified WHY as your model. That is possible. That is what I did for four years.

But maybe it's venturing outside your comfort zone and creating your own Golden Girls collaborative home. To that I say: "Make it happen!"

Marianne Kilkenny is a professional consultant, speaker, and educator who helps individuals and groups create supportive models for living and aging in community. She founded Women for Living in Community which offers conferences and workshops in North Carolina and nationally. She has been interviewed about the financial, safety, and social benefits of the shared home model on NBC Nightly News, CBS Early Show, ABC News, and NPR; has been featured in print articles in *Smart Money*, *Fox Business*, and *More* magazines; and has conducted numerous interviews for national print and electronic media outlets. She lives in a collaborative house in Asheville, NC, which she cofounded with four other adults. Visit her Web site: www.womenforlivingincommunity.com

Notes

[1]   This well-organized, well written how-to guide to cooperative living — full of practical checklists and excellent suggestions — is by three real-life single women — Louise Machinist, Jean McQuillin, and Karen Bush — who set up their own communal household. Find the questions to ask, boundaries to set, and other nuts and bolts of making this living arrangement work — often told through personal, humorous stories from their lives together. Used copies of the 2011 edition of the book, whose full title is *My House, Our House: Living Far Better for Far Less in a Cooperative Household*, are available from Amazon.com. A revised edition will be published in the summer of 2013. It is worth watching for! See their Web site at www.myhouseourhouse.com.

[2]   Annamarie Pluhar. *Sharing Housing: A Guidebook for Finding and Keeping Good Housemates.* Bauhan Publishing LLC, 2011.

A fabulous book for people who desire a good housemate and/or want to keep one. It is not just a resource to look at, but one to use regularly, as it is filled with handy worksheets.

[3]   See "Accessory Dwelling Units: Case Study." U.S. Department of Housing and Urban Development, Office of Policy Development and Research. June 2008. http://www.huduser.org/portal/publications/adu.pdf. This 26-page case study explores how the adoption of ordinances, with reduced regulatory restrictions to encourage ADUs, can be advantageous for communities. Following an explanation of the various types of ADUs and their benefits, the study provides examples of municipalities with successful ADU legislation and programs.

[4]   See the article on the AARP Web site: http://www.aarp.org/home-garden/housing/info-10-2010/adu_in_a_kit_fabcab.html.

[5]   See "In the Backyard, Grandma's New Apartment" by Susan Seliger (*New York Times,* May 1, 2012). http://newoldage.blogs.nytimes.com/2012/05/01/in-the-backyard-grandmas-new-apartment/.

[6]   Elaine Petrowski. "Prefab 'In-law' Cottages Mix High-tech Features, Comfort" (AARP, 2010), http://www.aarp.org/home-garden/housing/info-10-2010/abcs_of_adus.html.

Senior Cohousing: Taking Charge of The Rest of Your Life

by Charles Durrett

So many American seniors seem to live in places that do not accommodate their most basic needs. In the typical suburb, where the automobile is a de facto extension of the single-family house, individuals are essentially required to drive to conduct any business or partake in most, if not all, social opportunities. As we get older, as our bodies and minds age, the activities we once took for granted aren't so easy anymore. The house and yard become too big to maintain; a visit to the grocery store or doctor's office becomes a major expedition; handling the finances becomes more complicated, and the list goes on.

Of course many, if not most, seniors recognize the need to effectively take control of their own housing situation as they age. They dream of living in an affordable, safe, readily accessible neighborhood where people of all ages know and help each other. But then what? What safe, affordable, neighborhood-oriented, readily accessible housing choices actually exist?

With a liberal dose of anecdotes from senior cohousing pioneers, this essay provides an overview of how seniors can proactively take charge of their later years through designing and building a custom home and neighborhood designed to foster independence through a supportive and sustainable cohousing community.

A Danish Solution, Again

Imagine a living arrangement in which multiple, individually owned housing units (usually 20–30) are oriented around a common open area and a common house — a place where community is a way of life. Imagine residents who actively cooperate in planning the project, with one goal in mind — to recreate an old-fashioned neighborhood where you know each neighbor, you care about them, and eventually (usually sooner than later) you support them in some meaningful way.

A defining characteristic of cohousing is its **participatory process**. Here, prospective residents of Nevada City Cohousing participate in a design workshop led by Chuck Durrett.

A COUPLE OF YEARS ago I was in Denmark studying senior cohousing. Admittedly, I was there for somewhat selfish reasons. The agonies of placing my own mother in an assisted living facility were still fresh. Her story is, unfortunately, typically American: At 72 years old and determinedly, but detrimentally, living alone, she could no longer competently care for herself. Her children, doing their best, had reached the limits of their competence. Institutionalized assisted care, and eventually nursing care, were her only options. Or were they? After 20 years of designing, building, and living the cohousing life in the United States, I was certain there had to be a better way.

In Denmark, people frustrated by the available housing options developed a housing type that redefined the concept of neighborhood to fit contemporary lifestyles. Tired of the isolation and the impracticalities of traditional single-family houses and apartment units, they built housing that combines the autonomy of private dwellings with the advantages of community living. Each household has a private residence, but also shares extensive common facilities with the larger group, including kitchen and dining area, workshops, laundry facilities, guest rooms, and more. Although individual dwellings are designed for self-sufficiency (each has its own kitchen), the common facilities are an important aspect of community life both for social and practical reasons, in particular the common dinners. The common house is there to compensate for many of the things that the auto used to provide: bridge, dinner out, friends, singing, music, and so forth.

So I found myself back in Denmark, confident in my understanding of cohousing yet intent to learn all I could from my Danish elders. And what I found was completely unexpected and utterly refreshing. They were actually living the better life.

Some years ago I lost my husband and went through a difficult time. But I am glad that I lived here when it happened since it meant that I never felt unsafe. I was not together with other residents all the time but I knew they were there for me if I needed them. And when I came home at night I could feel the warmth approach me as I drove up our driveway.   (Møllebjerg in Korsør, Denmark)

PAUL AND KAREN:
A SNAPSHOT OF A DAY IN THE LIFE OF SENIOR COHOUSING

It's five o'clock in the evening and Karen is still going strong. After she puts away the last of the gardening tools, she picks up a basket of vegetables and freshly cut flowers. She feels energized to finish the day as strongly as it began. Her long-time neighbor and shade tree mechanic, Andrew, passes by to tell her that he successfully changed the wiper blades on her car. Grateful, Karen offers him a few of the choice flowers in her bunch. She knows his wife will love them. "All in a day's work," he smiles as he accepts.

Instead of rushing home to prepare a nutritious dinner for herself and her ailing husband, Paul, Karen can relax, get cleaned up, spend some quality time with Paul, and then eat with him in the common house. Despite his recent health troubles, Paul wouldn't miss a common dinner — it keeps his mind agile and makes him feel useful and wanted. It invigorates him on a daily basis.

Walking through the common house on the way home, Karen stops to chat with the evening's cooks, two of her neighbors, who are busy preparing broiled chicken in a mushroom sauce with new potatoes for dinner, in the community kitchen. The flowers and vegetables she brings to them couldn't be better looking, or better timed. Several other neighbors are setting the table. Outside on the patio, others are finishing a pot of tea in the late afternoon sun. Karen waves hello and continues down the lane to her own

The physical layout and orientation of the buildings encourage a sense of community. As in Nevada City, the clustered private residentces typically face each other across a pedestrian street or courtyard; cars are banished to the periphery.

71

house, catching glimpses into the kitchens of the houses she passes — here, a neighbor's grandchild does homework at the kitchen table; next door, George completes his ritual after-work crossword.

As Karen enters her house, relaxed and ready to help her husband with his medications and other needs, she thinks they will have plenty of time to stroll through the birch trees behind the houses before dinner.

Karen and her husband, Paul, live in a housing development they helped design. Neither is an architect nor a builder. Karen considers herself to be a semi-retired school teacher, as she volunteers in an afternoon reading program at a nearby elementary school. Paul is a retired lawyer. Ten years ago, recognizing the fact they were soon going to join the ranks of senior citizens, they joined a group of families who were looking for a realistic housing alternative to the usual offerings of retirement homes, assisted living facilities, and institutional nursing care. At the time, they owned their own home, drove everywhere, and knew only a few of their neighbors. But they knew that someday their house would become too difficult for them to maintain. They feared that one or both of them would lose the ability to drive. And if, forbid the thought, one of them unexpectedly passed away, how would the other manage? Would the survivor become a burden to their grown children?

One day, Paul noticed a short announcement for a meeting about cohousing in the local paper. Karen and Paul attended the meeting. They met other people who expressed similar concerns and fears about aging and their current housing situations, and they heard a zeal for the possibilities that

other options could afford. The group's goal was to build a housing development with a lively and positive social environment. They wanted a place where individuals would have a sense of belonging; where they would know people of all ages, where they would grow old and continue to contribute productively.

The **common house** typically includes a common kitchen, dining area, sitting area, children's playroom and laundry, and also may contain a workshop, library, exercise room, crafts room and/or one or two guest rooms. In elder cohousing developments these may be reserved for resident caregivers.

In the months that followed, the group further defined their goals and began the process of turning their dream into reality. Some people dropped out and others joined. Two-and-a-half years later, Karen and Paul moved into their new home situated in a community

Silver Sage VIllage in Boulder, CO, was one of the first elder cohousing communities constructed in the U.S.

of clustered houses that share a large common house. By working together, these people had created the kind of neighborhood they wanted to live in. And in all probability, they will live there for the rest of their lives.

Today, Karen and Paul feel secure knowing their neighbors care about them. If Paul becomes truly sick, people will be there to help Karen with groceries or will join her at the theater so she doesn't have to go alone. Common dinners relieve them of preparing a meal every night, and their children and grandchildren can stay in the community's guest rooms while they visit. They are members of a living cohousing community.

Senior Housing as Community

For Karen and Paul, and their neighbors, cohousing provides the community support that they missed in their previous homes. They downsized their liabilities and upsized their quality of life. Cohousing is a grassroots movement that grows directly out of people's dissatisfaction with existing housing choices. Based on democratic principles, cohousing communities espouse no ideology other than the desire for a more practical and social home environment.

Cohousing communities are unique in their extensive use of common facilities, and more importantly, in that they are organized, planned, and managed by the residents themselves. The great variety of cohousing community sizes, ownership structures, and designs illustrates the universality of the concept. And where cohousing has gone, so goes senior cohousing — each community has its own needs, and only the residents themselves know what is truly best for them.

We find cohousing communities immensely inspiring. Cohousing can be most effectively evaluated on its ability to create a positive and humane environment and meaningful and sustainable relationships. This is evident in the feelings of those who live there, the experiences of those who have left, and our own observations and comparisons among the various cohousing developments and other, typically more traditional, housing schemes.

After all, a home is more than a roof over one's head or a financial investment. It affects the quality of a person's general well-being — one's confidence, relationships, and even one's health. It can provide a sense of security and comfort, or elicit feelings of frustration, loneliness, and fear. A woman who worries about when to shop for groceries and get dinner on the table, while taking care of an ailing spouse, is often unable to concentrate on a job or reserve time to spend with friends or other family members, let alone take time for herself. This aspect of housing cannot be measured by cost, rates of return, or other traditional real estate assessments.

A more important concern for senior housing should be the people themselves and the quality of their lives and their emotional well-being. Seniors are used to watching out for their future financial needs, especially when they see retirement on the horizon. Cohousing affords them the opportunity to look out for their emotional well-being when kids have moved, friends have died, and spouses are infirmed or nonexistent.

I came to realize that seniors moving into senior cohousing are the ultraresponsible ones — they're looking at all of the horizon.

WHY COHOUSING JUST FOR SENIORS?

Dear friends, I have been home now for three days, recovering from the hospital visit. I was overwhelmed by the kindness and help I received, especially from Nancy and Roger. Nancy spent the night with me and looked after me, then they both took me to the hospital and spent many boring hours till I was admitted there. They are supplying me with food and go grocery shopping, folding my laundry, etc. I can hardly breathe before there is another good deed. Mike looks after my compost and garbage every day. My granddaughter Sonja, who came to visit me just when I needed it, was so impressed with all the wonderful people who keep showing up. There is no place like Wolf Creek Lodge! I hope I can be of use to you again sometime soon! (Magdalene in Grass Valley, California)

WHY WOULD SOMEONE WANT to create a cohousing community dedicated to seniors? There is no simple answer, since housing is an individual choice. Mixed-generational cohousing is an option for some seniors, but regular cohousing communities typically focus their energies in places where seniors have already been — building careers, raising families, and the like. While some seniors will find the youthful vigor of a regular cohousing community to be refreshing, others feel it's a case of "been there, done that."

As well, concerns of younger cohousers do not usually hinge on health issues. Due to limited resources, a community has to prioritize the design elements they want, and a reasonably priced project will likely not be able to provide a playground, soundproofed kids' rooms and baby pool as well as a meditation room, elevator, and caretaker's suite.

Since relationships are paramount in a cohousing community, residents live next door to their friends and, over time, their previous best friends (from life before senior cohousing) move in. These seniors live among people with whom they share a common bond

of age, experience, and community — a community they themselves built to specifically meet their own needs. These relationships provide purpose and direction in their lives and are as meaningful as any they have ever had. This is why many older adults choose to live in cohousing oriented toward seniors.

THE "AGING SUCCESSFULLY" SEMINAR: STUDY GROUP I

THE FIRST STEP TOWARD SENIOR COHOUSING — or any thoughtful transition to the next phase of retirement living — involves taking a hard look at the realities of aging. *How does one age in place successfully? As one ages, how does one effectively meet a host of changing logistic, social, and emotional needs?*

Stepping back and taking a good look inward and then ahead into the future is exactly what happens in McCamant & Durrett's 10-week Study Group I workshop, modeled after the seminar that initially led seniors to develop senior cohousing in Denmark. Participants discuss the issues of

aging in place with their peers, learn about their choices, and create a personal vision of what aging successfully entails. Through the course of the workshop, they gain skills and tools that can help them plan to age successfully. Upon completion, participants will know

if cohousing is for them. Some participants will choose senior cohousing; but all participants will begin to plan for successful aging, or at least to be conscious of what it means. Participants who decide to move forward with cohousing use *The Senior Cohousing Handbook* to guide them in the process.

The topics of Study Group I include:

1. Aging in place and aging in community
2. Group process
3. Realities of getting older
4. Co-care and outside care
5. Co-healing
6. The economics of getting older
7. Philosophy, spirituality, and mortality
8. Saging
9. Embracing risk
10. Case studies

The men and women living in senior cohousing communities are perhaps the most honest and clear-eyed people I have ever encountered. They completely accept the fact that they are aging. They admit they can't do everything they once did. They know the slope is downhill. That's life. But acknowledging this basic truth does not mean they are fatalistic. Rather, they have taken charge of their remaining years with the expressed intent of achieving the highest-quality life possible, for as long as possible. For them, this means choosing to build their own community where they live among people with whom they share a common bond of generation, circumstance, and outlook. And they have a great time doing it.

"Hey, we're getting older, and we're going to make the most of it. We've had a lot of experiences, and now we're going to have some more!"

Charles Durrett is an architect, author, and advocate of affordable, socially responsible, and sustainable design. He has made a major contribution in the last 20 years to multidisciplinary architecture and town planning — one that involves and empowers the inhabitants and enriches the sense of place and sense of community in both the urban and rural settings in which he works. He is principal of McCamant & Durrett Architects/The Cohousing Company and author of *The Senior Cohousing Handbook*.

HOW TO BUILD COMMUNITY

Turn off your TV
Leave your House
Know your Neighbors Greet People
Look up when you're walking
Sit on your stoop Plant flowers
Use Your Library Play together
Buy from local merchants
Share what you have Help a lost dog
Take children to the Park Honor Elders
Support Neighborhood Schools
Fix it even if you didn't break it
Have Pot lucks Garden Together
Pick up litter Read Stories Aloud
Dance in the Street
Talk to the Mail Carrier
Listen to the birds Put up a swing
Help carry something heavy
Barter for your goods
Start a tradition Ask a question
Hire young people for odd jobs
Organize a block party
Bake extra and share
Ask for help when you need it
Open you shades Sing together
Share your skills
Take back the night
Turn up the music Turn down the music
Listen before you react to anger
Mediate conflict Seek to understand
Learn from new and uncomfortable angles
Know that on one is silent though
many are not heard and
work to change this

This graphic, created by Syracuse Cultural Workers, may be purchased — as a poster or bookmark and in English or Spanish — through their Web site: http://syracuseculturalworkers.com/.

Lessons of an Accidental Developer

by Dene Peterson

My mother used to tell everybody that I've been "an administrator since the age of two." Chances are, the first time that occurred to her was in a moment of exasperation. From the beginning, I had a pretty good idea of how I wanted things to go. And I would insist in moving in that direction, organizing processes and people around me, no matter what the barriers.

As a child, those qualities probably didn't always endear me to adults. Nor was it always a plus in dealing with job supervisors as an adult. But it was exactly those traits, refined over the years by lessons learned working in collaboration with others, that served me well in my unexpected career as an accidental real estate developer. In fact, if there is one category of advice I have for those hoping to replicate our work in establishing what we believe is America's first affordable, mixed-use, elder cohousing community, it's the following.

To turn beautiful ideas into bold action, make sure that your leadership team:

- Possesses a high tolerance for risk;
- Prepares for steep learning curves;
- Keeps laser-like focus on long-range goals (so that they'll work their way through the inevitable frustrations to get there); and
- Understands the need to attract powerful allies and to build, nourish, and leverage networks of influence.

If reinventing communities for successful aging were easy, reinvention wouldn't be necessary.

From Convent to Community

The vision for what became the ElderSpirit Community in Abingdon, Virginia, had its foundation in 1967, when a group of us women working in Appalachia in areas of community service and development organized the Federation of Communities in Service (FOCIS). We had an advantage when it came to seeing both the big picture of service to others and the finer-grain responsibilities that come along with lofty goals. Core members of that founding committee were former nuns. For years, we had been committed to community development in Appalachian communities. When the Church hierarchy insisted we be more conventional than what we thought our work required, we chose mission over obedience, and we left the convent.

The FOCIS group expanded to include men as well as women. As some members approached retirement age, we thought about what it might take to create a retirement community that addressed our concerns for conscious, meaningful aging. We decided on the following goals:

- Create a model that allows older adults to share their wisdom with the larger community in such a way that younger people begin to look differently at old age.
- Create a community that builds personal relationships, as we believe that this is where we find much of our spirituality and meaning in life.
- Create a model that is affordable for all those people who have not made big salaries, but who have contributed to our society by the lives they have lived.
- Create a community where we are encouraged to face the fact we will die, and are supported to do what we need to complete our lives.

FINDING THE RIGHT PLACE FOR THE RIGHT IDEA

WITH THOSE GOALS IN MIND, the where and the how of the community became crucial. It would have to be a neighborhood within an existing community, so that even though we were planning a close-knit group of aging friends, we'd be surrounded by multigenerational families in the larger community. The way homes fit together, the balancing of private and public space — all of that called for expert design. And, toughest of all, the homes and maintenance responsibilities had to be within reach of incomes of ex-nuns and others who had not amassed huge nest eggs.

In 1995, we formed the FOCIS Futures committee to explore alternatives. We learned about the cohousing movement and chose that as a model. We found ourselves attracted to the later-life spirituality concepts of Drew Leder because of our background and missions orientation.[1] We chose the name ElderSpirit for our community, based on Leder's writings.

ElderSpirit Community is located on 3.7 acres alongside the Virginia Creeper Trail in Abingdon, Virginia. A mixed income development, 13 of the cluster houses belong to owners; 16 homes are for means-qualified renters.

Several people interested in the project lived in or near Abingdon in southwest Virginia, and they invited all who had expressed an interest to come to an "Immersion into Abingdon." Our friends gave us a tour of the town. They showed us the health, professional, and shopping resources for seniors and told us stories and experiences of living in Abingdon. The town has many features that make it attractive for retirees—a rails-to-trails walking, cycling, and running trail; the Barter Theater; several arts and crafts establishments; a fine health activities center with indoor pool; and an annual arts festival. It looked perfect.

I moved to Abingdon to look for property and found 3.7 acres bordering the Virginia Creeper Trail, a Rails-to-Trails success story and a popular recreational destination for visitors. To purchase the property, we borrowed $45,000 from 23 FOCIS members. The Retirement Research Foundation of Chicago awarded FOCIS a three-year grant for pre-development expenses, which provided salaries for a part-time staff.

In 1999, our group bought the 3.7 acres. Thanks to the grant, I had a job as project manager — and not a clue what was ahead.

Embracing the Challenges

Despite all my years as a born administrator, including fundraising and managing community development projects with budgets in the millions, I had to learn a whole new set of skills. Designing and implementing the kind of nurturing environment for aging the way we envisioned was an act of real estate development. That means overseeing teams of experts, not only in design and construction, but also in engineering, storm water management, landscaping, building and zoning codes, finance, sales, marketing, health regulations, and a long list of other responsibilities that folks who are not in the development professions can't imagine. It is also a political act, requiring allies in government at the local, state, and national levels.

The surest route to managing all those tasks successfully is to hire an experienced developer who will remove the day-to-day headaches of project oversight. But for us, and for most groups like us committed to affordability, renting the political and real estate development expertise we needed at market rate prices was likely to push costs beyond the means of many of those most open to the idea — and many of those most in need of the aging in community experience. What's more, even if we could come up with the money, there was no assurance we could find a developer with the right mix of political and real estate development experience AND the ability to apply that expertise to the goals of our project.

The simple fact is that, over the last half-century, the real estate development marketplace has become very good at delivering pretty much the opposite of what we wanted: car-dependent suburbs that tend to isolate people from workplaces, school, healthy exercise, and food — and from one another — at costs beyond the means of most family incomes. Choosing alternatives, including connected neighborhoods nestled within broader communities, often means paying a premium to others to face the political and technical headwinds. Because of those headwinds, even though elder cohousing is gaining traction throughout the U.S., the hassles make it tough for the movement to achieve growth on the scale necessary to make a difference in most seniors' lives.

What We Learned

Over the course of the decade-long effort that began with our initial meetings, followed by the purchase of the property — and thereafter the financing, design, and construction of our community — before finally moving-in in 2006, I had a series of revelations.

I, of course, renewed my gratitude for the gritty determination that seems wired into my head and heart, and for lifelong friends who have indulged and supported my ideas, even when the ideas seemed a little nuts. But I also grew to appreciate — more than anything, perhaps — the need to forge networks of support beyond our core group. At every stage, we could call upon well-placed experts, many of whom knew us from our previous lives as nuns and community development workers, and had no doubts about our competence and commitment.

There was no way that we could achieve our goals of affordability without help from nonprofit foundations and government agencies. Just when we needed them most, old and new friends from these networks of support stepped forward to help us with grant writing, with contacts with the right officials, and with coaching on design and engineering matters.

We ran into delays and dead ends. Construction was all but halted for 150 days because of rain, while the interest on our loans continued to grow. We negotiated and detoured our ways around unexpected barriers with regard to the site, and with environmental and public health requirements.

We had to rethink wish lists when costs threatened to bust our budgets. We hired and fired. We argued (respectfully) among one another. And we continually engaged with the broader community and our future next-door neighbors to prevent rumors of a "cult" moving into Abingdon from gaining traction.

The community gathers to celebrate the first five years of living in ElderSpirit.

Few, if any, of these tasks were anticipated in our initial, inspiring discussions of how we wanted to live with friends, new and old, for the rest of our lives. And I suspect the same goes for other groups just starting on this journey. This is why I wanted to spend so much time emphasizing the practical and often exasperating responsibilities that go along with making better places.

It's just as important, though, to stress that the struggle is rewarded. By the time we moved into our ElderSpirit homes, we were already a community, tested by adversity and made more confident by the ways in which we overcame the challenges. Our self-esteem went through the roof. As a result of managing all the practical necessities of building a physical place that enhances community, we've grown to be quite good at managing it. All the advantages we dreamed of when we first talked about aging in community have materialized, enriched by the experiences we've already shared. It just shouldn't be so hard to get to this point.

The tasks are made harder because of their against-the-grain ambitions. Many of the habits and rules of business-as-usual real estate development are unreasonable barriers, especially now that so many of us in America and the world are entering the last stages of our lives in places inhospitable to aging in community. So what I often stress in my talks to groups these days is that we all need to invest more energy into making changes in the way we shape neighborhoods.

That's my first recommendation: Let's lobby for change.

For those looking for more detailed lessons learned from the ElderSpirit journey, I offer these practical tips:

- Hire design and construction professionals with experience with affordable housing. Be honest about your intended price points. And understand how last-minute tweaks and amendments can radically alter costs.
- Get the best advice you can on how to make contracts clear and binding when it comes to what's expected of contractors. Be specific about who's responsible for absorbing costs for budget overruns and for missed deadlines. The "time is money" adage is never truer than in real estate development.
- Understand how real estate valuations and market rates in your locale affect financing and the perceived value of your project. Make homes affordable through compact, well-thought-out design, not through unrealistic discounts from market rates. If subsidies are part of your financial plan, make sure profits realized through later sales are at least partially recouped to continue supporting your project's affordability.
- Be aware of local building and zoning codes. Changing them to accommodate your project's needs can be a political ordeal. Be prepared for that, or adjust design to accommodate the rules.
- Take advantage of Universal Design, which address accessibility concerns in passageways, counter heights, bathrooms, etc. By itself, Universal Design doesn't assure successful aging in community. But if the place is right, in terms of neighborhood access to what seniors need for physical mobility and social interaction, then Universal Design completes the package.

To learn more about ElderSpirit, visit the community's Web site: www.elderspirit.org.

Dene Peterson, a former Glenmary Sister, is the founder and developer of ElderSpirit Community® in Abingdon, Virginia. Her professional background is in fundraising and administration of nonprofit organizations. She has won national recognition for her work with Head Start, community mental health, family planning, and neighborhood organization. Dene serves on the boards of the Aging in Community Network and Second Journey, and she has been honored with a Life-Achievement Award from the National Cohousing Organization.

Notes

1   Leder, Drew. "Spiritual community in later life: A modest proposal." *Journal of Aging Studies*, 10(2):103–116, 1996.

A painting by Walter Hurlburt, a resident of the Burbank Senior Artists Colony, from his grain elevator series. Photo by Tim Carpenter.

Aging in Community: It Takes a Village

by Ben Brown

My generation, the largest in world history, is about to write the last chapter in a life's work of disrupting business as usual, at least business as usual as it played out in the Depression and WWII eras. To go out in the same blaze of glory, we boomers better have one last act of revolution in us, an action plan that reverses the effects of our worst ideas over the last half century.

While we like to pat ourselves on the back for what we've created out of thin air, boomers' real clout is spending power. We put the *me* in *consume*. Markets for cars, homes, and all manner of toys and experiences responded to 74 million humans spending their way through life cycles from toddlers to geezers. The impact of our choices and the ways companies and governments organized to respond to them shaped the environment we must now navigate in our golden years. And it turns out it's a lousy environment in which to grow old.

Home and Community: The Boomer Effect

From the time of our birth, we've been moving markets for homes and neighborhoods. Before the end of the world war that defined our parents' generation, typical American neighborhoods were shaped by the limitations of an era that had barely emerged from the Great Depression before sliding into the home-front hardships of war. Walking, buses, and streetcars were principal options. Families with a wide range of household incomes clustered for convenience in compact, pedestrian-oriented neighborhoods with a mix of housing, shopping, and entertainment choices. "Traditional neighborhoods," we called them decades later when we found it necessary to reimagine the form.

After WWII, the GIs returned home to a nation soon to be transformed by government loan programs and unprecedented demand. Our baby boom hit, beginning in 1946, and the rush was on for more of everything — homes, schools, consumer goods, and cars.[1] The transformation of the American landscape was staggering. Between 1950 and 2000, the share of Americans living in suburban areas rose from 27 percent to 52 percent; the suburban population grew by 100 million, from 41 million to 141 million; and suburbia accounted for three-quarters of the nation's population change.[2]

We can blame our parents for launching the move to the 'burbs, but after brief flirtations with group housing, communes, and other variations of the old norm, we added our consumer clout to the migration farther and farther away from the walkable cores of the city and into the distant, disconnected 'burbs. Cars and cheap gas made everything seem possible, including the separation of the components of community into destinations linked by highways. No wonder, then, that so much of our built environment came to be designed at greater and greater expense for the accommodation of automobiles — ever-expanding roadways, never enough parking, and a dedication of portions of our homes for two-car garages.

What worked in the go-go days of building careers, families, and the delusions of an economy based on unlimited borrowing power doesn't look so great in an era with new rules for making ends meet and new pressures from changing demographics. After we work our way through the phases of denial about what's ahead of us, we boomers will find that what we want most — independence, prolonged health, and the rewards of social interaction — are tougher to achieve in the suburban environments we helped create. Especially if we have to work our way through this last phase of our consuming lives on a budget.

FIXING WHAT'S BROKEN

WE MAY HAVE ONCE SEEN the spacious lawns, the acre-lot McMansions, and the four-lane highways that allowed us to commute from houses we could afford to places we'd rather be as paths to the good life. But even as we began falling out of love with the long commutes, the energy and maintenance expenses of our dream houses, and the isolation of the 'burbs, the rules that legalized and financed all that stuff became the rules that stifle just about anything else — including beloved traditions we'd love to reclaim. Savannah's squares, Charleston's downtown, the historic neighborhoods of transit-served cities like Chicago, San Francisco, and New York City would be difficult to replicate under current suburban-focused zoning codes.

Finance and tax structures that privilege owning over renting, and 3,000-square-foot homes over cottages, restrict the choices we need as we age and struggle to manage incomes that have to last the rest of our lives. Infrastructure policy and funding on all levels conspire against the kinds of communities we want.

Suburban and exurban developments often require infrastructure subsidies in what Chuck Marohn, Jr., in *Thoughts on Building Strong Towns*,[3] calls a "growth Ponzi scheme" that demands endlessly accelerating new development to pay the freight for the previous round of water, sewer, and road construction. State departments of transportation, immunized against community push-backs by access to long-range funding, stamp out high-speed highways in places where true livability requires "complete streets" that accommodate bicycle, transit, and pedestrians as well as automobiles. At long last, officials at the tops of the federal bureaucracies that aggregate the bucks that filter down into states' and counties' coffers have seemed to embrace theories of smarter growth. But the memo doesn't always penetrate state agencies and affect local planning and development.

These barriers have to come down.

It Takes a Village

So here is the goal that deserves the most investment of our time and resources: making better, more connected and inspiring places that are secure, affordable places for growing old and for just about every other human activity.

To get the most bang for the buck, these places should be in close-in neighborhoods — "infill" neighborhoods, in the parlance of community development — where seniors have walkable access to services and amenities that already exist, whether we're talking about a medical clinic, a grocery store, transit options, or a coffee shop.

Every problem we'll face as we age is complicated by the way most Americans live — in car-dependent suburbs designed to separate the places we sleep from the places we work, shop, entertain ourselves, and gather with friends. Tons of research, much of it recounted in other essays in this book, document the positive relationship between human well-being and neighborhoods that offer multiple options for getting around, that encour-

Here are two adjacent neighborhoods in Ocean Springs, MS, perfect for aging in community. The Cottages at Oak Park (top) (center green looking toward two-story homes) and Cottage Square (one-bedrooms behind picket fences) benefitted by the post-Katrina exploration of safe, low-cost, in-town housing for people of all ages and incomes. On the two sites, totaling four acres, are 44 single-family units ranging from a studio of 250-square-feet to three bedroom homes of more than 1,300-square-feet. All are rentals, with some leased as offices. The cottage clusters are within walking distance of a full service grocery, schools, a YMCA, restaurants, hair salons and other daily needs. An across-the-street bus stop provides service to Ocean Springs' historic downtown, a half-mile away. Both sites and several of the units were designed by Bruce Tolar, who specializes in cottage neighborhood approaches to affordability, sustainability and aging-in-community challenges. (photos by Ben Brown and Bruce Tolar)

age social interaction, and that keep us in reach of daily needs without reliance on driving.

Hats off to those heroic folks, many of whom are featured in these pages, who are at the forefront of aging in community innovations that deliver just these kinds of opportunities. Every one of their best practices, from cohousing and in-home health care to the reinvention of skilled nursing, must be refined and expanded. But approaching the problem as do-it-yourself solutions, on the scale of a few committed individuals or even as self-sustaining communities that get most things right, will serve only a tiny fraction of the needs of an enormous aging population, most of whom can't pay the premium it will take to purchase the security they need on their own. We have to scale up.

To do that, it takes a village — and a town, a county, a state, and beyond — which means moving out of the cozy confines of private sector and nonprofit enterprise and into the labyrinth of government.

SOLUTIONS DRIVEN BY A NEW SENSE OF URGENCY

TWO REALITIES SEEM TO BE FORCING A CHANGE in the status quo and are worth leveraging on behalf of aging in community. One is the inexorable pull of austerity. The billions required to keep the clunky apparatus of sprawl going are diminishing. The other is a combination of the pull of market forces and the push of demographic change. Economists, real estate investment pros, and those sympathetic to Smart Growth tenets have been making the case for inevitable change for the last few years. But I'm struck by the recognition of these impacts in an unusual place — *Foreign Policy* magazine. In a January, 2013 article, Patrick Doherty presents a "Grand Strategy" for America leading a global reset in the wake of the Great Recession. Among the strategic components — walkable communities:

> . . American tastes have changed from the splendid isolation of the suburbs to what advocates are calling the "five-minute lifestyle" — work, school, transit, doctors, dining, playgrounds, entertainment all within a five-minute walk of the front door. From 2014 to 2029, baby boomers and their children, the millennial generation, will converge in the housing marketplace — seeking smaller homes in walkable, service-rich, transit-oriented communities. Already, 56 percent of Americans seek this lifestyle in their next housing purchase. That's roughly three times the demand for such housing after World War II.

The motivations are common across the country. Boomers are downsizing and working longer, and they fear losing their keys in the car-dependent suburbs. Millennials were raised in the isolated suburbs of the 1980s and 1990s, and 77 percent never want to go back. Prices have already flipped, with exurban property values dropping while those in walkable neighborhoods are spiking. Yet legacy federal policies — from transportation funding to housing subsidies — remain geared toward the Cold War imperative of population dispersion and exploitation of the housing shortage, and they are stifling that demand.[4]

It's encouraging that a national security specialist like Doherty and a journal dedicated to global policy issues recognizes the neighborhood design imperative. It underscores the cascading connections between international, national, state, and local strategies for improving the lot of humans and reducing the potential for conflict and suffering. Which means this is another of those opportunities to "think global, act locally."

Local, in fact, is where the principal action is when it comes to transforming less livable places into neighborhoods and communities that nourish meaningful living, regardless of what stage of life we're talking about.

Here's my list of strategies for speeding the transformation:

- **EDUCATE YOURSELF** on the relationship between healthy living and the built environment. The Centers for Disease Control and Prevention and its Livable Communities initiative is the place to start. Check out AARP as well. And for valuable case studies, consider the Atlanta Regional Commission's Lifelong Communities effort and the BARHII regional public health consortium.[*]
- **DON'T REINVENT THE WHEEL.** Just about everything you can think about when it comes to planning and implementing great places has been tested and refined somewhere else. Consult, collaborate, and customize lessons learned for your town or neighborhood. For the groups pushing the Big Ideas, look to the Congress for the New Urbanism and Smart Growth America.[†] For a case study of infill neighborhood solutions in service that apply to ag-

---

[*] For the CDC, see http://1.usa.gov/P5Bp74; for AARP, http://aarp.us/ O4Vckp; for the Atlanta commission, http://bit.ly/rrhn6V; and for BARHII, http:// bit.ly/13qwODI.

[†] For the Congress for the New Urbanism, see www.cnu.org; and for Smart Growth America, www.smartgrowthamerica.org.

ing in community, check out the cottage neighborhood movement that's found traction since the replacement housing crisis in the wake of Hurricane Katrina. I blogged about cottage options and and applied some of the lessons learned to the "geezer glut" (see below[*]).

- **EXPAND YOUR NETWORKS.** Look for connections with other advocates (for children's issues, transit, green building, community affordability, local food, accessible health care, etc.) and form mutually supportive, broad coalitions to multiply your influence.

- **ADVOCATE FOR SENSIBLE ZONING.** Lobby for rules that expand choices that build community and prevent development that undermines it. Mixing appropriately scaled commercial space with a diversity of housing is a good thing. So are small lots, accessory dwelling units (Granny flats, garage studios, etc.), liberal parking requirements, designed-in civic places. *Form-based coding*, which concentrates on the look and feel of buildings and public spaces, as opposed to building uses, is the new zoning tool.[†] The connection between zoning and community — including the implications for the spirit — is also a fertile area of inquiry.[‡]

- **BECOME A POLICY-MAKER.** Lobby on behalf of more connected, complete (mixed-use, transit-accessible, walkable/bikeable) communities. Get on citizen boards, especially the local planning commission. Run for office.

Ben Brown spent two decades as a staff reporter and editor for major newspapers and magazines, including *USA TODAY* and *Southern Living*. Since 1999, he's built a communications consulting practice focused on community development. A partner in the international consulting firm of PlaceMakers LLC (www.placemakers.com), Ben's advocacy work includes building on lessons learned from the Katrina Cottage movement to enable compact, sustainable, and affordable cottage neighborhoods. He blogs regularly on www.placeshakers.com.

---

[*] See: http://bit.ly/TzaIS4 and http://bit.ly/YxuwQ8.

[†] See www.formbasedcodes.org.

[‡] See http://bit.ly/RWIENg.

Notes

Segments of this essay have appeared previously in other articles and blog posts by the author.

[1]   The most popular summation of how post-WWII changes created the suburban era is in this manifesto of the New Urbanist movement: Andres Duany, Elizabeth Plater-Zyberk, Jeff Speck, *Surburban Nation: The Rise of Sprawl and the Decline of the American Dream,* 10th Anniversary Edition. North Point Press, 2000, 2010.

[2]   Analysis of real estate and U.S. Census data by Arthur C. Nelson, Presidential Professor and Director Metropolitan Research Center University of Utah.

[3]   Charles L. Marohn, Jr. *Thoughts on Building Strong Towns.* Charles Marohn, 2012.

[4]   Patrick Doherty, "A new U.S. grand strategy: Why walkable communities, sustainable economics, and multilateral diplomacy are the future of american power." *Foreign Policy* (online), January 13, 2012: http://atfp.co/101zYyk.

M_y name is Ann Zabaldo._

I'm 62 years old and I live in an intentional community in northwest Washington, DC.

Today I'm sad, vexed, and… cranky. I'm sad because my 61-year-old childhood girlfriend called to tell me she has "pre-frontal brain atrophy." I don't know what this is, but anything with "atrophy" at the end of it can't be good. My friend lives in a rural area of North Carolina — Asheville is 60 miles away.

She's having a difficult time trying to figure out how to get a ride to the doctor's office on a regular basis. She has friends, of course — one will be taking her to Asheville this week. But her friends have their own lives, as well as being scattered over a large geographic area. She can't depend on them ad infinitum. And she needs help with other things, too. She's having trouble making change. She forgets a lot of things. She's depressed. And she's scared. Very scared.

I'm vexed because she's having these difficulties, and because she doesn't know what to do. Neither do I. This makes me cranky. What makes me crankier is knowing it doesn't have to be this way.

How different it is for me, living in this intentional community called Takoma

Life in Takoma Park Cohousing

by Ann Zabaldo

Village Cohousing. We are a small-scale condominium, comprised of 43 privately owned homes. We came together because we saw the value of knowing our neighbors and pooling our resources to do more with less. By collaborating, we have all that we want and need without excess — we don't need 43 lawn mowers. We are NOT a commune. While we share a lot of things, income is not one of them.

Strangers to each other when we began 12 years ago, we have come to know firsthand the power of living in community which helps us live longer, healthier, more robust lives.

I was part of the development team that built Takoma Village. When I started the marketing and outreach campaign for the community, I was still walking 10 years after being diagnosed with multiple sclerosis. Over the last 12 years, I've gone from walking to using a power wheelchair. I suffer from extreme fatigue, especially in the heat. While I could live on my own in a single-family house or in a standard condominium, it would be so much harder. Most of my day would be taken up just maintaining my daily needs.

Instead, one of my neighbors buys my groceries every week of the year. I send her a list on Sunday night and Monday morning she delivers them, even puts them away for me. Another neighbor shops at the Farmers' Market so I can have fresh produce all year. Yet another neighbor picks up my prescriptions at the local drugstore. Several neighbors drive me to my appointments because I get so easily exhausted from driving these days.

I contribute my time and energy to our community through activities that I can do from home. I'm the point person for elevator maintenance and repair. I organize community events. On community work days, I'm the job-broker helping to match up people with work that needs to be done. I serve on a team that's overseeing refinishing the interior of our Common House — a community building, only bigger, with a lot more bells and whistles. It includes a living room with a small library/meeting area, a sun room, and at the center a very large dining room and kitchen, designed to host large community meals, parties, movie nights, and other community celebrations and events.

Living in community makes it possible for me to live an *interdependent* full, dynamic, passionate life in my own home. I am ever grateful to my neighbors.

Unlike my friend in North Carolina, I have 65 adult neighbors whom I can call for assistance if I need it. One of my friends in another cohousing community says you know you live in cohousing when you can call any neighbor at 2:00 a.m. — even the one with whom you have the least relationship — and they will come if you need help. That's the commitment that comes with the decision to live in cohousing. An example from my own life: One night fairly late, I fell in my living room. Luckily I had my cell phone, and I called a neighbor. In fewer than 30 seconds, three sets of neighbors showed up at my door. All of this makes this kind of community living a safe place for me.

My friend's situation would be so different if she lived in this kind of intentional community. The conversation wouldn't be "Who can I get to give me a ride?" but rather "Which one of my neighbors is going to get here first?" Ubiquitous in Europe, intentional community living can be the norm rather than the exception in our country.

You can do cohousing anywhere. While there are architectural design principles — front porches, central courtyards, or green spaces; parking relegated to the exterior of the community; core principles of spontaneous sharing, spontaneous support, commitment to neighborliness, bottom-up governance; shared work maintaining the community — all these can be practiced in any housing or neighborhood situation.

I've shared with you my experiences of how living in community has mitigated the effects of my disability. Living in community also mitigates limiting circumstances as we age. For those of us 80 million getting-ready-to-retire-baby-boomers, we would be wise to think in advance about what kind of community we want to be in as we age, before someone makes the decision for us. It's important to make that decision as early as possible so you have nurtured the relationships that will see you through difficult times. Waiting until you're 85 years old, in poor health and needing lots of assistance, is too late to form the relationships to age in community.

And now, I have to return to the vexing problem of helping my girlfriend find a ride to Asheville.

Ann Zabaldo, MA, is a national leader in the cohousing movement. She is past-president of The Cohousing Association of the United States and is a founder and current board member of Mid-Atlantic Cohousing, a regional nonprofit organization. A specialist in outreach, education, and marketing, Ann is a certified facilitator for McCamant & Durrett's Senior Cohousing Study Group workshops, and the co-executive producer of "Building Sustainable Communities for Today's Housing Market," a DVD and companion handbook created specifically for developers. Ann was also on the development team for both Eastern Village Cohousing in Silver Spring, MD, and Takoma Village Cohousing in Washington, DC, where she lives. Contact Ann at Zabaldo@earthlink.net.

The social architecture — or "social

software" — refers both to the informal activities, experiences, and interactions which foster a sense of belonging and interdependence among community members, as well as more formal structured programs, services, and activities that provide them support. The goal of social architecture is to encourage mutually supportive relationships that enhance quality of life and well-being, and ultimately contribute to the elders' ability to remain in their homes and connected to their communities.

One of the best-known innovative approaches, the Village model, is attracting enthusiasts across the country. **Candace Baldwin** and her colleagues at the Village to Village Network provide "A Little Help [to Their] Friends" (page 101) with a detailed overview and practical tips on how to jumpstart your own *village*.

Part 3
Creating the Social Architecture

In "The Circle of Care: Mobilizing Assets in the Community" (page 115), cultural creative **Joan Raderman** shows how her communal life growing up among a large extended family provided inspiration for an initiative that connected isolated seniors with cultural, arts, and educational resources in the community — a win-win for all involved.

Aging-in-community champions build bridges between generations because a strong community is by definition a good place for people *of all ages and abilities* in which to live, work, and thrive. Community activist **Kristin Bodiford**, who has worked at building community across generations, helps us imagine the "positive possibilities" in "Intergenerational Community Building" (page 123).

One of the key principles of aging in community is committing to a lifestyle that is economically, environmentally, and socially sustainable. In "The Sharing

Solution" (page 139), **Gaya Erlandson** and **Janelle Orsi** demonstrate how excitingly far one can take this principle.

Consumer demand for person-centered — and person-directed — health care has led to more creative in-home and community-based health and supportive services. Healthcare expert **Carol Barbour** shows how the continuum of care model has evolved, and she speculates on "Continuing Care Options: The Next Generation of Care" (page 153).

This section closes with the profile by **Susan McWhinney-Morse,** who helped create Beacon Hill Village, the model that's become the guiding light for the many villages now working to replicate it, in "Life at Beacon Hill Village" (page 165).

A Little Help from Our Friends

by Candace Baldwin, Judy Willett, Rita Kostiuk, and Natalie Galucia

How the Village Model is Transforming How We Age

FOR 60 YEARS, DOROTHY WEINSTEIN RAN a boarding house for medical students in Boston. Understandably, as she got older, it became more difficult for her to do the work on her own. At age 100, Dorothy finally decided she needed help making beds and cooking for the students. Dorothy's son, who worried for her health and safety, thought that it might be time for her to move to a retirement community. But for Dorothy, it would never be time to move.

Dorothy's story might be unique in that she was able to run an in-home business — and a labor-intensive one at that — for so many years, but her spirit and will to live independently is nothing if not normal. In fact, according to a variety of market research data, older adults today overwhelmingly prefer to age in place and are increasingly seeking options that allow them to continue to live in their own homes and communities.[1]

Consequently, many older adults purposefully seek out supportive communities reminiscent of a time when neighbors were a more signifi-

Neighbor helping neighbor — Ashby volunteer helps a member

cant part of each other's lives and provided a helping hand with no expectation of reciprocation. Today, the experience of aging could be viewed as a constellation — one that is multidimensional and interrelated as a result of recent healthcare policy trends and the realization that the "one size" approach to service delivery does not fit all.

Older adults — especially baby boomers who have experienced their own parents' aging — are searching for meaningful lifestyles as they retire and alternatives to nursing homes, assisted living, or continuing care retirement communities, which are increasingly perceived as lacking a sense of "community." It's been proven that aging in a community-based setting improves the quality of one's life and one's health.[2] In response, new models are beginning to emerge to support aging in the community that provide "one-stop shopping" through a single point of entry.

Community-based models support aging within the community among family and friends, where health care and social connections are provided within the community and an individual's home. Over the past 10 years, one of the innovative models to emerge is the Village model, which creates a wide array of support services and facilitates social connections so that older adults can enjoy a rich, independent, and healthy quality of life. This essay will provide an overview of the Village model and how this new approach to aging in community impacts the national discussion on health care.

The Village Model

Back to the story of Dorothy Weinstein: When she realized she needed help, she contacted Beacon Hill Village, a community-based membership organization that empowers older adults to remain active and engaged in their communities as they age. She told the Village staff how she was having trouble navigating the stairs at home — going up and down them backwards, sliding on her bottom. It's understandable why her son thought she should move to a retirement community, but Dorothy hoped there was another way.

There was. The Beacon Hill Village was able to coordinate neighborhood volunteers to provide Dorothy with companionship, light cleaning for the boarders, rides, home care services, and delivered meals and groceries — including pizza on some Fridays. On days Dorothy felt well, she joined lunch groups and lectures organized by the Village. This support meant that Dorothy was able to age in her own home, still actively engaged in the world around her. "At age 102, my mom died in her own bed, in her own home, with her family at her side," said Dorothy's son. "If it weren't for the Village, this might never have happened."

At the heart of the Village model is the focus on the individual as the core of the community. In this model, older adults are active members in the service delivery process and provide essential assistance in the planning and implementation of a wide range of programming offered through the Village. Villages offer members a network of resources, services, programs, and activities that revolve around daily living needs; social, cultural, and educational programs; ongoing health and wellness activities; and member-to-member volunteer support.

Built on cooperative principles, Villages facilitate access for community support services and connection to ongoing civic engagement. Most Villages are created and run by its members. Since the first Village, Beacon Hill Village in Boston, opened in 2002, 94 Villages have opened across the country, providing full-service programs to nearly 20,000 older adults. Membership levels range from 100–800 people, with an average membership of 200. Currently, at least 120 communities are in the development phase, which could result in an implementation of at least 75 new Villages within the next two years.[3]

Villages share the following "hallmark" characteristics:

- They are self-governing, self-supporting, grassroots membership-based organizations.
- They consolidate and coordinate services to members.
- They create innovative strategic partnerships that leverage existing community resources and do not duplicate existing services.
- They are holistic, person centered, and consumer driven.
- They promote volunteerism, civic engagement, and intergenerational connections.

Furthermore, Villages focus on expanding choice and access to their members; they create social networks within the community and provide assistance to secure long-term services and supports.

The need for this type of support is clear: Research shows that the most damaging threat to well-being in later life is not fear of absolute destitution or poor health, but loss of life purpose and boredom.[4] Villages address directly what recent research has documented as health-related problems caused by social isolation, including depression and increased risk of morbidity, mortality, cardiovascular disease, dementia, and Alzheimer's disease.[5] Real-life social networks decrease isolation, the likelihood of institutionalization, and mortality, and increase longevity. Villages' emphasis on volunteering not only provides manpower for Village programs, but, more importantly, provides an organized way to engage members in their community and improve their morale by "making a difference."

How Villages Work

Members contact their Village and ask for anything that they want or need that will help them to remain connected to their community. Villages are mindful not to replicate or replace services and supports that already exist in the community; thus each Village crafts their member services and programs based upon their community's unique needs. While every Village organization is a bit different, every Village provides three core services:

1. concierge or referral to providers or volunteers for anything the member might want or need;
2. health and wellness programs and services to allow members to stay in their homes for as long as possible (e.g., exercise programs, home health care, meals and groceries delivered); and
3. social and community-building programs, including seminars and wellness and prevention activities developed and administered by the members themselves.

Member requests can vary from day to day, and Village staff ensure these are met either through a referral to a preferred provider or with a volunteer. Transportation is the most frequently coordinated service for Village members, constituting an average of 60 percent of service requests. Transportation is provided through vetted and trained volunteers — both member and non-member — and Villages use private vehicles to offer rides to the grocery store, faith-based activities, or simply a ride to visit with a friend across town.

Flowchart for Village Member Requests

Services organized by the Village for their members vary widely depending on the member's request and availability of volunteers and/or providers to fulfill the request. The practice of referring members to outside service providers is a core feature of the Village model. Villages will "vet" providers (e.g., plumbers, home care agencies, handymen, dog walkers, etc.), including performing background checks, verifying business license/bonds, conducting reference checks, and conducting personal interviews. The Village maintains a list of these providers and adds to the list based upon recommendations from members. Similar background checks are conducted on every volunteer, and many Villages provide volunteer training as a requirement to participate.

Elliot, aged 75, is a prime example of how Village services can fill the gap between healthcare delivery and managing daily life in the community. When Elliot was diagnosed with cancer, he contacted his Village in Newton, Massachusetts, in hopes of getting a ride five days a week to radiation therapy. Newton at Home Village found volunteers for every ride. While Elliot was very grateful for the transportation help, he realized, much to his surprise, that he was most grateful for the new friendships he made with the drivers. Friendships and social connections are at the core of all interactions at Villages. If someone needs computer help, a ride to meet their granddaughter to ski, or an advocate at a hospital discharge, Villages work hard to fulfill these requests. This "whole person" approach highlights the Villages' commitment to helping make meaningful connections to the people, organizations, and activities that are important in a person's life.

Although all Villages differ in what services and member benefits they offer, the diversity of programs and services is member-driven and reflective of the community. Research indicates that 51 percent of the members volunteer with their Village — making the "neighbor helping neighbor" concept a foundation of the model.[6] Volunteers not only provide services to the members but also are "in service" to Village operations: serving as founders of newly developing Villages, providing governance oversight on the Village board and committees, conducting classes or organizing social activities, assisting in local marketing and member recruitment, or simply supplementing paid staff in the Village office to respond to member requests. Many Villages use volunteers as an essential part of the fabric of the organization, as well as to help offset the expense of paid staff, thereby assisting in financial sustainability.

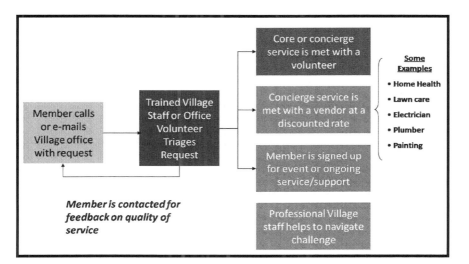

Based on research by the University of California, Berkeley and Rutgers University, the average annual fee to be a member of a Village is $429, and $573 per household. A majority (67 percent) of Villages offer discounted memberships to members who have incomes that are in the low and moderate range.[7] Villages typically operate as nonprofit, stand-alone organizations and derive their revenue from a variety of sources. With an average annual budget around $80,000, these organizations rely upon membership fees as a large portion of their revenue. The balance of the organizations' funds comes from a combination of individual donations, private foundation grants, and corporate sponsorships.[8]

As with most nonprofit organizations, sustainability is of critical importance to Villages. Consequently, the Village to Village (VtV) Network was launched in 2010 as the movement's national hub. Established as a peer-to-peer network of Villages, the VtV Network brings Villages and like-minded organizations together to create a national learning community to support replication in communities across the country. Since its launch in 2010, the VtV Network has 220 member organizations located in 38 states and three countries. The VtV Network is the "go-to" hub for the Village movement; its mission is to enable communities to establish and effectively manage aging-in-community organizations initiated and inspired by their members. The goals of the VtV Network are to:

- Promote the Village model as a community approach to aging for replication;
- Assist new, emerging, and established membership-driven Villages to create sustainable organizations;
- Gather feedback on how the benefits and programs can be revised to meet the needs of individual Villages; and
- Research and evaluate the impact of Villages on a number of social and health factors.

VARIATIONS ON VILLAGE IMPLEMENTATION

VILLAGES VARY IN THEIR IMPLEMENTATION because they reflect the unique needs and culture of their communities. Although Villages are typically formed as newly created nonprofit, grassroots organizations, there are a number of variations on the business structure of the Village model that warrant some discussion. One of the key factors behind these derivative business models is that Villages harness existing community assets and build upon natural networks within the community. Four distinct implementation and business models are emerging as the Village movement expands across the nation: the grassroots model, the parent organization model, the hub and spoke model, and the timebank/Village hybrid model. These variations are detailed below.

GRASSROOTS/VOLUNTEER STAND-ALONE NONPROFIT

This business model is the most common structure for a Village where the organization is a stand-alone nonprofit that is administered through a combination of paid staff and volunteers. Members are encouraged to participate in the governance by serving on the board or committees. These Villages have a strong reliance on volunteers to coordinate and execute the needs of Village members. Examples of this type of model include Beacon Hill Village in Boston, Massachusetts, and Capitol Hill Village in Washington, DC.

VILLAGE UNDER A PARENT ORGANIZATION

Existing social service and aging service organizations are strong assets in communities that often view the Village model as an opportunity to expand the mission of their organization. Likewise, starting a brand new organization is often a long, cumbersome process, and local founders do not always have the capacity to do it. Within this business model, the parent organization can serve as a fiscal agent and support the Village organization by providing the back office support, legal and financial management, and office space. In addition, the Village can benefit from utilizing the par-

Beacon Hill Village member kayaking

ent organization's nonprofit status to support fundraising efforts. In this business model, the Village can be "seeded" under the parent organization's umbrella and then separate itself, becoming a nonprofit, stand-alone organization after a few years. This model also allows established social service organizations to expand their services to a new market of older adults and offer more diverse programming. Good examples of this business model include the Avenidas Village in Palo Alto, California, and the SAIL Village in Madison, Wisconsin.

Hub and Spoke

The "hub and spoke" business model brings together multiple communities or neighborhood enclaves to share costs and back office support in order to serve a wider area. This model allows multiple smaller villages ("spokes") to be created in an area with a central Village ("hub") that handles the IT, database management, accounting, and other support roles ("back office") for the "spoke" Villages. This Village Model has emerged as communities prefer to create their own "spoke" Village to coordinate their unique programs and services with support from the "hub." The best examples of this new model of Village implementation include Marin Village serving Marin County, California, and WISE Connections located in Santa Monica, California.

Villages with Time Bank Component

The reciprocity model (also known as the "time bank") is based on neighbors exchanging skills, talents, and resources for time rather than money (one hour volunteered is equal to one time-bank dollar). Time banking is truly a local model that is based upon individuals helping each other, one-on-one or with group projects. Time dollars are exchanged for services or donated to a community pool to benefit those unable to provide a service. Members join the time bank for a small fee and schedule service exchanges online.[9] While volunteerism is crucial to the success of any Village, this business model takes coordination of volunteers to a new level, where members can "exchange time" and earn time dollars for volunteering. This concept, combined with the Village model, is beginning to emerge as a way to create a lower fee structure for Village membership where time "banked" is provided as a part of the membership fee. Tierrasanta Village located in San Diego, California is the only current operating example of this model.

Impact on Middle Class

The downturn in the economy that began in 2009 has impacted the ability of many middle-income homeowners to be able to secure the equity they need to retire. Many who had planned to use their home equity as a source of retirement income are now left with limited options to realize financial security. This also has impacted the ability for older adults to sell their homes for a windfall income to be used to move to a retirement or other such community. Thus, many older adults are staying put and looking for options, like the Village model, to allow them to remain in their homes and connected to their communities.

Villages are far less expensive than traditionally built place-based retirement settings, and allow people to contribute their skills, keep neighborhoods diverse, and contribute economically to their neighborhoods. In these intentional communities, people are working together to create mutually supportive neighborhoods to enhance the well-being and quality of life for older people at home and as integral members of the community.[10]

In addition to the connection, care, and social supports that Villages provide, they can impact cost savings to state and federal government healthcare systems through three core preventions:

1. Delaying or preventing unnecessary "spend down" for low-to-moderate income seniors in order to access Medicaid benefits. Because Villages provide comprehensive services to members, including non-medical wrap-around services to increase the effectiveness of clinical care, middle class individuals who remain at home need not deplete all of their assets simply to get medical and non-medical supportive services (transportation, wellness classes, social networking) coverage.

2. Decreased hospital admissions and readmission through services focused on health, wellness, and medical intervention. In the Affordable Care Act, focus was placed on supporting patients beyond hospital and physician office settings with the recognition that patients can't recover and thrive if their day-to-day and social support needs aren't met. Data further suggests the medical relevance of social relationships in improving patient care, increasing compliance with medical regimens, and promoting decreased length of hospitalization.

3. Delaying or preventing short- and long-term nursing home stays through services that provide high-quality, low-cost care through volunteers and discounted service providers. Villages provide critically necessary additions to traditional aging network services that build on progress toward person-centered and participant-directed support. Multitiered service consolidation combines service provisions with peer supports and consumer engagement to allow Villages to provide a comprehensive set of services and supports to their members. The Village model combines the characteristics of

an information and referral service, a care management approach, an aggregated consumer review list, and a collective bargaining unit for group purchasing options.

WHY VILLAGES ARE VALUABLE TO THE NATIONAL HEALTHCARE DISCUSSION

VILLAGES FOCUS ON EXPANDING CHOICE and access to their members and provide assistance to secure long-term services and supports and navigate the healthcare system. The current system drives individuals with moderate incomes to Medicaid; the Village model works to keep that from happening. Coordination of local resources, programs, and volunteers can round out the reach of primary care physicians and medical interventions that may lead to positive health impacts and decreases in hospital recidivism. As Villages continue to evolve, major nationwide savings in healthcare costs should be realized as the number and duration of emergency room visits

Beacon Hill Village founders discussing the formation of the Village

and hospital stays are reduced. No other model has as its focus social supports, practical day-to-day assistance, and partnerships with existing organizations. Villages can help weave together the delivery system for their own members, as well as help educate community residents about the availability of all services in a community.

Recently, the medical system has begun to embrace the value of social supports and non-medical components of health care. In a recent report from the Robert Wood Johnson Foundation, primary care physicians felt strongly about the connection between social needs and good health. Furthermore, 76 percent of physicians surveyed "wish the healthcare system would pay for costs associated with connecting patients to services that address their social needs."[11]

A unique longitudinal research project conducted in Australia has shown that "greater social networks with friends and confidants had significant positive impacts on longevity." Real-life social networks of elders and friends were shown to be more valuable than family relationships.[12] An earlier U.S. study showed that older adults who had active social networks decreased their risk of institutionalization by almost one-half.[13]

Maintaining independence is important for older adults, which means we must overcome the barriers that decrease functional capacity. With moderate levels of support and formalized coordinated efforts that could help older adults avoid or delay nursing homes admission, Villages may well be the model of the future. Yet understanding where this model fits into the overall aging infrastructure is critical. Villages currently fill gaps in existing health and social service programs, such as hospital-to-home support, early care management, 24/7 call lines, and "crisis teams" of retired volunteer social workers to help members resolve health access, program eligibility, and other issues.

WHAT'S NEXT?

THE VILLAGE MOVEMENT IS COMING at a critical time when the expanded older adult population is beginning to experience the gap between what they (and often their parents) will need to maintain their lifestyle and what their retirement savings will afford. With little hope of state and federal financing for direct services and supports, the Village model provides a strategy for communities, neighborhoods, and older adults to come together to create solutions. As the Village model continues to evolve, the Villages and the VtV Network will seek to strengthen the sustainability of this promising model and identify critical impacts of the Village model on members' lives.

The reality is that people need and want a variety of services and supports as they age. Choice, convenience, and customization increasingly characterize consumer expectations. Successful aging of older adults who wish to age in their homes and communities requires these "whole person" models that address essential needs related to safe, affordable, and accessible housing; community engagement; health and well-being; independence; and autonomy. Quite simply, the Village movement represents an expanding collective voice among older adults who are seeking — and creating — alternatives to the antiquated aging service delivery system.

From L to R — Candace Baldwin, Natalie Galucia, Judy Willett and Rita Kostiuk

As the Director of Strategy for Aging in Community, Village to Village Network, **Candace Baldwin**, MCED, assists communities, states, and the federal government to develop adequate long-term supports options, systems, and infrastructure to expand choice and independence for older adults. Ms. Baldwin was recently appointed to the board of the National Family Caregiver Association. She holds a BS in Public Policy from Indiana University and a Masters in Community Economic Development from Southern New Hampshire University.

National Director of the Village to Village Network, **Judith G. Willett**, MCED, is a seasoned professional with 30 years' management, marketing, and administrative experience in elder services and related fields. She was the Founding Executive Director of Beacon Hill Village and is the National Director of the Village to Village Network. She has a BS from the University of Michigan and an MA from Boston University's School of Social Work in Administration and Planning.

Rita Kostiuk brings her expertise in database management systems, marketing, national event planning, and member services administration as the Program Manager for the Village to Village Network. In this capacity Ms. Kosituk works directly with open and developing Villages to build and sustain their operations. She holds a BA and MSW from Boston College.

Natalie Galucia, MSW, serves as the Member Services Coordinator of the Village to Village Network and provides one-to-one assistance to Villages and communities seeking to replicate this model to support aging in the community. She received her MSW from Washington University in St. Louis in May 2012.

Notes

[1]   MetLife Mature Market Institute. Profiles of Americans 65+, America's Older Boomers, America's Middle Boomers, America's Younger Boomers.

[2]   S. Kaye, M. LaPlante, and C. Harrington. "Do noninstitional long-term care services reduce Medicaid spending?" *Health Affairs*, 28(1): 262–272, 2009.

[3]   E. Greenfield, A. Scharlach, C. Graham, J. Davitt, and A. Lehning, A National Overview of Villages: Results from a 2012 Organizational Survey, December 2012 Rutgers University, School of Social Work.

[4]   H. Moody. "The Experience of Aging," undated.

[5]   J. Holt-Lunstad et. al. "Social relationships and mortality risk: A meta-analytic review." *PLOS Medicine*, 7/10/10. Accessed January 16, 2013, http://www.plosmedicine.org/article/info percent3Adoi percent2F10.1371 percent2Fjournal.pmed.1000316 .

[6]   Greenfield et al., *ibid.*

[7]   *Ibid.*

[8]   *Ibid.*

[9]   What is a time bank? www.timebanks.org.

[10]   W.H. Thomas and Janice Blanchard. "Moving beyond place: Aging in community." *Generations*, 33(2):12–17, Summer 2009.

[11]   Robert Wood Johnson Foundation. (2011.) "Health Care's Blind Side: the overlooked connection between social needs and good health."

[12]   L. Giles, L. et. al. "Effect of social networks on 10-year survival in very old Australians: The Australian longitudinal study of aging." *British Journal of Epidemiology and Community Health*, 59: 574–579, 2005.

[13]   U. Steinbach, "Social networks, institutionalization, and mortality among elderly people in the United States." *Journal of Gerontology Social Sciences,* 47(4): S183–90, July 1992.

turn your ears on

A Poem by Kit Harper

cole porter's music drifts in the air
a fire in the metronome
fasten your hairnet earphones
sequester the bubble wrap adventure
where jersey cows sing gospel
surfing onto the rocks
at half moon bay

on the pier a grey terrier barking
conducts the bovine rigmarole
singing vivaldi, old bob marley tunes

come listen to the mustard garden
where bees go about the work of bees
queen anne's lace plays melodious allegros
with open red peonies sonata variation

turn your ears on
to hear the falling snow
ladybugs humming debussy

Kit Harper is a resident of Burbank Senior Artists Colony and a participant in its Poetry Café, a creative writing group which is facilitated by
Hannah Menkin.

THE CIRCLE OF CARE:
MOBILIZING ASSETS IN THE COMMUNITY

by Joan Raderman

Call it a clan, a tribe, a network or a family, whatever you call it, who-
ever you are, we all need one.

— Jane Howard, *Families*[1]

FAMILY ROOTS

I GREW UP AT THE HEM of my grandmothers' aprons. Two fiercely strong, yet loving, guardians, they were dedicated to nurturing me, as well as my siblings, through a turbulent childhood. Their love and steadfastness in our lives grounded us while our musician parents were busy trying to make a living.

Every weekend I would go stay with my Hungarian grandmother in the Bronx. From the moment I stepped off the elevator at her apartment building, I was transformed by aromas that seemed to be created by the gods. She would welcome me with a warm hug and steaming pots of culinary surprises simmering on the stove. With every bite I felt her love and care.

My Russian grandmother was a healer, highly educated and trained as a nurse. Back in Russia, people journeyed for miles to seek her help during times of sickness or transition. Whenever I was sick growing up, she was there to nurse me back to health.

My large, extended family was a Bohemian mix of academics and musicians. We all lived together on a bucolic, 50-acre farm in Rockland County, New York, near the Hudson River. We were only a short 30 minutes' drive from New York City, but it felt like we were worlds apart from the noise, hustle, and bustle of urban life.

My Russian grandparents bought the farm property in the late 1940s to escape the city and to give their children and grandchildren a good life. The farm was home to 18 of us — aunts, uncles, cousins, and, of course, our grandparents. I remember them as regal and wise, and the keepers of our family traditions. And there on the farm we were embraced by nature, music, art, learning, food, and love… across generations.

The farm was an exciting, enriching blend of familial dysfunction, creativity, and colorful friends. Our childhood days were spent playing in the woods and by the creek, climbing trees and fighting for who would get to swing in the hammock. When we got hungry, we could always find a delicious pot of something cooking to satisfy our bellies.

Every day we waited for the milk truck to climb up our long gravel road. We couldn't wait to cool off from the summer heat by jumping into the back of the truck and grabbing a piece of ice. When a milk bottle was opened, we would cry to be picked to be the one who got the cream floating at the top. It was Grandma Cima, the nurse, who would decide who needed it or deserved it most that day.

Every day, one of the grandchildren was picked by my Grandpa Leo to tutor him in English. In a strong Russian accent he would call me "Jawnee, help me to say my rrrrrrrrrrr's." After helping him to pronounce English words correctly, which usually ended up in big belly laughter, he would dig deep into his suit pockets, remove the pocket watch and the small journal in which he used to write down every funny or bright comment his grandchildren said, and then hand us a pack of candy charms. We were allowed to pick one in our favorite flavor and color. We felt honored when Grandpa picked us to tutor him. He enjoyed giving us the role of teacher. Even though we were just small children, he allowed us the opportunity to feel valued and important. Grandpa was a physics professor in Russia but could not use his degree here in America. He was always saddened by this.

Today only my cousins and I remain. Our parents and grandparents are long gone. We are all in our 60s and 70s now, and the farm was sold to a developer 45 years ago. You can drive by Kings Highway in Valley Cottage and find my cousins' names on the street signs: Reina Lane, Charles Court, Daniel Drive. The memories from the farm have framed our lives and shaped who we are today. Our children and our grandchildren know that when we gather together for family weddings and celebrations, stories from the farm and their great-grandparents will fly excitedly across the dinner table and dominate our conversations. We share stories from our unique upbringing, our youth, and the gift we shared being raised together on the farm, thanks to the wisdom of our grandparents.

The Epiphany

AT 50 YEARS OLD, I FOUND MYSELF DIVORCED and alone after a 25-year marriage and raising two children. It was Christmas 2003, and I was invited to sing at a large nursing home outside Boulder, Colorado. It was dark outside. I sat in the dayroom as the aides wheeled one person after another close enough to hear me. Soon there was what seemed like a sea of elders sitting in wheelchairs gazing at me. As I looked at their beautiful faces, they looked broken and sad. When I started to sing, they used their feet to move their wheelchairs closer and closer until there were only inches between them and me. One of the women reached out to hold my hand. As I sang, I saw tears coming to their eyes. Beautiful faces with broken hearts. When I got to the line in Silent Night that says, "All is calm, all is bright," it seemed to me that there was precious little left that was bright in their world.

When I got to the parking lot, I broke down. It wasn't like anything I had ever experienced before. My heartache and sadness at witnessing their pain and suffering gave way to outrage that we are warehousing our elders in institutions when it becomes too difficult for them to take care of themselves. Possessed by an idea, I was ultimately driven to a solution. I was determined to change how we live, grow, and age in our country. Thus, the Circle of Care Project was born.

Build It and They Will Come

OLDER ADULTS DO NOT BELONG SEPARATED and corralled in old people places. They belong here, at this concert hall, at this theater and play, in this college class, in this coffee house, in this park, in this restaurant, at this comedy show, at this dance, on this stage, volunteering in this Head Start program, and walking on this trail. We need each other, at every stage of our lives. The longing we all share for community and a sense of social belonging is fulfilled every time we gather. Community can be experienced whether you live in a yurt, cabin, your own home, cohousing, or a senior living community. The power of social and civic engagement to mobilize the arts, culture, and lifelong learning as a means to transform communities is boundless.

For three months I obsessively worked to design a model — the Circle of Care community design model — that would not only keep older adults active, engaged, and integrated into the fabric of community life, but would also unite the generations and help all people, regardless of age, income, or ability. My solution was to build partnerships with the arts, cultural, and educational organizations, transportation, and the business commu-

nity sectors in order to mobilize and reconfigure the resources that already existed within the community. I wanted the program to have a positive impact in the lives of senior participants, as well as the volunteer drivers/cultural companions.

To start, I focused on developing a program, Access to the Arts for Elders, designed to enable homebound seniors and those living in senior facilities to attend arts and cultural events. A "volunteer with benefits program," the volunteers who drove and/or accompanied elders on outings were compensated with a free ticket or admission. This win-win approach provided an opportunity for others in the community who might not otherwise be able to afford or be motivated to go alone to be and have a companion and free admission to a quality cultural event.

While the program was designed to target low-income, frail, and isolated elders, we made it inclusive and accessible to anyone who wanted to join us. In our first year, Circle of Care served 400 senior residents. Since that time, we have become a permanent, city-funded initiative that serves each year about 1,200 seniors throughout Boulder County and engages more than 2,500 registered volunteers.

In those early days I made calls from my dining room table to arts and cultural organizations for ticket donations. Our first partner was the Colorado Music Festival, who wanted to expand its reach in the community — and to fill its seats. They gave us 600 free tickets, and in six weeks we filled those seats, creating another win-win situation — a full house for them, and full and grateful hearts for our seniors and their volunteer companions benefiting from attending the performance.

Today, we have over 50 "Cultural Partners" — community arts, educational, and cultural organizations — in our network. Access to the Arts is our signature program, and the largest, with over $650,000 of annual in-kind ticket donations for seniors and the volunteers who are their "performance companions." Our Cultural Partners have benefited from a new model of audience development and community outreach for arts organizations, while our seniors and volunteers benefit from a culturally enriching activity, which goes beyond the opportunity to hear great music or be entertained by a theater performance for a couple of hours. It brings people out of their homes and into each other's lives. People that have been living as strangers begin to have a common bond, a social connection beyond sharing the same hallway. Volunteers find that they, too, come away with more than a free ticket. They become friends, engaging in the art of being human. They find that their world becomes a bit bigger, and a lot brighter.

BACK TO SCHOOL AT ANY AGE

WHILE PERFORMING IS ONE PERSON'S DREAM, returning back to school is another's that provides multiple health benefits. Research shows that by staying active through lifelong learning activities, older adults can improve their memory, increase their skills and knowledge, and build up their self-confidence. In addition, whether it's learning how to speak a new language or how to ballroom dance, learning new things offers opportunities to meet new people, have new experiences, and expand one's awareness in positive ways.

Charlotte Schatz, 85, heard through the grapevine that Circle of Care was creating a pathway for seniors to attend college through its Senior Audit Partners program. Mrs. Schatz was very interested — she had made it to her senior year at the University of Florida, in 1947, when other life events took precedent. It had always been her intention to complete her college education, but it was a dream deferred to raising a family, and later, caring for her husband and her own failing health. There were so many obstacles — mobility challenges, health issues, and even if she could get to the class, how would she be able to afford it?

We encouraged Mrs. Schatz to not be deterred — where there was a will, we would help to find a way. We found a scholarship to pay for the transportation to and from the University, as well as for the registration fee and books. We also found a student volunteer to escort Mrs. Schatz to the classroom, and another to assist in taking class notes. When stairs became an obstacle to meeting with the professor, we arranged for an alternative meeting site. Mrs. Schatz now has the confidence to complete what she started so many years ago. Next semester, instead of auditing the class, Mrs. Schatz plans to attend as a paying student and will finally have the opportunity to accomplish her dream of receiving her bachelor's degree.

Colorado University and its Senior Audit Program are not unique. Most colleges and universities offer a similar program that allows older adults and alumni to attend courses on a space-available, non-credit basis. Most schools, however, do not provide any special assistance such as financial aid or transportation support to attend classes, and many do not widely advertise their program. What truly makes our program unique, however, is the special attention we give to cultivating intergenerational and community relationships. In partnership with the University of Colorado, we have launched the Study Buddies program that recruits community volunteers to help seniors with assorted tasks, from guiding them through the registration process, to carrying their books and helping with class notes. In exchange, volunteers receive free enrollment to audit college courses.

Library Access Partners is another of our lifelong learning programs in which we partner with the Boulder Public Library system. Trained Circle of Care volunteers work to improve access for seniors, particularly those with disabilities and mobility challenges, to a wide array of library events.

Our Elder Adventurers program is also designed to help those with disabilities and mobility challenges to get out into the great outdoors and learn about nature. In partnership with Boulder and State of Colorado parks, recreation, and open-space organizations, we are able to provide a variety of fun and varied activities, from picnics to educational programs to nature strolls, whether by foot or in a wheelchair.

Making the World Bigger For Elders

As we grow older, one constant across racial, ethnic, economic, and social lines is the experience of loss. Whether it is something we voluntarily give up or it is something unexpectedly taken from us, we experience many losses — physical and mental functioning, job identity and income security, our homes and our neighbors, and most of all, our spouses, family members, and friends. With each loss, our world grows smaller, until without a loved one, the ability to drive, or the opportunity to make new friends at a different life stage, we become captives in our own homes, whether independent in the community or a senior facility.

At 78 years old, Lois Ilseman's experience of growing older is not unique: "I have suffered so many losses in recent years. My husband was in a nursing home for years — and that cost all of our money. When he died in 2000, I moved from my lifelong home in Pennsylvania to come to Colorado to be with my daughter, who was diagnosed with breast cancer. I know it is to be expected, but I was so depressed, so lonely."

Intergenerational social and cultural enrichment programs such as Circle of Care provide elders the opportunity to have new experiences, to make new friends, to enjoy the good things in life. These cultural opportunities serve to make the world a bit bigger at a time that many elders need it the most.

Mrs. Ilseman is a strong and enthusiastic advocate of the Circle of Care program: "It (Circle of Care) changed my life! I hadn't participated in music for so many years, I couldn't afford the tickets. But when I was young, my mother was a concert singer in Allentown, she sang in German — Schubert and Schumann — and I have always loved good music, but in recent years I've had so few opportunities to be around it. And along comes Joan, with free tickets and transportation to these wonderful places! There are so many talented young musicians, right here in Boulder! I feel like I am in my second life, I have been given a second chance. I have met so many new friends — because we share a common interest, it gives us something to talk about."

MOVING FORWARD

SINCE THE BIRTH OF THE CIRCLE OF CARE project, we have received a best practice designation from the MetLife Foundation and Partners for Livable communities in Washington, DC. With the release of the publication, *Stories for Change*, we are being contacted by cities across the country interested in starting Circle of Care communities — cities which shared our commitment to building sustainable solutions for aging in place, aging in community, and livable community design that address the needs of elders.

Circle of Care continues to strive to meet community needs through programming which is always inclusive and inspires multigenerational participation. Circle of Care programs such as Arts for Elders, Senior Audit

Partners, Intergenerational Voices, Elder Adventurers, Library Access Partners, and Elders Without Borders are all designed to remove the barriers to people, places, and programs that change lives.

As we gather several times a week to connect socially and share the arts, learning, social, and community engagement time, we build ties that bind us. We create a safety net to serve needs. Relationships build and foster the love, care, and sense of social belonging we all need, no matter how old we are.

Joan Raderman is the founder and community architect of Circle of Care Project, an award-winning social innovation project that provides sustainable solutions for aging in place, aging in community, and livable community design. For questions about or support in implementing a Circle of Care model in your city, e-mail joan@ circleofcareproject.org or visit www.circleofcareproject.org. To learn more, go to Stories for Change from the MetLife Foundation and Partners for Livable Communities: www.livable.org/storiesforchange.

Intergenerational Community Building: Imagining Positive Possibilities

by Kristin Bodiford

 IN MY WORK AROUND CREATING more aging-friendly communities, Anne, a woman in her eighties, sent me an e-mail to remind us to create whole communities. I hold stories like Anne's central in my work.

I live in a gated senior community with all the amenities one could dream of — workshops, handicrafts, exercise, etc. — you name it, we have it. And yet I am longing, longing, to walk to the corner coffee shop, to hear the sound of children playing, dogs barking. I want to eat at the corner cafe, see young people in love, walk to the library, catch the train into the city, watch mothers with their children in the park, young families, teenies in the latest, wildest outfit. Yes, I'm lucky to have what I do and I never forget that. But, I am excluded from the mainstream of life.

Please consider in your conversations that there are many of us who do not want to be maintained. We want to belong, not only to each other, with whom we may have only one common denominator, age, but to society. We want to be "just like everyone else." Think about building communities that are whole. We need each other, we can learn to care about each other, support the young and the old, give what we have the energy to do, not what society has assigned to us. Instead of a multi-million-dollar resort where every need is met and everything is planned for the generic aging American, think up something daring, something challenging, something creative. (Anne Leitch, February 21, 2008)

To inspire our thinking, I thought I would share a couple of stories that I see as daring and creative examples of communities working to build whole communities with greater connection between generations.

In 1996, a group of citizens from Austin (a neighborhood in Chicago) participated in a program called Citizen Leaders that was part of the Imagine Chicago initiative.[1] Their initial project was an intergenerational softball league, so teenagers and older residents could get to know each other. The softball league inspired block clean-ups before the games and team barbecues after them. Ultimately, conversation among neighborhoods led to the creation of block clubs, community gardens, intergenerational sports programs, and a youth club. In addition, people began to come together to collectively address important issues in their neighborhoods.[2]

In Cleveland, young people gathered oral histories from the elders in their community. While the youth were listening to their elders, they were also doing things to help them around their homes. In one instance,

 a group of youth painted their storyteller's front porch and planted flowers while he shared stories and photos from his life. As teens listened to older residents talk about how to make the community better, they began asking what they could do to help.[3]

These are the stories that inspire me.

In 2005, I had the opportunity to work in the community that I grew up in, where my parents still live, to better understand the challenges and opportunities residents face as they age. Over the last 50 years, the city of Lake Oswego, Oregon, grew as a community of young families fueled by the demographic wave of baby boomers. The city councilors realized that how the community responds to the changing needs of their community is critical to the success of the city. The city also recognized the tremendous strengths and contributions that citizens in this demographic group make to the community. A process was developed called the "Lake Oswego 50+ Community Dialogues" that mobilized and engaged the strengths of their community. The process was based on the belief that individuals have a strong stake in creating the future of their community and a desire to participate in shaping that future. Through active dialogue, community members created a vision of what a vibrant community would be for them as they age.

An important element in this vision was that residents wanted members of every generation to be able to remain connected to other generations living in Lake Oswego. They also wanted the focus and vision of creating community to be on creating a "community for all ages." They created a vision statement for what they envisioned for their community:

Lake Oswego is a community that honors and values every stage of life and encourages interaction between all ages. This community will be one where the knowledge of all individuals is shared to form a harmonious and compassionate link to benefit the social, physical and mental health of each citizen.

Foundational to this vision were social interactions that create a sense of community. Importantly, they wanted these connections for all generations, to encourage interaction among all age groups and to avoid segregation that can isolate generations. Many residents communicated that they wanted more intentional connection across generations. In particular, they wanted more structured opportunities that were designed specifically to interact with youth. They wanted activities and programs to bring youth and adults together to develop relationships and help form a better understanding of each other. Residents advocated for planning and policy development that recognizes the needs of individuals along the entire life span.

So how do we build more intergenerational connection in our communities?

We can begin with programs and initiatives in our communities that bring generations together. A major initiative by Harvard School of Public Health and MetLife Foundation states:

Community-based initiatives that bridge the generations should receive special attention, by integrating the old with the young, transmitting knowledge and experience to future generations and re-enforcing the value of people of all ages.[4]

Intergenerational programming refers to activities or programs that increase cooperation, interaction, and exchange between people of different generations. Through intergenerational programs, people of different generations are also able to share their talents and resources to support each other in relationships that benefit both the individual and their community. These programs provide opportunities for individuals, families, and communities to enjoy and benefit from the richness of an age-integrated society. This takes planning from a lifespan or multigenerational approach to an intergenerational approach. As Marge Schiller and Juanita Brown would say, "Multigenerational is the *who* and intergenerational is the *how*."

As we work to bring generations together, what *questions* might we ask that help us to explore what a vibrant intergenerational community looks like?

The seeds of change — that is, the things people think and talk about, the things people discover and learn, and the things that inform dialogue and inspire action — are implicit in the very first questions we ask. It may well be that our most important task is continuously to craft the unconditional positive question that allows the whole system to discover, amplify and multiply the alignment of strengths in such a way that weaknesses and deficiencies become increasingly irrelevant.[5]

A question that drives my work is how we build community where we have opportunities to care about and for each other. Intergenerational community building embraces this relational orientation. When we encourage generations to come together, our mutual understanding is enhanced; our capacity to care for each other, expanded; and our shared effort of addressing community issues, empowered.

Imagine a community in which the wisdom of the different generations is harnessed to care for and grow the community. (David Peters, Co-Coordinator, Communities For All Ages in New Rochelle, NY)

Communities for All Ages (CFAA) offers an alternative, intergenerational lens to create communities that are good for people in which to grow

up and grow older, and it intentionally engages multiple generations to work on issues. They stress that intergenerational community building is most successful when it engages individuals from all stages of life and intentionally focuses on fostering meaningful relationships from the outset. We often hear from multiple generations how much they learn about each other, when they are able to develop and strengthen their relationships.

I think older people are afraid of young people... but when you mix them up together... it's not as scary, is it? Young people are like everybody else... just have to get used to them... have to reach out to them, embrace them. (Older adult resident, Communities for All Ages)

I learned when adults understand the place youth come from, it can be really fun to work with them to make changes in our community. I learned that I can be on that level with adults and that they bring fun, wisdom, and knowledge when we learn from each other at a deeper level. I didn't understand this before. I never thought that would be possible. Now I know that anything is possible. (Youth, Antioch, CA)

As we engage in intergenerational dialogue, we have the opportunity to bring forward the best of what has been and what is, to spark our imagination for what could be, what is possible. It also allows for community values and history to be shared and passed on.[6] I am left wondering, how can we do this when we live in age-segregated communities? When we live in intergenerational communities, we have more opportunities to rub shoulders and be in relationship with each other.

As we work to bring generations together, we might ask ourselves, *who else might be included?*

Nancy Henkin from Communities for All Ages reminds us to consider, "Who is not at the table? Whose voices are included? Whose voices are left out? Kids who have left school, older adults who don't speak English or who are physically frail? How can the building of relationships be part of what we do?" She proposed an intentional focus on relationship building and social capital as a critical foundation to intergenerational community building.

Social capital is generated through trustful, reciprocal relationships and through creating social connections as a means of facilitating collective agency.[7]

Intergenerational community building demonstrates possibilities for cultivating caring in our families, neighborhoods, schools, and communities. This type of high-empathy caring is at the heart of a relational responsiveness through which communities and societies develop strengthened social capital and resilience in the face of adversity. Through engaging with each other in this relational way, we build our capacity to get along and work together to better meet the needs of all community members.

In this important move from fragmentation to interconnection, relational approaches offer resources to cultivate compassion for self and others, caring, empathy, and spontaneous action to help others. Kiwi Tamasese from Family Centre of New Zealand proposes that a sense of interconnection can result in a reciprocity or mutuality that the future is ours together, and with our rights we have a collective responsibility for each other and our world.

> *We intend it as an exploration, a call for greater awareness, conversation and broad debate about what we believe is our fundamental interdependence on one another and the crucial role of human relationships in the health of societies.*[8]

Building intergenerational relationships and partnerships can also be a challenge and requires investing in preparing different generations and groups of people to work together. This essay explores how we might draw upon important relational resources with an attentiveness to building our collective capacity for dialogue, storytelling, listening deeply, and social action.

DIALOGUE

INTERGENERATIONAL DIALOGUE CREATES OPPORTUNITIES to challenge thinking, develop relationships, revisit assumptions and beliefs, and consider new approaches to address important issues in our communities. Not  only will this benefit youth and older adults, it will benefit the whole community, all generations. I will share a specific story about a group of youth from Antioch, California, in a project called Choppin' it Up that expanded their learning in transformative dialogue methods to their community. This was part of a countywide adult/youth partnership to address teen dating abuse in Contra Costa County, California, including a Teen Dating Abuse Policy Summit sponsored by Senator Mark DeSaulnier (in photo) and Assembly member Susan Bonilla.[9.]

PRINCIPLES OF TRANSFORMATIVE DIALOGUE

- Examine the assumptions and judgments that we hold.
- Create a safe space by developing and committing to shared agreements.
- Speak from our personal experiences.
- Inquire into and be reflective of our reactions and responses.
- Be curious about and work to understand different viewpoints.
- Continue to expand the dialogue and engage more voices.
- Search for local meaning and relevance, and construct knowledge through social processes.
- Imagine the future and positive possibilities. Move towards and support social action. These new understandings and ways of seeing and knowing carry a number of possible actions or responses. In other words, knowledge and social action go together.

In one particular dialogue, the youth were exploring what they could contribute in their community if they were to weave their strengths together. Ideas ranged from creating activities downtown for all ages to come together and revitalize what was once the heart of the community, to addressing important issues in their community like gang violence and homelessness. They then envisioned a possible future if they were to put these ideas in place, and they imagined a community where young people are valued for these contributions and looked upon positively by other community members. They  discussed things that would need to happen to help make their future vision a reality. One young man raised his hand and said, "2015 is too soon. We need help from others, adults in our community to achieve this vision. To do that, we need to change their perception of us."

This started a new conversation from the one we had been having, focusing on how others might perceive them, how critical support from adults in the community was to achieving their vision, and what they could do to begin changing the way they might be viewed in their community. The youth decided to expand voices involved through hosting a community dialogue to support a collective imagining of the future. They also invited elders in the community to advise them in their efforts.

STORYTELLING

WHEN THE YOUTH MET WITH THE LOCAL ELDERS, the elders shared their experiences growing up in Antioch. The youth were energized to capture

the memories of their elders. The young people were discovering the importance, as Phil Stafford writes, "to employ story to sustain that connection to our past. Old people, as the *rememberers*, represent a treasure we must protect. They re-member our communities."

The elders also shared how people viewed them as "youths" in their communities and drew connections between what the youth shared about how they thought their community might view them. In some cases elders and youth connected on being seen as a "hoodlum," "up to no good," which they felt affected their participation in the community.

There are many ways that our stories about youth or about older adults increase the distance between generations. We can work to create new stories that reinforce our interconnectedness and build bridges to understanding. Narrative practices provide a road map for reauthoring problem-saturated dominant stories that lead to new stories and positive possibilities.

> *I am fed up with the media affecting me on a daily basis. I wear a black hoody and people see me as a hoodlum, a troublemaker. I enter the store and all eyes are on me. But I bet those people don't know that I average a 3.86 GPA in high school. And I also bet you that those people don't know that my intentions aren't to destroy the community, but to restore it.* (Antioch Youth)

Narrative practice provides a way for us to identify events or stories that lift up positive aspects of our lives that include messages of purpose, values, hopes, and dreams. By sharing these stories with each other, between generations, our communities become more richly storied or narratively resourced, providing alternative options for meaning-making and social action.

Joe Lambert from the Center for Digital Storytelling shares that "story-work is a tool for healing, helping us reweave our connections to each other, strengthen communities, and heal societies through listening, making stories, and marking places with narrative." In doing so, storytelling renews and changes everyone in the process. When we listen, deeply listen, to what others are saying, magic happens.[10] It is transformative.

LISTENING

LISTENING PLAYS AN IMPORTANT ROLE in both remembering and creating new stories. Listening carefully with great respect to someone as they tell their stories creates a space in which transformation can occur.[11] At times, people share their deepest experiences and sometimes great pain in these stories. Charles Waldengrave from the Family Centre in New Zealand talks about this as a great honor and sacred encounter. The elders in Antioch shared that being able to listen to another person's story and contribute to their well-being is an act of love. In this act of listening, memories are carried on, and people have a chance to be heard that builds a sense of belonging.

> Listening is an act of co-narrating — as listeners respond and interact with
> the narrator, they play a role in the shaping of the story.[12]

As the youth listened to the wisdom of their community elders, they began together building a positive image for the future based upon the best of the past. The youth learned more about the lives of community elders, stories about the history of Antioch, and visions for how the elders would like to leave Antioch for future generations. Edward Sampson states, "…our lives must be a shared story, never entirely ours alone."[13] How we create shared stories carries many possibilities.

Jerome Bruner uses a metaphor of map-making for how people might (re)construct stories of their lives as a journey. We might borrow from the metaphor for intergenerational community building through listening to others' stories to find our way and create a map of the journey.

> It is as if they were embarking on a journey without maps — and yet, they
> possess a stock of maps that might give hints, and besides, they know a
> lot about mapmaking. First impressions of the new terrain are, of course,
> based on older journeys already taken. In time, the new journey becomes
> a thing in itself, however much its initial shape was borrowed from the
> past.[14]

The journey forward illuminates the possibility of contributing to a collective narrative about how we develop a sense of shared purpose that promotes resilience and creates positive change in communities.

SOCIAL ACTION

HOW WE PERFORM SOCIAL ACTION together offers powerful possibilities for transformation in our communities. Intergenerational community building stresses the importance and possibilities of all people working in partnership with each other and amplifying each others' strengths to ensure that young people, old people, and those in between receive the critical support and opportunities that promote healthy development throughout the lifespan.[15]

> *Every single person has capabilities, abilities and gifts. Living a good life depends on whether those capabilities can be used, abilities expressed and gifts given. If they are, the person will be valued, feel powerful and well connected to the people around them. And the community around the person will be more powerful because of the contribution the person is making.*[16]

A key element of intergenerational community building is the role of youth/adult partnerships. Developing youth and adult advocates that know how to think across a lifespan in community planning is key to ensuring that more voices are heard, in a way that respects and supports all of the generations. Intergenerational civic engagement, bringing generations together around social issues that impact communities, helps to broaden voices and bring more perspectives into social agendas and dialogue. This might look like an intergenerational council, in which youth and adults serve together to ensure that there is an intergenerational lens and priority in policy and programmatic decision-making. This approach also engages the strengths and builds the capacity of all generations to be active community contributors, where youth and older adults can serve as facilitators to bring people together in their communities, dissolve boundaries, and include more voices.

Strengthening youth–adult partnerships by participating in ongoing opportunities to engage in collaborative social action helps us to develop new ways of working together that are opening a way forward to radically different possibilities. These different possibilities are growing out of strengthened relationships where youth and adults are seeing each other in new ways. A colleague, Michelle McQuaid, shared a quote from *My Stroke of Insight* where the author explains how, after she lost her ability to speak, she longed to communicate: "Whatever my age, whatever my credentials, reach for me. Respect me. I am in here. Come find me."[17] What if we were to think that each human being might be deep inside chanting, "Reach for me. Find me. I am here. Find my greatness." This great power to be seen, heard, and to discover and care for each other is to be alive in our fullest, with connection at our core. Maybe the first step to creating good intergenerational relationships is to reach for each other with respect — to find each other.

IMAGINING POSITIVE POSSIBILITIES
SOMETHING DARING, SOMETHING CHALLENGING

WHEN WE IMAGINE POSSIBILITIES, we create new stories and realities that lead to new understandings and relational practices. When addressing social injustices and adversity that people face in their lives, a new story of relational responsibility speaks to the importance of the process of relating itself.[18] When we bring this attentiveness to issues of social justice, we find that it is imperative that we not only address the specific needs and engage and build upon the strengths of children, youth, families, and older adults within the communities in which they live, but that we also address the context of people's lives. The notion of social injustice is greatly underestimated and underaddressed in our conversations about youth and older adults and the challenges they face in their lives. These injustices include poverty, lack of housing, unemployment, violence, abuse, and racism. We must work together to build more social, gender, economic, and cultural equity. Reflecting on the privileges and rights that come with being part of a dominant culture or group encourages relational responsibility to work for increasing equity between people in our worlds, with a significant focus on those most marginalized by dominant cultures.[19]

> *A resilient community recognizes the interconnectedness of all its citizens and understands the well-being of children and youth is connected to the well-being of other age groups — and vice versa.*[20]

Through developing and strengthening our connections among each other, we can address important social issues of marginalization, inequity, and injustice in this world through compassionate action. Through these relationships, conditions of spontaneous compassion and action are created, like the left hand stopping the bleeding on the right, where people naturally care about each other and do what they can to help each other to thrive throughout the lifespan. Jerome Bruner wrote in his book, *On Knowing: Essays for the Left Hand*, that the left hand traditionally represents the powers of intuition, feeling, and spontaneity.[21]

When we work to deepen our understanding of each other, and have

striking moments where our view has shifted and we see things anew, we almost cannot help but move towards social action.[22] In this respect, community capacity building is about generative intergenerational relationships that demonstrate caring, respect, acceptance, and personal and social power. This thinking has inspired my learning journey about how we can build this type of deeper understanding and connection with each other that results in compassionate actions in our relationships, neighborhoods, and communities. As we do this, we also move a way of thinking about "those people/those children" to a collective responsibility and to "our children/our people."

My concluding proposal is this: When we consider what type of community we want to live in, we can also ask, what type of community do I want to contribute to and to build? How can we bring our vision, knowledge, and skills to create connected and caring communities that engage the strengths of all generations? Through our relationships with each other this vision begins to take shape. The resource is our conversations with each other. We can begin with conversation — one conversation at a time.

Whatever you can do, or dream you can do, begin it. Boldness has genius, power, and magic in it. Begin it now." [23]

Kristin Bodiford is Principal of Community Strengths offering expertise in dialogue models and other transformative strategies to support community and systems planning for positive change. Kristin is co-founder of *Creating Aging-Friendly Communities*, an international community of practice with more than 3,000 members focusing on creating more aging-friendly communities in partnership with UC Berkeley and the CDC Healthy Aging Research Network (www.agingfriendly.org). In addition, Kristin's work includes a federal demonstration project — called Families Thrive (www.familiesthrive.org), whose goal is to create a more responsive system for children and youth exposed to domestic violence — and a collaborative inquiry — called Choppin' it Up (www.choppinitup.org) — which encourages youth to participate in and host dialogues and conversations that promote positive change in their schools and communities. Kristin is a Taos Institute Associate and holds a PhD in Social Sciences from Tilburg University and an MBA from University of California at Davis. To learn more about her work, please visit www.communitystrengths.org.

Resources and Notes

Generations United works to improve the lives of children, youth and older adults through intergenerational collaboration, public policies, and programs. www.gu.org.

Communities for All Ages is a national initiative that helps communities address critical issues from a multigenerational perspective and promote the well-being of all age groups. www.communitiesforallages.com

Creating Aging-Friendly Communities is an online resource to support people, organizations, and communities who are working to make their communities more aging-friendly. www.agingfriendly.org

[1] Imagine Chicago is a nonprofit organization that has been working since 1992 to cultivate hope and civic engagement in a variety of cross-cultural and intergenerational initiatives, projects, and programs. www.imaginechicago.org

[2] Imagine Chicago Ten Years of Imagination Report, http://www.imaginechicago.org/docs/publications/ Ten%20Years%20of%20Imagination.pdf, p. 24.

[3]   Cleveland State University professor Dwayne Wright created the project, "Our Stories," which produces oral histories from elders in exchange for painting and planting flowers. http://blog.cleveland.com/metro/2008/06/oral_histories_paint_a_picture.html

[4]   Harvard School of Public Health — MetLife Foundation Initiative on Retirement & Civic Engagement. http://harvardschoolofpublichealth.net/chc/reinventingaging/report_highlights.html

[5]   J.D. Ludema, D.L. Cooperrider, and F.J. Barrett. "*Appreciative inquiry: The power of the unconditional positive question.*" *Handbook of Action Research*, P. Reason and H. Bradbury (Eds.), pp. 189–199. Thousand Oaks, CA: Sage Publications, 2001.

[6]   Sheila McNamee and Kenneth J. Gergen. *Relational Responsibility: Resources for Sustainable Dialogue*, p. 64. Thousand Oaks, CA: Sage Publications, 1999.

[7]   Ross Deuchar, "Urban youth cultures and the re-building of social capital: Illustrations from a pilot study in Glasgow." *A Journal of Youth Work,* 1: 7–22, 2009. www.youthlinkscotland.org/webs/245/documents/JournalYouthWork.pdf

[8]   Maia Szalavitz and Bruce Perry. *Born for Love: Why Empathy Is Essential — and Endangered*, p. x. New York: William Morrow, 2010.

[9]   Choppin' it Up was developed in partnership with the Youth Intervention Network, the Antioch Unified School District, and Families Thrive of Contra County. To view videos produced by the youth, please go to www. choppinitup.org.

[10]   Joe Lambert. *Digital Storytelling: Capturing Lives, Creating Community,* pp. xvi, 86. Berkeley: Digital Diner, 2002. Check out the Center for Digital Storytelling Storylab project "All Together Now" that is based on two generations' stories about lifting their voices in community at http://www.storycenter.org/all-together- now/.

[11]   Charles Waldegrave and Taimalieutu Kiwi Tamasese. Keynote Presentation: Enriching Collaborative Practices across Cultural Borders Conference. Merida, Yucutan. March 20, 2012.

[12]   Janet B. Bavelas, Linda Coates, and Trudy Johnson. "Listeners as Co-narrators." *Journal of Personality and Social Psychology,* 79(6): 941–952, 2000.

[13]   E.E. Sampson. *Celebrating the Other: A Dialogic Account of Human Nature,* p. 139. Chagrin Falls, OH: Taos Institute Publications, 2008.

[14] Jerome S. Bruner. *Actual Minds, Possible Worlds,* p. 36. Cambridge, MA: Harvard UP, 1986.

[15] Bonnie Benard. *Resiliency: What We Have Learned,* p. 105. San Francisco, CA: WestEd, 2004.

[16] John P. Kretzmann and John McKnight. *Building Communities from the inside Out: A Path toward Finding and Mobilizing a Community's Assets,* p. 13. Evanston, IL: Asset-Based Community Development Institute, Institute for Policy Research, Northwestern University, 1993.

[17] Jill Bolte Taylor. *My Stroke of Insight: A Brain Scientist's Personal Journey.* New York: Viking, 2008.

[18] McNamee and Gergen, *Relational Responsibility.*

[19] Waldegrave and Tamasese, Keynote Presentation.

[20] Benard, p. 104.

[21] Jerome S. Bruner. *On Knowing; Essays for the Left Hand.* Cambridge: Belknap of Harvard UP, 1962.

[22] Arlene Katz and John Shatter. "Social poetics as a relational practice: Creating resourceful communities." Construction of Health and Illness, at Social Construction and Relational Practices Conference. Durham: n.p., 1999.

[23] W.H. Murray. *The Scottish Himalayan Expedition.* Quote attributed to Johann Wolfgang von Goethe. London: Dent, 1951.

"The Room," a painting by Suzanne Knode, a resident of the
Burbank Senior Artists Colony. Photo by Tim Carpenter.

The Sharing Solution

by Gaya Erlandson and Janelle Orsi

I HAD ENTHUSIASTICALLY TOUTED her book, *The Sharing Solution,*[1] for nearly two years, so it was a real pleasure to meet Janelle Orsi last October at a conference in Colorado on Collaborating for Social Change. Janelle is founder of SELC (the Sustainable Economies Legal Center) in Oakland, California, a firm which trains lawyers, law students, and citizens in what's called sharing law. Like real estate or family law, sharing law is emerging now as a specialized area of legal practice. Janelle is taking a lead in promoting sharing law in part by coauthoring *The Sharing Solution* written for the general public.

The Sharing Solution is a treasure trove of ideas and tools for sharing goods, services, wisdom, space, etc. — almost anything you can think of! — with our neighbors. Its surveys and forms help us be clear about what we have to share and what our expectations are. The useful legal advice details, for example, how to craft agreements that include ways to end the arrangement cleanly when that becomes desirable. The end result of such agreements is that we have more while buying less.

The benefits of sharing with people who live in close proximity are obvious: We save money, reduce resource consumption and thus landfill, and live more sustainably. Less obvious, perhaps, is how our interactions and shared interdependence help create a caring community. Sharing becomes a way to break through the isolation and illusion of independent living.

What To Share

HERE'S A QUICK INVENTORY OF THINGS we use only rarely: hand tools, lawn and garden equipment, ladders, long extension cords, vacuum cleaners, cars, washing machines, clothes lines, wheel barrows, bicycles and pumps, folding tables, irons and ironing boards, extra TVs, binoculars, telescopes, camping gear, back packs, canopy tents, folding or plastic chairs for special events, car or bicycle racks, inflatable boats or swimming inner tubes, special kitchen ware (crock pot, Vitamix juicer or blender, electric mixer, yogurt and bread makers, picnic baskets, thermoses, coolers, etc.), musical instruments, piano, holiday or special event decorations.

Another category is office extras: dry erase easel, flip chart stand, tripod, FedEx service, 3-hole punch, paper cutter and shredder, pencil sharpener, microphone, karaoke device, loud speaker, clip boards, extra computer, fax machine.

Space also can be shared. Plots of land can become common vegetable and herb gardens or children's playgrounds. Garages can be used to fix cars, support work projects, or maintain a tool-lending library within a neighborhood community.

We also can share information and skills and create a neighborhood food or business co-op, a barter network, community energy projects, ride sharing, shared food gardens, etc. Time itself can be shared for fun purposes such as going to the movies, sharing meals, a BBQ or holiday gathering, block yard sale, music events, neighborhood talent shows, or birthday celebrations, just to name a few.

I hope this quick catalog opened your eyes about the possibilities of sharing. To delve more deeply into the matter, get a copy of *The Sharing Solution*.

As is unfortunately too often the case, existing public policies will need to be changed if we are to maximize the social benefits of sharing. The three excerpts below are taken from articles by Janelle Orsi which are published in http://www.shareable.net/, "a nonprofit online magazine that… covers the people and projects bringing a shareable world to life."

- The focus of the first is on **urban agriculture** and how cities should be doing everything in their power to facilitate localized food production.
- The second is about using **homes as sharing hubs.**
- The third is on how to make our **neighborhoods more sharing environments**.

All three are guaranteed to stretch your thinking with concrete recipes for creating community within the neighborhoods where we live.

Urban Agriculture[2]

CITIES SHOULD BE DOING EVERYTHING in their power to facilitate localized food production, and a key component of that is enabling urban agriculture and community gardening. Peak oil, the breakdown of our industrial food system, the high cost of sustainably produced food — these and other factors lend an urgent need to use every plot of available city land for food growing.

Sharing is a critical component of urban food growing. First, food growing is labor intensive and requires that community members collaborate and share skills and knowledge. Sharing is also critical to land access; the people who will suffer the most from a food crisis are the urban poor who have less access to resources and tillable land. Much of the land that could be cultivated is owned by middle- or upper-class urban residents, private vacant lot owners, and government entities. A key question for cities is: How can the city incentivize the sharing of land resources to ensure that everyone is nourished?

Here are a few suggestions for ways that cities can adopt policies to facilitate the growth of urban agriculture and community food growing spaces:

Mike Lieberman in his New York City fire escape garden. Photo credit: Urban Organic Gardener.

1. **OFFER PROPERTY TAX INCENTIVES FOR VACANT PRIVATE LOTS THAT ARE USED FOR URBAN FARMING:** Cities should offer private land owners a property tax discount during years when an otherwise empty lot is used for food growing. The Williamson Act in California[3] already provides property tax incentives to preserve land as agricultural in rural areas, and a similar policy should be applied in urban areas. Generally, land has higher income earning potential when it is built up with strip malls and housing developments. But it doesn't always make sense to assess a property based on this potential value when the land is actually being used for a more modest activity, like

agriculture. Even if a piece of land will eventually be developed, landowners should be rewarded for putting it to productive agricultural use in the meantime. Such a tax incentive could dramatically multiply the amount of available land for community gardening and urban farming.

2. **CONDUCT A LAND INVENTORY AND PRIORITIZE THE USE OF CITY-OWNED LAND FOR URBAN FARMING:** Cities should conduct inventories of land available for urban food growing, and prioritize the use of public lands for food growing. In 2009, Mayor Gavin Newsom of San Francisco, California, asked the city "to conduct an audit of unused land[4] — including empty lots, rooftops, windowsills, and median strips — that could be turned into community gardens or farms." (Yes, he even asked for a survey of windowsills!) In other cities, private groups have conducted such inventories. In Brooklyn, New York, an organization called 596 Acres has identified and created a map of 596 acres of vacant publicly owned land.[5] In Oakland, California, geographer Nathan McClintock published a report and interactive map of public lots available for urban farming.[6]

Conducting land inventories for urban food growing is not a new idea. During WWI and WWII, to relieve burdens on the railroads and reduce demands for materials used in canning and processing, the U.S. government encouraged the cultivation of yards and unused plots of land. Up to 44 percent of the country's vegetables were produced by individuals and families in small "victory gardens" during WWII. Community organizers were sent out to survey available land for urban and suburban food growing. The National War Commission used the slogan "put the slacker lands to work," implying that any tillable lands not being used for food production were, basically, slacking off.

3. **CREATE DEFINITIONS OF "COMMUNITY GARDENING" AND "PERSONAL GARDENING" IN THE ZONING CODE AND ALLOW SUCH ACTIVITIES IN EVERY CITY ZONE:** Many cities simply do not know where to fit community gardens into the zoning picture and, as a result, sometimes community gardens have had to jump through extensive legal hoops to get a permit for operating. Cities should recognize that individuals and communities that produce food for their own consumption or for charitable/educational purposes are providing a public good. Cities should create definitions of "community gardening" and "personal gardening" in the zoning code and specify that such uses are a permitted activity in every city zone. For example, community gardens

in Oakland are now permitted in nearly every zoning except certain industrial zones.

4. **CREATE A SIMPLE PERMITTING PROCEDURE AND ALLOW COMMERCIAL FOOD GROWING IN EVERY CITY ZONE:** The next logical step after enabling food growing throughout a city is to allow people to sell the veggies they grow. In some cities, urban farmers growing produce for sale have had to pay thousands of dollars to obtain conditional use permits. However, given the low margins of urban food production and the high social value of localized food systems, a city should require no more than a simple administrative use permit and charge no more than $100 or $200 in permit fees for someone wishing to engage in commercial food growing. For example, in Oakland, it is now possible to get a $40 home occupation permit to sell produce grown in one's backyard.[7]

5. **ALLOW PEOPLE TO PLANT VEGETABLES IN SIDEWALK/PARKING STRIPS:** It is often illegal for people to plant vegetables in the strip of land between a sidewalk and the street, or a permit is required to do any landscaping other than grass. Seattle, Washington, recently changed this law, allowing anyone to plant vegetables in the sidewalk strips in front of their homes.[8] A sidewalk strip could become a micro-community garden for neighbors to enjoy together.

6. **AND, FOR HEAVEN'S SAKE, ALLOW PEOPLE TO PLANT VEGETABLES IN FRONT YARDS:** Front yards are another ideal spot for community food growing, and cities should not fine and penalize people for planting front yard veggies. A Berkeley, California, resident was fined $4,500 for his front yard veggies,[9] and an Oak Park, Michigan, resident was charged with a misdemeanor for planting a front yard veggie garden.[10] An outright ban on front yard vegetables is bad policy. If a city is worried that front yard vegetable gardens could give the appearance of blight if neglected, the city should simply impose requirements that front yard vegetable gardens be reasonably well-kept and that a significant amount of dead plant material may not be left in the yard for too long.

7. **SUBSIDIZE WATER FOR URBAN FARMS AND COMMUNITY GARDENS:** Water is typically subsidized for rural farmers, and the same should apply to urban farms. Cities should at least offer water discounts to organizations that designate land for publicly accessible community food gardens. Cities could

also offer rebates and subsidies to urban farms that make use of recycled grey water or that capture and store rainwater that would otherwise drain to the sewer system. Such incentives could make water access more affordable to urban farms, while reducing the impact on the city's fresh water resources and stormwater run-off.

8. **CREATE REASONABLE POLICIES FOR URBAN LIVESTOCK RAISING:** The ability to raise one's own eggs, milk, and meat is critical to a more sustainable food system, since the majority of such products are currently produced by large-scale factory farms. Cities should give residents the right to raise their own livestock, within reasonable limits to ensure the well-being of animals and to ensure a low impact on surrounding neighbors. A group of students and faculty at the University of Oregon have produced a very helpful guide to Local Land Use Laws to Allow Urban Microlivestock which includes a sample ordinance for cities. Cities should also create guides and resources for urban livestock raisers, such as the helpful resource created by the Ontario Ministry of Agriculture.[11]

9. **EXEMPT CERTAIN CHICKEN COOPS AND GOAT SHELTERS FROM BUILDING AND ZONING PERMIT REQUIREMENTS:** It can be unclear at what point a small chicken coop or goat shelter has become a "structure" or "building" subject to regulation and permitting requirements from the local building and planning departments. Most people build their own simple coops and shelters and are sometimes surprised to learn that a local building department would have required a permit for such a building, or they may be surprised to learn that the planning department must approve the size and placement of the construction. Cities should define the size and placement of certain small chicken coops and goat shelters, such that residents can construct them without obtaining any permits.

10. **LIMIT THE RIGHT OF HOMEOWNERS' ASSOCIATIONS TO PREVENT HOME FOOD PRODUCTION:** Currently, most homeowners associations have the right to make rules about how homeowners use their properties. Some homeowners' associations have been known to tell residents that they cannot keep chickens and bees, or that they cannot grow edible plants in their front yards. Although it would be preferable to make state laws to curtail homeowners' associations' powers in this regard, each city can also pass laws that allow people to grow and raise their own food as a right.

11. **DE-PAVE PARADISE AND PUT A TAX ON PARKING LOTS:** The City of Philadelphia[12] imposes a tax on properties based on the size of impervious space on the property. This tax serves to prevent stormwater floods and incentivizes capture, storage, and percolation of rainwater. Because urban farms allow almost all rainwater to percolate, Philadelphia's tax system creates a huge incentive for property owners to replace paved spaces with urban gardens. Although most residences and commercial properties are required to provide some parking areas, such a tax would encourage property owners to at least remove any unnecessary pavement and replace it with gardens.

HOMES AS SHARING HUBS[13]

OUR HOMES ARE THE MOST OBVIOUS HUBS for the sharing and collaborative consumption movements. After all, we live in them, and so does most of our stuff. Sharing our car, sharing our vacuum cleaner, borrowing and lending household goods, offering our homes as a temporary place for others to stay — these are all activities that make a great deal of sense — from economic, efficiency, and ecological standpoints. Generally, there are almost no legal barriers to these sharing activities, so long as they are happening on a casual, occasional, and uncompensated basis.

Community organizations partner to construct an urban vegetable garden in Ft. Myers, Florida.
Photo credit: Gabriel Kamener. Used under Creative Commons license.

But what if we want to get more organized about our sharing, and maybe even share the costs of things like owning a car and certain household goods? Perhaps we want to earn a profit. As the folks at Collaborative Consumption have pointed out, there is HUGE potential to make money by sharing what is in our home.

Unfortunately, legal barriers begin to kick in when we turn our household sharing activities into money-makers. We have already discussed these barriers in our article on Collaborative Consumption's Legal Paradox.[14] To sum up the barrier: In most residentially zoned areas of a city, residents are very limited in the types of businesses they can engage in at home. Home offices tend to be okay, as do some tutoring activities; but any businesses that involve more than a few visiting customers, or that involve keeping an inventory, tend to be disallowed.

Here are a few suggestions for ways that a city can encourage people to share what they have in their homes. We encourage readers to post additional suggestions in the comments area:

12. **ALLOW COMMUNITY GATHERING ACTIVITIES IN HOMES:** Cities should consider expanding the list of allowable community gathering activities in residential areas. In most cities, zoning barriers could arise if someone wanted to use their home as a community gathering space — for example, to host cooking, garden, or yoga classes; to hold house concerts; to host regular food swaps or underground restaurants;[15] or to offer the yard as a community garden. While we are all allowed to hold a reasonable number of gatherings in our home, cities do tend to object when such gatherings become regular or involve money making. In many residential zones in Oakland, California, for example, residents would need an expensive conditional use permit in order to engage in activities defined as Community Assembly, Recreational Assembly, and Community Education activities.[16]

13. **ALLOW PEOPLE TO SELL PRODUCE GROWN IN BACKYARDS:** Our food system probably cannot get any more local than a neighborhood-based vegetable delivery service. Sophie Hahn of Berkeley, California, began selling weekly vegetable boxes to a few of her neighbors, only to learn that the city zoning prohibited such activities.[17] Cities should follow in Oakland's footsteps and allow people to sell produce they grow in their backyards.

14. **EXPAND ALLOWABLE GARAGE AND YARD SALE ACTIVITIES:** Many cities put a cap on the number of yard sales that a property can host each year; for example, in Dallas, Texas, the limit is two per year. Other cities impose limitations that prevent a person from turning their garage sale into a regular retail location.[18] For example, a city might specify that you can only sell your own belongings, and not things you bought for the sole purpose of reselling. Maybe it's time to open up the way we think about yard sales and consider that yard sales could be an important site for increasingly localized econo-

mies, within limits, of course. One suggestion would be to allow people to sell their home-grown vegetables in a yard sale, and to allow sales of baked goods, in those states where cottage food production is legal.[19]

15. **EXEMPT RESIDENTIAL CHILDCARE COOPERATIVES FROM PERMITTING REQUIRE-MENTS:** When parents make cooperative arrangements to provide care for their own and others' children, they are often exempt from state childcare licensing requirements. For example, in California, a cooperative home childcare arrangement involving 12 or fewer children is exempt from state licensure, if it meets the statute's requirements.[20] Cities can likewise encourage such cooperative arrangements by offering permit exemptions or lowering the permitting barriers for such cooperative arrangements.

16. **ALLOW PERSONAL VEHICLE SHARING IN HOME DRIVEWAYS AND GARAGES:** Getaround and Relay Rides[21] are two San Francisco-based services offering car owners the opportunity to share their vehicles through a car-sharing program. Yet, these services could potentially face a barrier, which is that cities may not allow personal residences to essentially be used as car-rental hubs. To reduce traffic and parking problems, cities should clarify that each residential property is allowed to regularly rent at least one car, if not an unlimited number of cars from their property. Furthermore, cities should allow people to park such vehicles anywhere in the driveway, and not just in the legally designated spots on the property map.[22]

17. **ALLOW A LIMITED NUMBER OF SHORT-TERM STAYS IN PEOPLE'S HOMES:** Currently, many cities have a blanket prohibition on charging guests for short-term stays (usually defined as shorter than two weeks or a month). To charge a guest for such a stay would mean the host is operating a hotel, which is not legal to do without a permit. This is a problem that peer-to-peer rental service AirBNB is facing,[23] as some cities are calling attention to the unpermitted home stays. Ideally cities would allow this to happen, at least on a limited scale, since such activities not only reduce the cost of living for local residents, but also make it more affordable for travelers to stay in the city.

SHAREABLE NEIGHBORHOODS[24]

A CITY'S SAFETY AND ECONOMIC STABILITY can be greatly enhanced if a spirit of community and sharing is fostered in every neighborhood.

Here are a handful of suggestions for ways that city policies and programs could foster community-building in neighborhoods:

1. **CREATE A STAFF POSITION FOCUSED ON NEIGHBORHOOD COMMUNITY ACTIVITIES:** Each city should hire at least one staff person dedicated to facilitating community-building activities in neighborhoods. This staff person would communicate regularly with neighborhood groups and associations, facilitate permitting and offer supplies for block parties, help organize emergency preparedness meetings, and give neighborhoods other support and resources. For example, in the city of Albany, California, there is a Community Services Manager that facilitates a handful of community-building activities such as neighborhood veggie swaps and block movie nights, for which the city lends neighborhoods a giant screen and projector.

The Collaborative Home as drawn by Collaborative Consumption. Used under Creative Commons license

2. **FACILITATE SHARING AND EMERGENCY PREPAREDNESS SIMULTANEOUSLY:** In many respects, sharing and building community are the most important things we can be doing to prepare for emergencies. The City of Berkeley has a great tactic for getting neighborhoods organized: Give them free stuff to share. The city awards caches of emergency supplies[25] to neighborhood groups that have demonstrated that they have gotten organized and done some emergency preparedness planning and training.

3. **DESIGN NEIGHBORHOODS FOR SHARING:** The layout and physical features of a neighborhood can greatly influence the ways that neighbors interact with each other.[26] For example, social interaction is enhanced in neighborhoods with walkable spaces, plazas, parks, and narrower streets. Cities can enhance neighborhoods[27] with initiatives to redesign streets, sidewalks, and intersections, and by imposing shareable design requirements on new planned communities.

4. **OFFER NEIGHBORHOOD SHARING SHEDS AND PODS:** In the same way that the City of Berkeley has offered special containers to neighborhoods for storing emergency supplies, a city could offer special containers or sheds where neighbors could store other shared items, such as the neighborhood lawn mower, vacuum cleaner, badminton set, and so on. It would be like having a mini tool library in every neighborhood. Cities could, for example, supply a container that is 6x6x6 feet (something similar to a POD),[28] and designate a street parking spot for that container. The neighborhood group could complete an application with the city that demonstrates that it is organized and has a plan for managing the shared stuff.

5. **ADOPT A NEIGHBORHOOD SOCIAL NETWORK PLATFORM:** Recently, companies like NextDoor, rBlock, and OhSoWe[29] have developed social network platforms for neighbors, and California cities like Redwood City and Palo Alto have begun to adopt these platforms on a citywide basis or actively encourage neighborhoods to use them as a community-building tool. With such platforms, users get daily updates from their neighbors with information like: "Free plums from my tree!" "Has anyone seen my orange cat today?" "Can someone lend me a bicycle pump?" These platforms could grease the wheels of sharing in a neighborhood, and also give cities a more effective platform for communicating with residents.

6. **HELP NEIGHBORS REMOVE FENCES:** At least one city that we know of, Elgin, Illinois, has created an incentive program to help people remove chain link fences from their front yards.[30] Removing fences from front or back yards helps to increase everyone's access to open green spaces and facilitates connection between neighbors.

Gaya Erlandson, PhD, is a psychologist, writer, teacher, social architect, and community consultant. Certified in Imago Relationship Therapy, she loves to coach couples, facilitate groups, and offer trainings related to conscious relationships and living in community. Gaya lives in Lotus Lodge — a unique community of 9 people near Asheville, NC, which is situated on 2.5 acres of land with a pond, stream, and organic gardens. Lotus Lodge was the subject of a recent news "Golden Girls" segment on "CBS Early Morning" — an experience which in part has inspired the project she is now working on, a how-to book on creating and maintaining shared households as well as one on aging in place. Contact her via gerlandson.phd@gmail.com, LotusLodge.com or (828) 581-9036 and read her article at www.secondjourney.org/itin/12_Win/3Sum/CBS.htm.

Janelle Orsi, founder and director of the Sustainable Economies Law Center, is an attorney and mediator focused on helping individuals and organizations share resources and create more sustainable communities. She works with social enterprises, nonprofits, cooperatives, community gardens, cohousing communities, ecovillages, and others doing innovative work to change the world. In 2010, Janelle was profiled by the ABA as a Legal Rebel, an attorney who is "remaking the legal profession through the power of innovation." In 2012, Janelle was one of 100 people listed on The (En)Rich List, which recognizes individuals "whose contributions enrich paths to sustainable futures." Her most recent book, *Practicing Law in the Sharing Economy*, was published in 2012.

Notes

[1] Orsi, Janelle and Emily Doskow. *The Sharing Solution: How to Save Money, Simplify Your Life and Build Community*. Berkeley, CA: Nolo Press, 2009.

[2] Go to http://www.shareable.net/blog/policies-for-a-shareable-city-11-urban-agriculture to post comments to this article on Urban Agriculture and add to the collection of policy suggestions. To view a 9-minute YouTube cartoon on urban agriculture and city policies produced by the Sustainable Economies Law Center entitled "Citylicious," go to http://www.youtube.com/watch?v=fYUr0GKWWX8.

[3] http://www.conservation.ca.gov/dlrp/lca/Pages/Index.aspx

⁴ http://www.motherjones.com/blue-marble/2009/07/san-franciscos-latest-eco-innovation-city-effort-grow-produce-almost-everywhere

⁵ http://www.596acres.org/

⁶ http://www.urbanfood.org/

⁷ http://www.sfgate.com/homeandgarden/article/Oakland-allows-urban-farmers-to-sell-produce-2328189.php

⁸ http://www.cityfarmer.info/2010/02/02/vegetable-gardens-crop-up-in-seattle-parking-strips/

⁹ http://sf.streetsblog.org/2009/06/04/food-bad-lawns-good-berkeley-bureaucrats-target-transition-activist/

¹⁰ http://www.huffingtonpost.com/2011/07/08/julie-bass-jail-vegetable-garden_n_893436.html

¹¹ http://www.omafra.gov.on.ca/english/livestock/urbanagricul.html

¹² http://www.mmwr.com/home/publications/default.aspx?d=2793

¹³ "How else might a city further enable the use of our homes as sharing hubs? Please post your thoughts at the link below and help us build this collection of policy proposals. Thank you!" — Janelle Orsi
Go to http://www.shareable.net/blog/policies-for-a-shareable-city-6-homes-as-sharing-hubs to post comments to this article on Homes as Shareable Hubs.

¹⁴ http://www.shareable.net/blog/airbnb-uncovers-collaborative-consumption-legal-paradox

¹⁵ http://shareable.net/blog/the-shareable-food-movement-meets-the-law

¹⁶ http://library.municode.com/HTML/16490/level3/TIT17PL_CH17.10USCL_PT2CIACTY.html

¹⁷ http://www.berkeleyside.com/2011/04/15/urban-homesteader-challenges-city-on-sale-of-edibles/

¹⁸ http://www.eastbayexpress.com/ebx/where-the-garage-sale-never-ends/Content?oid=1369823

¹⁹ http://www.cottagefood.org/

²⁰ http://daycare.com/california/state5.html

²¹ http://www.getaround.com/ and http://www.relayrides.com/

[22] http://www.shareable.net/blog/policies-shareable-city- percent25231-carsharing-and-parking-sharing23

[23] http://www.shareable.net/blog/airbnb-uncovers-collaborative-consumption-legal-paradox

[24] "How else might a city encourage sharing in neighborhoods? Please post your thoughts below and help us build this collection of policy proposals. Thank you! !" — Janelle Orsi
Go to http://www.shareable.net/blog/policies-for-a-shareable-city-7-shareable-neighbor

[25] http://www.ci.berkeley.ca.us/uploadedFiles/Fire/Level_3_-_General/2011 Community Emergency Supply Program Application.pdf

[26] http://shareable.net/blog/how-to-design-a-neighborhood-for-happiness

[27] http://shareable.net/blog/the-suburbs-aint-what-they-used-to-be

[28] http://www.pods.com/Storage/Storage-Containers-101.aspx

[29] http://www.nextdoor.com/; http://www.rblock.com/; and http://www.oh-sowe.com/

[30] http://www.cityofelgin.org/index.aspx?NID=322

CONTINUING CARE OPTIONS: THE NEXT GENERATION OF CARE

by Carol A. Barbour

IT'S NOT ALL ABOUT GENES. Most people can vastly improve their chances of a healthy old age by making better lifestyle choices throughout their lives. As much as 70 percent of physical decline past the age of 65 is related to modifiable factors. Smoking, poor nutrition, lack of physical activity, and failure to access preventative health services are just a few examples of poor health choices people make that contribute to the prevalence of chronic diseases such as heart disease and diabetes. Chronic diseases are the leading cause of death and disability in the U.S.[1] According to the World Health Organization, 80 percent of heart disease and 40 percent of cancers could be prevented with a healthy diet and lifestyle. Social interaction is another element of a healthy lifestyle, and one that is often overlooked. Scientific research conducted by the National Institutes of Health demonstrates that older adults are happier and healthier if they participate in groups that seem meaningful to them.

WHAT IS LONG-TERM CARE?

Long-term care is a range of services and support you may need to meet your health or personal needs over a long period of time. Most long-term care is not medical care, but rather assistance with "activities of daily living" such as bathing, dressing and using the toilet.[2]

FOR INDIVIDUALS WANTING TO REMAIN in their own homes as an alternative to institutional long-term care, planning for this likelihood is prudent. Even when blessed with good genes, a strong circle of family and friends, and a lifetime of good healthy choices, one day we are still likely to need long-term care services. Indeed, 70 percent of individuals over the age of 65 will require at least some type of long-term care services during their lifetime, and over 40 percent will need care in a nursing home for some period of time. On average, someone age 65 today will need these services for 3 years (women: 3.7 years; men: 2.2 years); 20 percent will need care for more than 5 years.[3]

A comprehensive long-term care plan for aging in community should include strategies to both access and pay for home health care and supportive services, should the need arise. This type of planning for the future is especially important for middle-income Americans. People with significant assets can consider self-insuring for their long-term care needs, while low-income Americans may qualify for health and supportive services through Medicaid. It's the people in the middle of the income spectrum who are likely to have assets to protect, but not necessarily the financial resources to cover the costs of care. Long-term care services can add up quickly and are not usually covered by Medicare. The average costs for a home health aide or homemaker services is $20 an hour, and for a registered nurse, it can be two or three times that amount. Just 4 hours a day from a home health aide adds up to nearly $30,000 a year; and a round-the-clock home health aide would cost nearly $175,000 a year — almost twice the cost of the average nursing home!

Who pays for long-term care?

Many people mistakenly believe that Medicare will pay for long-term care services. However, Medicare only pays for long-term care services if skilled services or rehabilitative services for a short period of time are required. Most long-term care expenses are covered out of pocket, by long-term care insurance policies or other private payment options such as a reverse mortgage, and by Medicaid for those who qualify as low-income or when other financial resources are exhausted.[4]

Regardless of income level, it is important to think about where to turn for long-term care services should they be needed. For some types of assistance, such as transportation to the doctor or store, balancing the check book, and doing household chores, family, friends, and neighbors (informal caregivers) may be willing and able to assist — and you may be comfortable in asking or accepting their help. Other tasks, such as assistance in the shower, toileting, or with medications may be beyond their, or your, comfort level.

Another factor is time. Some family and friends may be willing to help out occasionally or for a short period of time, but may not be able to commit to helping out over a longer duration.

Finally, whether informal caregivers are willingly or reluctantly assisting with care, over a long period of time the costs to their own well-being can be enormous. For example, according to recent studies.[5]

- 47 percent of caregivers use up all or most of their own savings in providing care;
- 23 percent who care for a loved one for more than 5 years report their own health as being fair or poor;
- the stress of caring for persons with dementia impacts the caregiver's immune system for up to 3 years after the caregiving ends;
- 40–70 percent of caregivers have clinically significant symptoms of depression.[6]

While informal caregivers can be instrumental members of a long-term care team, relying on their sole support as a long-term care strategy has a variety of potential pitfalls for all involved. In recent years, new models have begun to emerge to help elders and their families find and pay for long-term care services in their own home. One of these new models, "Continuing Care at Home" also known as "Continuing Care Retirement Communities (CCRCs) Without Walls" is an option designed to help older adults plan for a future where they are able to stay in their own homes, even as their need for levels of care increases.

EVOLUTION OF THE CONTINUING CARE CONCEPT

CONTINUING CARE AT HOME (CCAH) grew out of the Continuing Care Retirement Community (CCRC) model which was brought to the United States over 100 years ago from Europe. Early CCRCs were charitable organizations affiliated with religious or fraternal organizations to care and shelter their aged or disabled members and other dependents. Some, such as Masonic Homes and Methodist Homes for the Aged, still carry on this mission.

Today, Continuing Care Retirement Communities are both nonprofit and for-profit organizations that provide housing, supportive services, and healthcare options usually spread out on a single campus. The size of the campus, number of residents, and types of housing, amenities, and services range widely between communities. Most CCRCs offer a range of housing and care options, from the most independent to the most intensive of care (referred to frequently as the continuum of care).

For the residents needing the least amount of care, there are independent living units, ranging from small cottages and apartments to luxurious condominiums and houses. Basic services most often included at this level of care include transportation, meals, laundry, housekeeping, security, maintenance, and access to community amenities (pool, golf course, fitness center, etc.). Other services, such as occasional home healthcare assistance, are available for an additional fee. Usually the residents living in independent housing are healthy and able to live at home with minimal assistance.

Assisted living facilities are the next step in the continuum of care and are designed for residents needing an increased amount of help with activities of daily living such as getting dressed, bathing, medication supervision, and personal assistance. Depending on the financial arrangement made in entering the CCRC, this level of care may cost a higher monthly fee.

Skilled nursing facilities, such as a nursing home or rehabilitation center, are reserved for residents needing a high level of skilled nursing and/ or around-the-clock care. This can be temporary, as in the case of recovering from a broken hip, or long term, such as residents with advanced Alzheimer's or Lou Gehrig's disease. Again, the higher the level of care in some agreements may result in a higher monthly fee.

The costs to live in a CCRC range according to the contract agreement. The most comprehensive (and the most expensive) is the *extensive agreement* also known as a *life care agreement*, which covers all housing, resident services, amenities, and long-term care services for the life of the resident. A *modified agreement* differs in that it offers only a limited number of long-term care service days — beyond that the resident has to pay out of pocket if Medicare does not cover the costs. The third is called a *fee-for-service agreement*, which differs in that residents are assured access to health and long-term care services but must pay the prevailing rates. This is usually the least expensive of the three types of contracts, but it puts the resident at risk if they can no longer afford to pay for health or long-term care services out of pocket to continue living there.

Of all the senior housing options, CCRCs are among the most expensive and least subsidized by government (Medicare or Medicaid) or long-term care insurance. Most of the 1,900 CCRCs across the nation charge a substantial entry fee in addition to monthly payments. As the U.S. General Accountability Office report below illustrates, the costs vary widely by the type of aforementioned contract, as well as other factors such as the geographic region of the country and the level of services and amenities.

While the costs to live in CCRCs are substantial, residents benefit in a number of ways. The accessibility of the continuum of care, as well as care coordination on site, assures that residents can easily access the level of care they need, when they need it. This type of supportive health environment lessens trips to the emergency room and allows those who need acute care to often get it on the campus where they live, making health care less disruptive and difficult. In addition to providing medical support,

TABLE 1: 2009 CCRCs ENTRANCE AND MONTHLY FEES BY CONTRACT TYPE

	Extensive (Life Care)	Modified	Fee For Service	Rental
Entry Fee	$160,000 – 600,000	$80,000 – 750,000	$100,000 - 500,000	$1,800 – 30,000
Independent Living Monthly Fee	$2,500 - 5,400	$1,500 - 2,500	$1,300 - 4,300	$900 - 2,700
Assisted Living Monthly Fee	$2,500 - 5,400	$1,500 - 2,500 [a]	$3,700 - 5,800	$4,700 - 6,500
Nursing Care Monthly Fee	$2,500 - 5,400	$1,500 - 2,500 [a]	$8,100 – 10,000 [b]	$8,100 - 10,700 [b]

Fee ranges reflect different size living units among the CCRCs that the GAO visited, with smaller units being less expensive. The entrance and monthly fees above were for single occupancy. Additional fees may apply for double occupancy, additional meal service, or other amenities.

[a] Agreement provides 60 days of assisted living or skilled nursing care, after which the prevailing rate for either assisted living or skilled nursing services, less a 10 percent discount, is charged.

[b] One CCRC noted that their facility would bill Medicare Part A, Medicare Advantage plans, or any other available insurance for any qualified skilled nursing stays before billing the resident for nursing care, when available.

The table, whose source is a GAO analysis of information obtained from eight selected CCRCs (California, Florida, Illinois, Ohio, New York, Pennsylvania, Texas, and Wisconsin) appears in United States Government Accountability Office (GAO), *Older Americans: Continuing care retirement communities can provide benefits, but not without some risk*. GAO-10-611, June 2010, p. 7. http://www.gao.gov/assets/310/305752.pdf.

CCRCs provide a socially supportive environment. Most communities have a strong emphasis on social interaction and community involvement that greatly reduces social isolation, boredom, and inactivity. CCRCs also provide residents with a sense of security and assurance that, no matter what happens, they will be cared for in a community where they are known and know others.

Two of the major challenges to the CCRC model are that a high percentage of Americans are unable to afford the fee structure and/or they want to remain in their own homes. As noted by Stephen J. Maag, JD, Director of Residential Communities at LeadingAge, "The real strength of a CCRC is the ability to provide an active and engaging lifestyle in a way which enhances the health and well-being of the resident. However the nature of a CCRC has limited this benefit to only those who choose to move onto a CCRC campus. Many seniors prefer to stay at home, some can't afford either or both the entrance or the monthly fee for a variety of reasons."[7]

CCRCs "WITHOUT WALLS" OR CONTINUING CARE AT HOME: THE NEXT GENERATION OF CONTINUING CARE OPTIONS

IN THE 1980s, a forward-thinking group of Friends (Quakers) in the Philadelphia area became concerned that the financial and healthcare security benefits provided by a CCRC were out of reach for most moderate or low income seniors. Neither were there alternatives that provided these guarantees for the vast majority of seniors who desired to age in their own homes and community. Motivated with a mission, the group successfully secured over $2M in grant funding to develop an alternative known as a "CCRC Without Walls" or "Continuing Care at Home" (CCAH). Primary funders for this innovative venture included The Commonwealth Fund, Robert Wood Johnson Foundation, and The Pew Charitable Trusts.

Throughout the 1980s the group conducted market research and worked with actuaries to develop a fee structure to support a continuing care program designed to help people age in community rather than move to a campus-based setting. The original fee structure mirrored the campus-based CCRC and included an up-front entrance fee and ongoing monthly fee. Without all the expenses related to bricks and mortar, entrance fees for the CCAH models are significantly lower, ranging from $10,000 to $44,000, with monthly fees ranging from $400 to $1400.

The first CCAH plan in the nation was launched by Friends Life Care and became operational on July 1, 1990. Today, Friends Life Care serves over 2,300 individuals in southeastern Pennsylvania, New Jersey, and Delaware.

The CCAH plan is designed to work much like the campus-based CCRC. Enrollees (called members) in the plan are screened as part of the admission process to ensure that they are in relatively good health and capable of living independently (a similar evaluation is conducted for prospective CCRC residents). Services included in the plan are designed to help members move along the continuum should their health change. As previously noted, in a CCRC the continuum consists of independent living units, an assisted living facility, and a nursing home, all on one campus.

For CCAH, the continuum of services is designed to support the members' independence in their own home and community. The continuum generally includes:

- **CARE COORDINATION** — A professional who assesses the member's potential health risks and keeps track of medical conditions, prescriptions, advance directives, and any other important information needed in an emergency. If the member's health changes, the care coordinator will manage and oversee all the **home care and support** services required, supervising the caregivers and monitoring member satisfaction.
- **PERIODIC HOME SAFETY REVIEW** — Taking any limitations the member may have into account, the care coordinator comes to the home periodically to help identify and correct safety issues and to recommend adaptive equipment.
- **EMERGENCY RESPONSE SYSTEM** — Members receiving care and members at risk are eligible to receive a medical alarm. An emergency response system allows the member to reach emergency medical services around the clock with the touch of a button.
- **HOME CARE SERVICES** — Caregivers provided to assist members with the activities of daily living (ADLs), such as bathing, dressing, eating, moving about, and using the bathroom are an essential component of the CCAH plan. Caregivers also help with meal preparation and light housekeeping and provide socialization, occasional transportation, and companionship for the member.
- **NUTRITIONAL SUPPORT** — Grocery shopping, food preparation, or home delivered meals in accordance with any dietary restric-

tions are provided for those members who are unable to meet nutritional needs on their own.

- **Adult day care** — If needed, attendance at an adult day care center can be arranged in order to help prevent or delay assisted living or nursing home placement.
- **Health & wellness programs** — Programs include opportunities to recognize, learn about, and improve behaviors that can affect long-term health and resilience.
- **Access to assisted living facilities and nursing homes** — CCAH programs make every effort to help members stay at home for as long as safely possible; however, there are occasions when members require the specialized care of a nursing home or an assisted living facility.
- **Referral service** — In addition to health-related services, CCAH plans maintain a list of reliable, prescreened providers who can be hired by members to assist with home maintenance, housekeeping, snow removal, lawn services, legal services, and financial planning.

CCAH is sometimes compared to long-term care insurance, another form of financial protection for individuals who understand the importance of planning ahead for long-term care. Unlike long-term care insurance, CCAH is "high touch." Care coordinators develop a relationship with the members from day one, regardless of their age. CCAH programs do far more than pay for the care needed by the membership; they assess the members' need for care, make all the arrangements, and oversee the implementation of the care plan. Care coordinators identify health risks early on and assist with preventive measures. In addition, resources are provided to help members develop and maintain healthy lifestyles. This includes opportunities for social engagement both in person and as part of exclusive online communities.

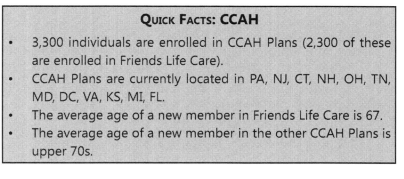

Quick Facts: CCAH
- 3,300 individuals are enrolled in CCAH Plans (2,300 of these are enrolled in Friends Life Care).
- CCAH Plans are currently located in PA, NJ, CT, NH, OH, TN, MD, DC, VA, KS, MI, FL.
- The average age of a new member in Friends Life Care is 67.
- The average age of a new member in the other CCAH Plans is upper 70s.

CHANGING WITH THE TIMES

AFTER MORE THAN A DECADE of steady, robust enrollment in its CCAH Plan, Friends Life Care experienced a sharp decline in the rate of new membership in the early 2000s. This sent them back to the drawing board to better understand the decline and to figure out how to restore the appeal of the program. Lessons learned reflected a new set of demands by the boomer population. First, the relatively large, up-front entrance fee was an obstacle to enrollment. Second, consumers wanted to design a plan for financial protection that met their personal budgets. Third, health and wellness programs were considered essential to this population.

In response, Friends Life Care adjusted the business model to significantly reduce the need for an up-front entrance fee and to allow for consumer choice regarding plan coverage. The plan continues to offer all the services included in the original plan, but shares the cost of the services with the member based on a predetermined daily and lifetime limit selected by the member at the time of enrollment. The result is significantly lower annual fees (averaging approximately $3000 per year per member). Rather than entrance fees in the tens of thousands of dollars, the entrance fee is equivalent to the first year's annual fee and can be paid over time.

Friends Life Care also introduced its VigR (Vitality, Independence, Growth, and Resilience) program in response to consumer demand. This proactive, research-based program helps participants understand and improve these four essential elements that maximize overall health. Open to all Friends Life Care members, the VigR program includes an ever-evolving array of interactive opportunities for improving body and mind. VigR Enrichment Workshops provide an ever-changing selection of expert-led mini courses on diverse health- and lifestyle-related topics. VigR Benchmarks gives residents an assessment tool for examining current habits and quality of life and for tracking positive change. VigR eMeetinghouse offers residents a Web-based health-information resource and online social community.

There has been a good deal of interest in the CCAH business model in recent years. In addition to Friends Life Care, about a dozen other programs have been implemented by campus-based CCRCs across the nation. Currently, these programs are all based on the entrance fee model originally established over 20 years ago by Friends Life Care. Many of these newer entry fee programs struggle with enrollment and have yet to achieve critical mass.

Baby Boomers Change the Landscape

Boomers started turning 65 beginning January 1, 2011 at the rate of 10,000 per day; this trend will continue for the next 19 years. Life expectancy at age 65 is at an all-time high of 18.5 years; the age 60+ population is projected to grow by 70 percent between 2005 and 2025.[9]

The Urban Land Institute's senior fellow for housing, John McIlwain, author of *Housing in America: The Baby Boomers Turn 65*,[10] believes that personal preferences and limited resources will keep older adults away from institutional settings, including CCRCs, in the coming decades. He predicts that future generations are more likely to age in place. AARP has long reported results of surveys that indicate that as many as 90 percent of seniors prefer to remain in their own communities.[11]

While there are many views and predictions about the landscape in the future for the latter part of life, there is generally consensus that baby boomers are changing the face of retirement. Creative alternatives that help people age in community while addressing the physical and health challenges that can accompany the aging process will continue to evolve as the boomers continue their journey and break new ground.

Carol A. Barbour serves as president of Friends Life Care System and its subsidiary corporations: Friends Life Care (operating in Pennsylvania, New Jersey, and Delaware); Life Care at Home Partners, the consulting division of Friends Life Care; and Intervention Associates, a care management company. In 1986, Carol joined the team that pioneered the continuing care at home business model. She is a frequent speaker at national professional associations. Contact her at cbarbour@friendslifecare.org or 215-628-8964.

Notes

[1] Gerontological Society of America, "The State of Aging in America," 2007.

[2] U.S. Department of Health and Human Services, National Clearinghouse for Long-Term Care Information.

[3] *Ibid.*

[4] *Ibid.*

[5]   MetLife study based on 2008 National Health & Retirement Study; reported in "ElderLaw Answers," June 14, 2011.

[6]   Studies cited by National Family Caregiver Association.

[7]   Steve Maag, Director Residential Communities. "CCRCs without walls: Care models of the future." *LeadingAge* online newsletter, February 2012.

[8]   Carol Barbour, Dianna Rienstra, and Robert Yee. "Continuing Care at Home: The Emerging Regulatory Environment," presented at the LeadingAge Annual Conference and Exposition, October 2012.

[9]   U.S. Census Bureau.

[10]   John McIlwain. *Housing in America: The Baby Boomers Turn 65.* Washington, DC: Urban Land Institute, 2012.

[11]   Geralyn Magan, "Where will future seniors live? Not in retirement communities." *LeadingAge* online newsletter, November 29, 2012.

Sleepless

A Poem by Dolly Brittan

Unable to sleep
I look out my window
Surprised
Expecting total darkness
I see optimistic lights
glittering here and there
I watch a thieving cloud
Pocket the silver coin moon
Then just as quickly
Regretting its larceny
Surrenders
Its stolen treasure

©2012 by Dolly Brittan

Dolly Brittan is a resident of Burbank Senior Artists Colony and a participant in its Poetry Café, a creative writing group which is facilitated by Hannah Menkin.

I *have belonged to a "village"*

— that new *aging in community* concept — in downtown Boston for over 10 years. Beacon Hill Village is a member-driven organization for local residents 50 and older, which provides programs and services so that members can lead active, vibrant, and healthy lives while living in their own homes and neighborhoods as they age. For many, that will be for as long as they live. For others less fortunate, the choice to stay at home may become more complex, sometimes impossible. But the fact remains that most of us want to be autonomous, linked to our own neighborhoods and able to pursue our own lifestyle as we age.

The elements that enable us to thrive — and I believe most village members feel they do — vary greatly from person to person and from month to month.

Life at Beacon Hill Village

by Susan McWhinney-Morse

I rarely avail myself of all the opportunities and services that our village has to offer. I am healthy, happily married to an active retired lawyer, and surrounded by wonderful family. Life is good. Yet I depend on our village in a very deep sense. And, I really love our village.

I love our village because it espouses community engagement, healthy lifestyles, and intellectual stimulation; it is run by and for our members; but it mandates nothing, and it has no requirements or restrictions other than paying an annual fee.

I love our village because it is reflective of the neighborhood in which I live. With nearly 400 members, it is a magnetic combination of the vigorous and the frail, the new old and the very old, the rich and the urban poor. (Contrary to myth, Beacon Hill and Back Bay, the neighborhoods our village covers, is not just an enclave for the wealthy. Twenty percent of our population over age 65 live near or at the poverty line.) We are a diverse group representing a variety of backgrounds and interests. We meet in both structured meetings and casual settings, in large groups as well as small, informal gatherings. Some members attend stretch classes, walking groups, and tai chi, while others meet informally for a cocktail or potluck. At any gathering, one finds canes and walkers, running shoes, and high heels. Some members are actively involved in the life of the village; others rarely or never appear at any gathering nor request any support or services. They are just happy to know that the village exists and is there if and when they should need it.

SEARCHING FOR A BETTER WAY

The prospect of aging, particularly in our culture rampant with ageism, is disconcerting, even frightening to many people. These feelings were the impetus for a small group of us to gather in 1999. Each of us had witnessed firsthand the distress our relatives experienced as they aged: a mother in a retirement community in Florida who felt lonely and abandoned; a parent in a nursing home, marginalized and overdrugged; an uncle with very limited means and no immediate family to help out. We found these prevalent scenarios shocking and unacceptable — and we were determined to find another way.

It did not take us long to discover that the conventional wisdom about aging well was deeply flawed and limited. The first piece of advice we all received was to MOVE: to a warmer climate, to continuing care retirement communities, to senior housing near our children. Why, we asked, should we have to pull up our roots from a community we love just to be "safe"? Why did we need to lose our history, our friends, our identity? Why did we have to compromise our lifestyles before it became absolutely necessary, just to fit into a pre-designed community? In my opinion, senior congregate housing is "warehousing the elderly." Why would we ask our children whose lives were already hectic with jobs and children to take us on, too? And what about financial considerations? Moving is an option available only to a small group of us who could afford it. Although we conceded that warmer climates and segregated communities were good choices for some people, they were not a viable or attractive option for us.

Sadly, the only other option for most people was to just stay put, to downsize, perhaps cut way back on expenses if necessary, and hope for the best. For those on very limited budgets there are community-based, government-sponsored programs, but that leaves the majority of us on our own. Alone. A pretty grim option for anyone.

Our small group of 11 neighbors spent two years studying all aspects of aging, dreaming of solutions. Though discouraged at moments, in the end we prevailed.

In the winter of 2002 our group came up with a plan for aging well that was so grounded in common sense, so available to all older people, and so responsive to our needs and wants, that we could scarcely believe that it did not already exist. It is a 21st-century update of the way things, in an ideal world, are supposed to be but with an important fail safe component: We form *partnerships* with health-care professionals and community organizations that help us advance our mission to remain at home and stay healthy and connected to our community.

In doing so, we totally rejected the hierarchical system of the past, which was designed to take care of us, make choices for us and keep us safe. That system is one that all too often patronizes and infantilizes us. It is also a system that is unaffordable for so many older people. The concept of partnership brought about a paradigm shift in the way we age. It has instant appeal. And most remarkable of all, it is affordable. As of this writing, there are 96 open villages stretched across 38 states, 4 villages internationally and over 100 villages in development. We are now all linked together by a Web-based network called the Village to Village Network — vtvnetwork.org/.

I love going to my weekly political discussion group. It is full of informed, articulate people with strong opinions. I love seeing how organs are made, how bronze is cast, how a totally green office building in Cambridge was constructed. I will be forever indebted to the caterer who served dinner to my family the day I came home from the hospital with a new knee. All this courtesy of Beacon Hill Village.

But what is most important to me is I have entered an older age still in control of my life, still a contributing member of my community, still a known member of my neighborhood. There are moments when all of us, as we age, search for new meaning in life. As children we learn; as adults we earn. What is it we do with this gift we have received — the gift of longevity? My friends and I, and all the baby boomers who are following us, must at some point confront this question. I believe that being a member of the village has left me free to explore my tomorrow in a healthy and informed way with little anxiety or worry about my future. I know where to find support and information and friendship when and if I need it. That is what villages are all about. I also know that it is up to me to forge a healthy and happy future. Beacon Hill Village is here to help me to accomplish this goal.

After a career in marketing and fundraising, **Susan McWhinney-Morse** was haunted when her mother-in law, after being placed in a nursing home, said, "Here, I'm just an old woman. I've lost my identity." In 2002, at age 69, McWhinney-Morse and a group of Boston residents created Beacon Hill Village to give people over 50 the support and services they need to retain their identities by "aging in community," in their own homes.

Research and policy data analysis

provides the critical information needed to encourage broad community support — and governmental action — on aging-in-community approaches to addressing social policy challenges.

Are we "Paddling Alone or Up the Creek Without a Paddle?" **Bill Benson** and **Nancy Aldrich** ask in their frank and (let's admit it) rather bleak analysis of the widening gap between needs of the aging middle class and the services currently available — or even contemplated — to address those needs (page 171).

Part 4
Research and Policy Considerations

Bridging the concepts of aging in place and aging in community, **Susan Poor** makes the case that for middle-class Americans, staying at home may be the only affordable and available option. Poor provides a detailed compendium of "Current Aging-In-Place Choices" (page 183 ff.), from institutional long-term care to innovative, grassroots models.

The AdvantAge Initiative is nationally recognized for its innovative approach of using consumer-derived data to inform community planning and action. **Mia Oberlink**, director of the Advantage Initiative, describes how the Internet and online surveys can be used as a tool to engage older residents as a first step towards involving them in the process of making their communities more liveable for all ages (page 197).

In, "Aging Together," internationally known aging researcher **Anne P. Glass** shares lessons learned from collecting data since 2006 on the first three senior cohousing communities in the United States (page 203).

Social capital and social networks are important components of successful aging and cornerstones for aging in community. **Tobi Abramson**, in "The Ties

That Bind" (page 211), defines these closely related concepts and illustrates how they work synergistically within aging-in-community projects.

The section concludes with the last of our four profiles. In "Getting Older Then and Now" (page 217), **Richard Bergman** describes the reaction he and his wife had to a "conscious aging conference" — and what they did about it. A new idea — Community Without Walls — was the result.

The Aging Middle Class and Public Policy

Paddling Alone or Up the Creek without a Paddle?

by William F. Benson and Nancy Aldrich

THE NATION'S HEALTH AND SOCIAL SERVICES safety net has never been adequate to meet the needs of all the low-income older adults it was designed to support. The growth of the older population and anticipated declines in funding over time will only serve to broaden the gulf between need and adequacy of services for this population.

For middle-class older Americans, the gulf is much broader and is likely to be vaster in the not-too-distant future. The latest research from the AARP Public Policy Institute's Middle Class Security Project indicates that if current economic trends continue, living standards in retirement will decline; that rising healthcare costs will pose a significant threat to middle class security; and that Social Security will be the main source of income for all but the wealthiest retirees in the future.

This gap between need and support is likely to be especially true with respect to the ability of middle-class aging boomers to afford the long-term services and support (LTSS) they will need in the future. LTSS encompasses a broad array of supportive services to help older adults and persons with disabilities accomplish their daily tasks. The need for LTSS is assessed based on a person's ability to perform activities of daily living (ADLs), such as eating, bathing, showering, using the toilet, dressing, walking across a small room, and getting in or out of a bed or chair. A broader array of LTSS is needed by those who need assistance with what are called instrumental

ADLs, such as preparing meals, managing money, shopping for groceries, doing housework, or taking medications.

The social safety net that has existed for prior generations — Older Americans Act (OAA) programs and services, Medicaid, Medicare, and the Social Services Block Grant, among others — are rapidly changing and will likely face increasing pressure to cut costs as boomers age. All of these programs are facing budget restraints, along with others that serve vulnerable older adults — low-income home energy assistance, Section 202 elderly housing, and food stàmps, to name a few. Even Social Security, arguably one of the most important domestic policy successes of the twentieth century, providing essential retirement income to millions of beneficiaries, is under assault from some quarters and will face increasing pressure to change and reduce future projected expenditures.

The simultaneous growth in the number of older adults and a decline in dollars available to support and assist them present a major public policy paradox. No doubt, policy makers will believe they face an endless list of "Hobson's choices." In 2011, the first baby boomers — those born between 1946 and 1964 — reached age 65, and by 2030 there will be more than 70 million older adults (twice the number as in 2000). By 2030, older adults will comprise nearly one in five Americans. The oldest of this group, those 85 and over, will grow from 5.3 million in 2006 to nearly 21 million by 2050. This is the group most likely to need intensive LTSS.

To compound matters, as a result of the economic recession that began at the end of 2007, many boomers find themselves with lower levels of savings and fewer assets than they had planned on. Many middle-class boomers are unlikely to significantly make up for their losses. Many people, especially women, face a serious risk of running out of money in retirement, according to the Women's Institute for a Secure Retirement (WISER), a national nonprofit organization that runs the federal government's National Resource Center for Women and Retirement. Women are particularly at risk due to a combination of lower lifetime pay and time lost due to caregiving responsibilities. Half of all women work in traditionally female, relatively low-paid jobs without pensions; three out of five working women earn less than $30,000 per year; and female retirees receive only half the average pension benefits that men receive, according to WISER.

Meanwhile, healthcare costs continue to rise, along with the cost of living in general, taking a huge bite out of the budgets of retirees living on fixed incomes. Over the past decade, the healthcare portion of household budgets rose by 51 percent — nearly double the growth in household average income (30 percent) and more than three times the rate of spending growth for all other products and services, according to AARP's Public Policy Institute.

States and municipalities are not likely to offer much relief, as many are cutting their budgets for aging services and other programs, just as the aging population has begun to soar. Nonprofits and charitable organizations have seen their revenue drop as well. Even if economic recovery replenishes state and local coffers, it is unrealistic to think they will provide major resources for the economic well-being of middle-class boomers as they age or to cover their LTSS costs.

There's another chasm that further compounds the challenges — the gulf between what people know and what they believe about what they and their loved ones face in meeting LTSS costs. While an estimated 70 percent of those over age 65 will need LTSS at some point in their lives, according to the Administration on Aging (AoA), a 2009 survey by Metlife Mature Market Institute found that only 36 percent of respondents thought they might need long-term care someday. A 2006 AARP survey found that almost 60 percent of Americans believed that Medicare pays for long nursing home stays and assisted living. The 2009 Metlife Mature Institute survey also found that people mistakenly believe that the majority of long-term care is received in a nursing home when, in fact, most long-term care is provided at home.

More than 90 percent of persons age 65 and older with disabilities who receive help with daily activities are assisted by unpaid informal caregivers (family, friends, or neighbors), and 66 percent receive no paid care at all, relying entirely on informal caregivers, according to AARP's Public Policy Institute. There are about 34 million informal caregivers providing care at any given point in time, and 52 million providing care at some time during the year, according to AARP. Many of these caregivers are the aging baby boomer middle class, who see an impact on their own health and on their pocketbook as they struggle to take care of aging parents. AARP estimates the economic value of this unpaid care coupled with lost income due to care provided by informal caregivers at $375 billion in 2007.

THE RISE OF THE "MIDDLE-CLASS POOR"

THE TERM "MIDDLE-CLASS POOR" has been used to describe those impacted by dwindling savings, unemployment, the rising cost of living, and the recent economic recession. Middle-class incomes generally range between

$20,000 and $100,000 a year, according to Leading Age, an organization of nonprofit aging-services providers. The median 2010 income of households with householders 65 and older was $31,408, compared to $49,445 for people of all ages, according to Census Bureau statistics. The middle-class poor are generally not qualified, based on their income, for public assistance. Yet, they cannot afford to pay privately for nursing home care or LTSS in their homes and communities.

Only 14 percent of Americans are "very confident" that they will have enough money to live comfortably in retirement, according to the annual retirement confidence study conducted by the Employee Benefit Research Institute. The study found that 60 percent of workers report that the value of their households' savings and investments, excluding the value of their primary home and any defined benefit plans, is less than $25,000. Those

President Lyndon B. Johnson signing the Medicare Bill at the Harry S. Truman Library in Independence, Missouri. Former President Harry S. Truman is seated beside him.

without adequate retirement savings will be unable to pay the estimated $6,500 a month cost for nursing home care or even $1,700 a month for in-home assistance, according to the AoA. Census data show that more baby boomers will enter their retirement years below the poverty level (10.1 percent of those ages 55–59, compared to 9 percent of those currently age 65 and older), although the 85 and older age group continues to have the highest poverty rate (12.3 percent).

Middle-class elders seem to be particularly vulnerable to the impact of a multitude of factors on their retirement well-being. Many will not be able to afford supportive services to remain in their homes, but will not qualify for Medicaid programs for supportive services or be able to tap into Older Americans Act programs (e.g., meals on wheels). These programs must target or prioritize services to older adults with the greatest economic and social needs, including those who (1) are living below the poverty threshold; (2) have physical or mental disabilities that pose risk for institutional placement; or (3) are culturally, socially, or geographically isolated, including isolation caused by language, race, or ethnic status.

While there are adequate supports for health care as boomers age, there are few good choices available for the aging middle class members who need LTSS other than private long-term care insurance or spending all their money until they qualify for Medicaid. According to the Kaiser Family Foundation, seven out of ten nursing home residents are on Medicaid in large part because they depleted their savings.

AVAILABILITY AND LIMITATIONS OF EXISTING PROGRAMS FOR MIDDLE-CLASS OLDER ADULTS

MEDICARE IS A FEDERAL HEALTHCARE PROGRAM for people age 65 and older, and certain people with disabilities, who have contributed to the program throughout their working years. As noted earlier, it is commonly, but erroneously, believed by many that Medicare will cover LTSS costs. A 2009 long-term care survey by Metlife Mature Market Institute found that only one-third (34 percent) of respondents realize that health insurance, disability insurance, or Medicare will not pay for expenses associated with LTSS. Nearly 20 percent of survey respondents believe disability insurance will cover their long-term care costs. One-third (33 percent) said Medicare/Medigap will cover them, while 14 percent said their health insurance provider will do so. Similarly, a large number of caregivers (76 percent) are unaware which insurance or programs pay for long-term care, the Metlife survey found. Another survey, conducted by the SCAN Foundation and the University of California–Los Angeles found that 60 percent of California's residents mistakenly believe or are unsure if Medicare pays for long-term care needs.

Medicare and private supplemental health insurance ("Medigap") do not cover most long-term care expenses, leaving Medicaid as the "safety net" for many middle-income persons. However, to receive Medicaid long-term care services, older individuals must become impoverished and spend almost all of their assets (see "Medicaid," below). In fact, Medicare only covers short-term care for certain rehabilitative services. Medicare covers medically necessary home health care for homebound beneficiaries who need skilled care. Medicare also pays for 21 days of skilled rehabilitative nursing home care for beneficiaries with skilled care needs who had a prior hospital stay of at least three days, as well as a very limited amount for days 21–100.

Furthermore, Medicare is expected to be a target of future budget-cutting and deficit-reduction efforts by Congress; it seems unlikely it will be expanded to cover LTSS for the aging population, at least not before the boomer population is gone. An estimated 96 percent of Medicare spending and 83 percent of Medicaid spending is for people with chronic conditions, according to Partnership for Solutions, a project of Johns Hopkins University and the Robert Wood Johnson Foundation. Chronic diseases such as heart disease, cancer, and diabetes are the leading causes of disability and death in the United States, and their prevalence as the boomers age will contribute to growing financial demands on the Medicare program.

Medicaid covers long-term care services for certain adults who have become impoverished as a result of disabling illness or injury. Unlike Medicare, it is a shared responsibility of the federal government and states. As federal and state dollars dwindle, lower funding levels likely mean that states will constrict programs and eligibility. Thirty-three states and the District of Columbia allow the "medically needy" — those with high medical bills — to spend down to a state-set eligibility standard, and because few people can afford the high cost of nursing home care, 38 states allow people needing nursing home care to qualify with income up to 300 percent of the Supplemental Security Income ceiling ($2,094 per month in 2012), according to the Kaiser Family Foundation. An important part of the Affordable Care Act passed in 2010 is that it has incentives for states to offer more home- and community-based services under Medicaid, and it encourages better coordination of services for individuals who are eligible for both Medicare and Medicaid.

In recent years, Congress has amended Medicaid policy to cut costs and discourage older adults from reducing assets in order to qualify for Medicaid nursing home care. This means that Medicaid officials can examine how beneficiaries spent their money over the past five years, the so-called five-year "look back" period, to ascertain if it was done to qualify for Medicaid. This is a rigorous — many would say onerous — test for middle-class elders. Fortunately, for married couples where one spouse is on Medicaid and in a nursing home and the other spouse remains living in the community, there is a "spousal protection" provision that allows the spouse to retain a certain amount of income for his/her living expenses in the community. All of these restrictions and complexities, not to mention state-by-state variations in eligibility and services, make it difficult for older adults to know whether they are eligible for Medicaid.

The importance of Social Security to middle-class boomers and older adults cannot be overstated. For many boomers, that importance may be even greater down the road. The average Social Security benefit is $13,800 a year. Women on average receive $2,000 less, according to the Older Women's League. Informal caregivers, primarily women, are likely to see lower Social Security benefits because of years when they had no earnings or when they worked part-time due to their caregiving responsibilities.

A total of 36.8 million older Americans — 89 percent of all people age 65 and older — receive Social Security. More than 19 million older Americans rely on Social Security for 50 percent or more of their family income, and almost half of beneficiaries rely on Social Security for 90 percent of their family income, according to the AARP Public Policy Institute. More than a quarter of older women depend on Social Security for nearly all of their family income. Social Security kept 38 percent of older adults out of poverty in 2010.

President George H.W. Bush signs the Americans with Disabilities Act on the South Lawn of the White House on July 26, 1990.

On the surface, the Older Americans Act (OAA), enacted into law in 1965 along with Medicare and Medicaid, would seem to hold considerable promise for middle-class older adults. Although created in spirit to provide services and information to all Americans age 60 and older, in reality the OAA cannot do so due to its limited funding. The dual mission of the OAA is (1) to fund the development and implementation of comprehensive and coordinated systems to serve older adults, and (2) to provide for advocacy on behalf of older adults. The act created a nation-wide infrastructure of national, state, and local programs. Since 1984, funding has been targeted to those individuals with the greatest social or economic need, with particular attention to low-income minority individuals, rural older people, and the frail and disabled.

There are, however, some OAA programs that do serve middle-class elders as well as some boomers. For example, the long-term care ombudsman program investigates the complaints of residents of nursing homes and assisted living facilities regardless of the economic status of the resident. Another is the Aging and Disability Resource Center (ADRC) Program discussed later in this essay.

Unfortunately, federal OAA funding, now hovering at around $1.9 billion a year, has shrunk over time in proportion to the growth in the number of older adults. OAA funding has seen few increases in recent years. Although it has so far been subjected to few cuts, this so-called "flat funding" in fact erodes the ability of agencies to continue, let alone grow, programs and services. Federal funding for the portion of the OAA that provides for home-delivered meals and other nutrition services, for example, has not kept pace with inflation or the growth in the older population. OAA funding increases have lagged behind increases in the cost of living, even as the demand for OAA services rises. Waiting lists are common for home-delivered meals and other vital services. Unless state and local agencies can raise additional monies, the absence of funding increases means a decline in meals served, support services, family caregiver support, and other OAA programs.

President Obama just signed the Patient Protection and Affordable Care Act on March 23, 2010, the cornerstone of the most significant regulatory overhaul of the U.S. healthcare system since Medicare.

Between 1993 and 2012, there was a 39 percent increase — about 2 percent per year — in funding for the core OAA supportive services and elder protection programs. Some of the OAA programs, such as elder abuse prevention, only saw a 16 percent increase in funding over that time period — less than 1 percent annually.

The population age 65 and older will increase 79 percent between 2010 and 2030, according to Census data, growing from 40.2 million in 2010 to 72.0 million in 2030. In order to keep up with the growth in the aging population and the increased cost of services, national aging organizations believe that the OAA budget would need to see sizable increases each year.

The AoA funds several grant programs specifically focused on supporting older adults to remain in their homes and communities rather than go to long-term care facilities to have their needs meet. For the most part, programs such as Community Innovations in Place and the Naturally Occurring Retirement Communities (NORCs)serve low- to moderate-income individuals. The middle class is largely left out.

The Social Services Block Grant (SSBG) is a source of direct funding to states to help meet the needs of vulnerable populations. Although funded annually at $1.8 billion, roughly the same as the OAA, states have the freedom to use the funds for a broad array of groups, such as children, people with disabilities, the homeless, and others. For older adults, it can be used to fund services to help keep people in their homes and communities such as adult day care, personal care, and other home-based services. It is also currently the only source of federal dollars to support states' adult protective services (APS) programs that respond to cases of abuse of older and other disabled adults. Thirty-four states rely on SSBG to support their APS program. Services for vulnerable older adults accounted for 27 percent of SSBG expenditures in fiscal year 2009, according to the Center for Budget and Policy Priorities. Although SSBG programs serving older adults are not restricted to only those who are low-income (APS responds to reports of abuse regardless of victims' ages), the reality is that SSBG funds are spread very thinly over numerous vulnerable populations, and the program has been a constant target of budget cutters. The so-called Ryan Budget in the House of Representatives calls for eliminating SSBG, and there was a proposal to eliminate SSBG as part of negotiations on the American Taxpayer Relief Act of 2012. It is likely that SSBG will again be a target in upcoming deliberations over further deficit reduction and program cuts.

The one new federal program that held the promise of providing relief to the middle class in meeting their LTSS costs and needs was the Community Living Assistance Services and Support Act, the CLASS Act, passed in 2010 as part of the Affordable Care Act. It would have provided a mechanism for people of all incomes to purchase long-term care insurance as part of a large actuarial pool. However, due to the law's requirement that the program be "actuarially sound" — that is, not rely on government funding — there was enough concern about its financial sustainability that Congress repealed the CLASS Act on January 1, 2013, before it even started, as part of the American Taxpayer Relief Act.

In lieu of the CLASS Act, Congress authorized a Commission on Long-Term Care to develop a plan for creating and financing a comprehensive, coordinated, and high-quality system that ensures the availability of LTSS for individuals in need of such services and supports, including the elderly and other individuals who require assistance to perform activities of daily living. While the vision and goals are lofty, practical reality is causing many to be skeptical that the Commission's work will result in tangible improvements for the elderly and boomers. Individual commissioners were to be appointed within 30 days of enactment, and the Commission's work is to be completed by the end of June 2013. It has no budget and is to be staffed by borrowed federal employees. Despite these obstacles and the skepticism, others believe that the Commission could make a substantial contribution by helping explain to policy makers and the public alike the magnitude of the need for LTSS and that the problem isn't going away. It could also provide a realistic set of possible solutions — especially for the middle class — for having their LTSS needs met in a person-centered and quality way without breaking the bank of either individuals or the government.

Shoring up Programs to Protect the Middle Class

Despite the limits of the OAA in meeting the needs of the middle class, the established infrastructure of its national, state, and local aging services can serve as a base to build access to services for middle-class older adults and their informal (nonpaid) caregivers. Aging network programs bring three decades and more years of experience working in their communities and planning for and delivering a wide array of services. The OAA-funded Aging and Disability Resource Centers (ADRC) serve as a one-stop shop in each state for people of all ages, incomes, and disabilities to get information on the full range of long-term services and supports. These centers provide information and assistance to individuals needing either public or private resources, to professionals seeking assistance on behalf of their clients, and to individuals planning for their future long-term care needs. ADRC programs also serve as the entry point to publicly administered long-term supports, including those funded under Medicaid, the OAA, and state revenue programs.

A unique feature of the OAA is its requirement for advocacy at all levels of government to improve the lives of and services for older adults. This underutilized aspect of the OAA could provide a natural path for leaders to encourage the development of a sound aging infrastructure.

There are some encouraging trends in Medicaid, according to a 2012 analysis by AARP. AARP found that more states are showing interest in Medicaid-managed LTSS — 12 states have such programs; 11 states have planned to implement them in 2012 or 2013. The study also found that more states are focusing on ways to better integrate Medicare and Medicaid for people who are eligible for both programs. AARP found that fewer states were planning on cutting their aging and disability budgets, and four states increased their aging and disability budgets. The Affordable Care Act includes important improvements related to home- and community-based services through the Medicaid program.

Efforts to improve disease prevention and health promotion and public health systems can go a long way to reducing chronic illness among future older adults, and reduce or delay the need for LTSS. More than 75 percent of healthcare costs are due to chronic conditions, according to the Centers for Disease Control and Prevention (CDC). A growing body of evidence indicates that preventive services can postpone or prevent disease and disability, maintain or improve health status, contain costs, and enhance the quality of life of older adults. The use of evidence-based interventions — those supported by good research — for chronic conditions are strongly supported by AoA, CDC, and the Agency for Healthcare Research and Quality.

William F. Benson introducing Kathy Greenlee, Assistant Secretary of the Administration on Aging, at the NAPSA conference in San Antonio in October 2009.

As a result, there has been a significant increase in OAA services' use of evidence-based interventions such as physical activity and chronic disease self-management, along with closer collaboration with the public health world. Recent Medicare changes provide more coverage of preventive services and an annual wellness visit for beneficiaries. More work in the area of disease prevention and health promotion could result in a healthier and less-costly older population, better able to cope with their own aging.

Rather than increased funding or major new programs for social services or for LTSS to serve the middle class, which seems unlikely in the foreseeable future, policy makers could use tax policy for the benefit of middle-class boomers as they age. For example, tax-based approaches for writing off a portion of LTSS or the cost of long-term care insurance may make these services more affordable for middle-class older adults. However, even these modest proposals, which are not new, would be considered in an environment where even the long-cherished home mortgage deduction, which has benefited the middle class enormously, is being questioned in the debates over deficit reduction and tax reform.

Communities can provide leadership in promoting healthy living for older adults, encouraging elders to engage in meaningful and vital action, creating elder-friendly communities, and encouraging new consumer-driven models of living and receiving services, such as the Village Model begun in Boston. In many areas, elders are already "voting with their feet," by moving into elder-friendly communities such as Naturally Occurring Retirement Communities, cohousing, intergenerational communities, and other supportive retirement communities.

As AARP's Public Policy Institute's Middle Class Security Project study has just concluded, public policy solutions to help shore up the middle class include increasing access to affordable healthcare coverage, slowing the growth of healthcare costs, addressing the costs of LTSS, and ensuring that Social Security continues to provide the foundation for a secure middle-class retirement and is improved for those most vulnerable.

And so it seems that our current system — or non-system as many believe — for shoring up the middle class as they age is untenable and unsustainable. Without further public policy support and other innovation, given contemporary currents, the middle class may have to paddle alone, or find themselves up a creek without a paddle.

Bill Benson is Managing Principal for Health Benefits ABCs (HBABCs), an organization offering health and aging policy, educational, and strategic planning consulting services. Benson has worked on health and aging issues for nearly four decades including in various leadership positions in the U.S. Congress and senior appointee positions at the U.S. Administration on Aging, including Acting Assistant Secretary for Aging, prior to starting a consulting practice in 1998.

Nancy Aldrich has more than 30 years of journalism experience in the health care and aging policy fields. She was the editor of the acclaimed Older Americans Report for nearly 20 years, reaching a vast professional audience with essential news, information, and analysis. She now works as a writer for Bill Benson at Health Benefits ABCs.

Connected to Community: Current Aging-in-Place Choices

by Susan Poor

As we age, our needs and interests evolve and change, so our choices of housing should be wide ranging, as should be the spectrum of activities and services.[1]

Most older adults wish to remain in their homes and communities as they age. Today, just 10 percent of older adults live in supported environments of some kind, with the remaining 90 percent living in "traditional" housing with no external assistance.[2] By choice and perhaps economic necessity, the large majority of older adults will continue to live as independently as they can for as long as they are able — and will need a range of services and supports to achieve this.

Successful aging in place requires coordination — and ideally integration — at the intersection of housing, health care, non-medical long-term services and supports (LTSS), and technology. LTSS components are the services and practical supports that, when absent, may limit peoples' ability to live independently or encourage them to neglect their medical plan of care, which can lead to poorer health. The supports include such things as caregiving assistance, transportation, grocery shopping, home modification, prepared meals, connection to the larger community, and social capital. This essay profiles a number of options that are allowing older adults to age in place, connected to their communities.

Aging — The Big Picture

The American population is aging and living longer. Baby boomers — the oldest of whom began turning 65 in 2011 — can expect to live into their 80s and 90s, giving them a 20–30-year period of phased retirement, encore careers, volunteer activity, and perhaps roles in raising grandchildren, supporting their children, or being caregivers to family members and friends.

As they age, nearly all will have at least one chronic condition, and many will have several. If their health declines, it will likely occur gradually over time, with intermittent periods of inpatient care and more intense medical needs. Some conditions, such as high blood pressure and arthritis, which occur in half the population, will be readily managed in home settings. Advanced stages of other diseases (e.g., dementia, cardiopulmonary disease, stroke, cancer, diabetes, obesity-related conditions) will require intensive care management and a range of medical and non-medical services to support patients and their caregivers. These realities notwithstanding, 85 percent of Medicare beneficiaries with three or more activity limitations still live in traditional housing.[3]

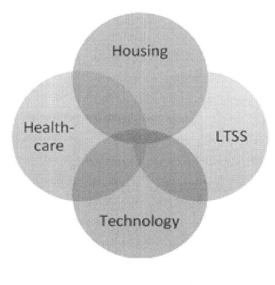

The majority of boomers, like their parents, own their own homes. Some will live with other people; some (primarily women) will live alone or become widowed or divorced during these years. Yet for many, homes have lost value, and retirement savings have diminished due to the 2009 real estate and economic crisis.

Homes may also need basic maintenance as well as modifications in response to owners' physical needs. While estimates vary, the Employee Benefits Research Institute reports that in 2012, 64 percent of retired Americans had less than $50,000 in their retirement accounts.[4]

Other data indicate that nearly half of middle-income workers will be poor or near poor in retirement.[5] Some may benefit from reverse mortgages, annuities, and other vehicles for increasing their economic security. But poverty will disproportionately impact the heath care, housing, and economic security of low-income and minority individuals and their families.

While nearly all will be covered by Medicare, many will be shocked to learn that Medicare does not cover either residential or community-based long-term services and supports (LTSS) and that their access to nursing homes or community-based alternatives means spending down to become Medicaid eligible. They will need, on average, three years of assistance, including one year in a nursing home (currently about $87,000/year) and two years of paid care at home (currently about $36,000/year).[6] As is true today, family and other informal caregivers (e.g., friends and neighbors) are likely to provide the majority of the care older adults will receive.

AGING IN PLACE CONSIDERATIONS

AGING IN PLACE HAS GENERALLY MEANT aging independently while living in the place of one's choosing for as long as possible. What the overview above makes clear is that aging in place, in the community, is not only the preferred choice of older adults; it may be the *only* affordable and available option for many seniors. While publicly funded systems and services exist for those with low incomes, the same supports do not exist for the middle class. Even if older adults wish to move, most will not qualify for subsidized housing and will find other options, such as Continuing Care Retirement Communities (CCRCs) and assisted living, costly. The challenge of the future is therefore to enable *affordable* independent living in peoples' own homes, as the need for services increases and at a time when it is clear that the federal and state governments are not going to lead these efforts for middle-income seniors.

Increasingly, aging in place incorporates the idea of "aging in community" and the necessity of "housing with services." Aging in community expands the concept of aging in place by including active engagement of older adults in planning and implementing services and supports, maintaining meaningful connections to the surrounding community, and having control over housing and other choices. We must weave together housing with health care, LTSS, and technology so that people have both a place to live *and* healthcare coverage and the non-medical services and supports that buttress independent living and enhance the success and efficacy of medical interventions.

The role of technology cannot be underestimated in achieving these goals. Advancements in technology for social connections, communication with medical personnel and family, brain fitness, arranging in-home services, diagnosis, medication management, health monitoring, receiving medical services at home, etc., will be groundbreaking in upcoming years. Finding balance in the "hi-tech/hi-touch" equation will play out over a long period of time.

A New Vision of the "Continuum of Care"

Today's seniors — including baby boomers who have experienced the aging of their parents — are searching for and creating alternatives to the traditional forms of long-term care (skilled nursing facilities, assisted living, or continuing care retirement communities). These settings are increasingly seen as institutional and out of sync with consumers' preference to age in their own homes and stay meaningfully connected to their communities. That said, there is a "culture change" movement afoot that is impacting institutional long-term-care facilities and encouraging a shift in focus from the needs and ease of the institution to those of the resident and family. Key to this transformational shift is emphasis on "person-centered care" or "resident-directed care."

> Person-Centered or Resident-Directed Care is an ongoing, interactive process between residents, caregivers, and others that honors the residents' dignity and choices in directing their daily life. This is accomplished through shared communication, education, and collaboration. Relationships developed as part of this process benefit all involved, creating a community that affirms the dignity and value of each individual who lives and works in the nursing home.[7]

The current and ever-expanding spectrum of choices for places and support services for aging — ranging from the medical model of skilled nursing facilities to emerging models of programs that support aging in place in one's own home — is almost mind-numbing. Following the conclusion of this essay, you will find a descriptive compendium that includes examples of transformational change occurring within the more traditional models of long-term-care settings as well as within the community.

Thinking About the Future

No sector of the U.S. economy will be untouched by the doubling of the age 65+ population over the next 30 years to 20 percent of the population — 80 million people, one in five of us. Twenty-two percent of the older population (19 million people) will be age 85+, half of whom will have dementia. Is the near universal desire of older adults to age in their homes and communities a pipe dream or the only affordable option we have as a society?

It is more affordable if we "operationalize" the value of non-medical LTSS. Vermont's Blueprint for Health recognizes the difference between evidence-based *medicine* and evidence-based *health*. Leaders there discovered that evidence-based *medicine* doesn't work, because physicians have limited, if any, knowledge about obstacles patients live with at home and in their communities that keep them from doing what physicians recommend. In an evidence-based *health* model, community health teams that include physicians, nurses, social workers, and behavioral health counselors help tie medical care together with real-life issues such as transportation, insurance problems, housing, and unemployment. Based on its evidence-based health approach, Vermont has seen reductions in hospital admissions, emergency department visits, and lower monthly costs per person.[8]

Isolation is another factor that, when left unchecked, can have a severe impact on health status and therefore costs. Data show that social connections — friends, family, neighbors, or colleagues — improve our odds of survival by 50 percent. Low social interaction is equivalent to smoking 15 cigarettes a day, equivalent to being an alcoholic, more harmful than not exercising, and twice as harmful as obesity.[9] Further, receiving social, non-medical supports decreases morbidity and mortality rates and increases life expectancy, self-efficacy, adherence to medication regimes, and self-reported health status.[10]

To extend the resources available to upcoming generations of older adults, it is critical that housing, health care, and LTSS models be linked (and enhanced by technology) to take advantage of low-cost "aging in place, connected to community" models such as Villages, NORC SSPs (Naturally Occurring Retirement Communities Supportive Services Programs), TimeBanks, grassroots caregiving models, neighborhood associations, block captain approaches, and church and other faith-based networks. All of these models have strong civic engagement, volunteers, and mutual assistance cultures that can strengthen communities while supporting the individuals who live in them.

We will need many innovative housing and LTSS choices for the burgeoning older adult population. We cannot ignore the need for consumer direction, safe dwellings, and holistic, humane settings for those needing skilled or custodial care in group environments. But we can greatly expand the range of non-medical LTSS by shining a brighter light on the wealth of social capital that exists in most communities and inspiring the creation of innovative ideas and solutions.

A Compendium of Options

SKILLED NURSING FACILITIES, formerly called nursing homes, are nursing and healthcare facilities licensed by the state which provide a residence for elders who need skilled nursing and assistance with LTSS. Many provide additional services such as dental care, mental health care, dementia care, pain management, and palliative care. Medicare covers short-term rehabilitation stays but does not pay for elders who have longer-term needs. For those with long-term acute or chronic healthcare needs, they will have to pay out of pocket until they "spend down" their assets to become eligible for Medicaid, which covers costs for those who are low-income. Long-term care insurance can also be a vehicle for covering costs for a time period specified in the contract. In 2011, the average annual cost of a private room in a nursing home was $87,235.

ASSISTED LIVING FACILITIES provide a residence to elders who need some support with such activities as dressing, bathing, or cooking, or who want a more supportive environment (e.g., dining room meals, planned social activities, transportation), but who do not require skilled nursing care. Smaller settings for up to six people may be called adult foster care, adult family homes, supportive care homes, and board and care homes. Most assisted living facilities only accept private pay or long-term care insurance. A few states offer fee-waiver programs for low-income elders. Assisted living costs in 2011 were about $3,500/month or $42,000/year.[11]

CONGREGATE CARE FACILITIES combine private living apartments with centralized dining services, shared common spaces, and some LTSS, including meal preparation, housework, and outside the facility shopping and healthcare appointments. Some contract for healthcare services, but congregate facilities are not licensed to provide care services such as bathing, dressing, and toileting. Congregate care is an industry segment between independent living and the health-related services of the assisted living facility. Costs are slightly less than those of assisted living.

CONTINUING CARE RETIREMENT COMMUNITIES (CCRCs) provide a continuum of care as a resident's health changes, from independent living apartments, to assisted living, to skilled nursing care, although not all residents move through the continuum. Most CCRCs require a one-time entrance fee ranging from $250,000 to upwards of $700,000 and monthly service fees of \$2,000–\$4,000 or more. CCRCs typically offer at least one of three contract types: 1) life care (Type A) where the entrance fee is nonrefundable (or refundable on a declining balance approach) while monthly fees are fixed regardless of the level of care the resident requires; 2) modified life care (Type B) where the entrance fee is usually refundable in part and the resident is entitled to some period of free care (e.g., 60 days) or at a reduced cost when the resident moves to a higher level of care; and 3) fee for service (Type C) where the entrance fee is almost always refundable but the resident pays market rate if a higher level of care is needed. Many CCRCs accept Medicare in the skilled nursing section of the community, and some are beginning to address residents with long-term-care insurance, but otherwise no third party reimbursement is available to cover the fees associated with CCRCs.

GREEN HOUSES®[12] are small, home-like, skilled nursing facilities for six to ten people that focus on a holistic approach to care and services. They are designed to provide an alternative to institutional long-term care, with an emphasis on honoring seniors' dignity, privacy, and autonomy by providing meaningful activity and relationships, independence, and improved quality of care. Green House architectural hallmarks are an open kitchen, a hearth, a single dining room table, and lots of natural light, creating a home-like atmosphere rather than the often more sterile environment of a large nursing facility. The organization and philosophy of care of these homes are transformative, with an emphasis on creating a small, intentional community and an emphasis on person-centered care. The costs are comparable to those of nursing homes; currently about half of Green House residences are covered by Medicaid.

ALTERNATIVE ASSISTED LIVING FACILITIES are a small but growing number of assisted living facilities that are embracing a more holistic care model in response to consumer demand for person-directed care. For example, in Oregon, Elite Care's Extended Family Residences provide resident-directed assisted living in a home-like environment. Embedded in their philosophy is a culture of mutual reciprocity, family involvement, and engagement of residents who might otherwise need to be in a skilled nursing facility due to high physical care needs or dementia.

SECTION 202 SUPPORTIVE HOUSING FOR THE ELDERLY is the only federally funded housing program specifically for low-income seniors, although other subsidized housing programs do include older adults. Section 202 Housing provides secure, barrier-free, and supportive housing that can accommodate residents as they become more frail. Services commonly available include transportation, assistance with housekeeping and meals, and some social and health services, usually provided in partnership with other community providers.

CCRCs WITHOUT WALLS — also called Continuing Care at Home (CCAH) models — are less expensive alternatives to "brick and mortar" Continuing Care Retirement Communities. Sometimes managed by staff affiliated with existing CCRCs, these home-based programs offer the continuum of care concept to community residents who do not wish to live in a CCRC or can't afford to, but who want access to services such as home health aides, visiting nurses, and transportation that could delay or even prevent the need to move away for care. Care coordination is a key aspect of these community-based plans. Like CCRCs, there are both "Type A" and "Type B" continuing-care-at-home plans. Type A plans typically offer unlimited lifetime coverage and require up-front entrance fees ranging from $20,000 to $70,000, and monthly fees from approximately $250 to $800 per month. In Type B plans, the subscriber shares some portion of the financial responsibility for care and, as a result, fees are significantly lower. The entrance fee, which can be paid over time, is typically equivalent to the total fees for a full year and ranges from $3,000 to $7,000 depending on age at enrollment. Type B plans are especially appealing because subscribers don't feel as though they are paying for something that they may never use. Like the Village model, most CCRCs Without Walls seek to promote a sense of community through organized events, from exercise classes and book clubs to theater nights and museum tours. There are currently CCAH plans operating in ten states, including the District of Columbia.

VILLAGES are consumer-driven, grassroots, membership-based organizations that empower older adults to remain active and engaged in their communities as they age. Villages offer members a network of resources, services, programs, and activities that revolve around community building; daily living needs; social, cultural, and educational activities; ongoing health and wellness; and member-to-member volunteer support. Ninety Villages are now in operation across the country. Villages average 150 members with annual membership fees ranging from $100–$1,200.

AGE-RESTRICTED COMMUNITIES, also called senior retirement or active adult communities, provide market rate housing to healthy, active seniors, generally age 55 and older, who wish to live among their peers rather than in mixed-age communities. Supportive services are not provided, and residents may need to move should their health conditions change requiring more care.

NATURALLY OCCURRING RETIREMENT COMMUNITIES (NORCs) is a demographic term used to describe typical communities or neighborhoods where a large number of residents have lived for a long time and have aged in place. AARP estimates that about 5,000 NORCs exist across the country; these concentrations of older adults can facilitate the organization of supportive communities. In some NORC communities, nonprofit organizations have partnered with other agencies to create Supportive Services Programs (SSPs) that include social services, healthcare services, and socialization, recreation, and volunteer opportunities for residents. NORC SSPs are designed to be responsive to individual and community needs, and they depend on resident involvement and community partnerships to maximize success.

ACCESSORY DWELLING UNITS (ADUs) are a type of housing created or added to a single family home or built separately on a lot. In-law units, "granny flats," and restored out-buildings are examples of ADUs. Consumers can lease and purchase ADUs (if their local zoning laws permit them) through such companies as MedCottages™,[13] which provide prefabricated 12-by-24-foot bedroom–bathroom–kitchenette units that can be set up as a free-standing structure in a back yard and include state-of-the-art technology features.

SHARED HOUSING is an arrangement in which a homeowner provides space for a tenant and, in return, receives income and/or needed assistance. It also includes individuals jointly sharing the housing expenses. Shared housing allows older adults to stay in their homes while benefiting from companionship, assistance, and mutual support.

COHOUSING OR CLUSTER HOUSING models create intentional neighborhoods by designing residential developments around shared and jointly owned common areas. Cohousing supports independence but promotes interconnectedness, mutual assistance, community interaction, and a degree of community management. Elder cohousing communities are built by midlife to older adults and focus on the unique needs of this population.

SENIOR COOPERATIVE HOUSING is a housing model popular in rural communities that provides apartments and townhomes that residents own and run cooperatively, although some hire a management company to assist in managing the property. Commonly owned amenities include a community room, kitchen, gardens, workshops, laundry facilities, and exercise room. There are usually a number of resident-directed social programs such as book and gardening clubs, potlucks, and games and activities in the common room. Like elder cohousing, because of density they make a good location for community partnerships that serve older adults, such as a congregate meal site or health clinics such as a flu vaccine site.

COMMUNITY-BASED SERVICES are an integral part of the network providing critical services to older adults and invaluable support and respite for family caregivers.

- **PACE (THE PROGRAM OF ALL-INCLUSIVE CARE FOR THE ELDERLY)** fully integrates Medicare and Medicaid financing as well as medical and social supports, with services delivered through Adult Day Health Centers and home care for individuals who are assessed to be eligible for nursing home care. About 20,000 people in 29 states are served by PACE programs.
- **HOSPICE** is an integrated, end-of-life medical/social model that supports families with a full range of skilled home health care and supportive services when a person is diagnosed with a terminal illness and has a life expectancy of six months or less. Hospice benefits are usually covered under Medicare, Medicaid in most states, insurance plans, as well as private pay, depending on individual circumstances.
- **SENIOR CENTERS** provide a wide array of services, including socialization/civic engagement opportunities, information and assistance, meals and nutrition counseling, transportation, options counseling, wellness programs, etc., often at very low cost or even free for qualified seniors. Over 60 percent are delivery sites for Older Americans Act programs and services. Many senior centers are reinventing themselves to appeal to a broader range of community residents. The country's 11,000 senior centers serve 1 million older adults every day.
- **ADULT DAY CENTERS** provide a range of services for older adults. Social centers provide meals, recreation, and some health-related

services. Medical/health centers provide social activities as well as more intensive health and therapeutic services. Specialized centers provide services to specific care recipients, such as those with diagnosed dementias or developmental disabilities. Adult Day Centers also serve as sites for Chronic Disease Self-Management Programs. About 4,600 adult day centers across the country serve over 260,000 people.

INNOVATIVE COMMUNITY MODELS

- **MATHER LIFEWAYS CAFÉ PLUS** model serves up fun and educational, wellness-related programs and activities in pleasant café surroundings. The Café Plus model has been appealing to senior centers looking at new ways to attract older adults.
- **EPISCOPAL SENIOR COMMUNITIES SENIOR CENTER WITHOUT WALLS** program is a nondenominational free telephone program connecting California elders through activities, friendship, and community. From the comfort of their homes, participants can access an assortment of classes and support groups, when going to a community senior center is difficult.
- **THE LIVING AT HOME NETWORK** in Minnesota coordinates local volunteers, health professionals, and a wealth of other resources to help older residents stay in their own homes and connected to their communities.

INNOVATIVE GRASSROOTS SUPPORT AND CAREGIVING MODELS represent an innovative wave of services and programs to support seniors living in their homes and their caregivers. These models harness the social capital within the community and utilize the individual assets of people willing to volunteer their assistance to provide care.

- **SHARE THE CARE** brings together friends and family in an organized network to provide supports and services for people who are chronically ill, terminally ill, or disabled.
- **LOTSA HELPING HANDS** provides a free, Web-based service that develops communities for organizing circles of community during times of need.
- **TIMEBANKS** represents "pay it forward" models that allow members to perform a service for another member, in the process earning a "time dollar" that can be redeemed for an hour of time volunteered by another member.

- **TYZE NETWORKS** provides private online communities centered around one person needing friendship, support, and connection.
- **THE TRANSITION NETWORK'S CARING COLLABORATIVE** provides member-to-member volunteer support for health-related needs.

Susan Poor, MPH, is the Director of Innovation and Business Development at On Lok in San Francisco. She is a specialist in community approaches to aging, the Village model, long-term services and supports (LTSS) for older adults, end-of-life care, family caregiving, health care reform, and managed care. Prior to joining On Lok, Susan worked with the Village to Village Network to replicate Villages nationwide. As Owner/Principal of Susan Poor Consulting, she worked with local governments and nonprofit providers on a wide range of aging and health-related projects. Susan is a Founder and Board Member of San Francisco Village, Co-Chair of the San Francisco Long Term Care Coordinating Council, and West Coast Director of Outreach for Share The Care. In her work with On Lok and the Village movement, Susan is a leader in focusing attention on the LTSS needs of middle-income seniors. Susan can be reached at susan@susanpoor.com or spoor@onlok.org.

NOTES

[1]   Henry Cisneros, Margaret Dyer-Chamberlain, and Jane Hickie, eds., *Independent for Life: Homes and Neighborhoods for an Aging America.* Austin, TX: University of Texas Press, 2012.

[2]   *Independent for Life.*

[3]   *Independent for Life.*

[4]   R. Helman, et.al., "The 2012 Retirement Confidence Survey," Employee Benefit Research Institute, March 2012. ebri.org/pdf/surveys/rcs/2012/EBRI_IB_03-2012_No369_RCS.pdf (accessed August 31, 2012).

[5]   Teresa Ghilarducci, "Our ridiculous approach to retirement," *New York Times*, July 21, 2012. nytimes.com/2012/07/22/opinion/sunday/our-ridiculous-approach-to-retirement.html (accessed August 31, 2012).

[6]   MetLife Mature Market Institute, "Market survey of long-term care costs" (New York: Metropolitan Life Insurance Company, October 2011). metlife.com/assets/cao/mmi/publications/studies/2011/Highlights/mmi-long-term-care-costs.pdf (accessed August 31, 2012).

[7]   Wisconsin Coalition for Person Directed Care. www.wisconsinpdc.org

[8]   Pauline Chen, "When doctor's advice is ignored at home," *New York Times*, March 10, 2011. http://well.blogs.nytimes.com/2011/03/10/when-home-life-trumps-health-care/ (accessed August 31, 2012).

[9]   Julianne Holt-Lunstad, Timothy B. Smith, and J. Bradley Layton, "Social relationships and mortality risk: A meta-analytic review," *PLoS Medicine*, July 10, 2010. plosmedicine.org/article/info percent3Adoi percent2F10.1371 percent2Fjournal.pmed.1000316 (accessed August 31, 2012).

[10]   Michele Heisler, "Building peer support programs to manage chronic disease: Seven models for success, " California HealthCare Foundation, December, 2006.

[11]   MetLife Mature Market Institute.

[12]   See thegreenhouseproject.org.

[13]   See medcottage.com/index.php.

Who are you?

A Poem by Karolyn Merson

Inspired by Billy Collins" poem "Litany"

You are the bread, the staff of life.
However, you are not the wind that is
fickle, that comes and goes.
It is possible that you are a fish, that
gives food and sustenance to all living things.
It might interest you to know that you are
spirit that is invisible but touches all
things.
You will always be just you
all the days of your life.

© 2011 by Karolyn Merson

Karolyn Merson is a resident of Burbank Senior Artists Colony and a participant in its Poetry Café, a creative writing group which is facilitated by Hannah Menkin.

Online Surveys Engage Older Adults in Community Planning

by Mia Oberlink

Among its many benefits, the Internet is facilitating direct communication across different sectors of society as never before. Anyone with a computer and an Internet connection has the opportunity to express his or her opinions and needs to a variety of audiences. Under the right circumstances, this can create positive change swiftly and effectively.

A recent *New York Times* article provides a good illustration of how female consumers are influencing cosmetic companies by participating in online conversations. In their efforts to stay fresh and up to date, cosmetic companies are constantly discontinuing old products and introducing new ones. The rub is that many women prefer the old products. Now, through company-run *Internet chat lines* and *social media sites*, women are expressing their preferences, and the cosmetic companies are listening. "Until recently, these consumers had little recourse other than to register complaints with manufacturers' service centers," writes the author. But now, thanks to the Internet, the companies are receiving timely input from customers and responding by reissuing the discontinued products. "It's literally reshaping how the market is driven," said one analyst. "The consequence of a poor decision could take 18 months to two years to filter back to the head office," said one executive. "With social media you can take an instant read."[1]

This concept works not only in commerce but also in the public arena, where the Internet is facilitating communication between groups that in the past rarely had direct, instantaneous access to one another. The Internet allows like-minded people to find one another, exchange ideas, and become a collective force capable of influencing decision-making. Voters can easily reach their elected officials and make their opinions known; community residents can easily alert local government departments about pressing community problems and needs.

AN INSTANT READ ON OLDER ADULTS' OPINIONS

ANOTHER EFFECTIVE, LOW-COST WAY TO ENGAGE older people in civic matters is the *online survey*. The AdvantAge Initiative has developed a survey tool and planning process which allows a community to measure — and improve — its "aging friendliness." Collecting older adults' perceptions of and experiences in their communities becomes the first step toward involving them in the process of making their communities more livable.

The philosophy driving the AdvantAge Initiative approach is that community planning needs to include roles for the people most affected by decisions and actions that result from the planning process. Once older residents weigh in with their thoughts and opinions, they then become active stakeholders who can help implement whatever plans emerge. While this may seem patently obvious to readers, it's surprising how often communities fail to take these important, necessary steps!

ADVANTAGE ONLINE SURVEYS REVEAL PROBLEMS

THE ADVANTAGE INITIATIVE TEAM recently conducted an online survey in two urban neighborhoods that illustrates many of the points made so far. Over 1,200 adults age 60 and above responded to the survey. An extensive marketing campaign encouraging people to take the survey was conducted with the assistance of many neighborhood associations, providers of health and social services, elected officials, and others. In promoting the survey, these same groups became stakeholders in the survey process and joined an advisory group that helped interpret the survey findings.

The survey asked older people their opinions about what they thought about their neighborhoods and how they could be made better places for older people in which to live. Demographic characteristics (age, gender, marital status, living arrangements, health status) of the respondents were also collected along with information about their social networks, care needs, activity levels, and knowledge of available services.

The answers to questions that asked residents how they got around the neighborhoods proved particularly useful to the sponsoring organization whose mission was to advocate for improvements in the built environment (e.g., housing, sidewalks, streets) in addition to improving older adults' knowledge of and access to existing services.

When all the responses were tallied, these key issues emerged: Over 71 percent of respondents cited heavy traffic as a big problem in their neighborhood, 27 percent thought streets and sidewalks in the neighborhoods needed repair, and 15 percent felt that traffic lights allowed too little time for pedestrians to cross the streets. A follow-up series of open-ended questions asking what changes they would make to improve conditions for older people in the neighborhood identified the same issues. Here is a small sampling of some of the comments we received:

I live in an area with streets that permit truck traffic. Although there are recent changes that give pedestrians some more protection from autos and trucks, I am loath to cross the streets at night.

I would work to reduce traffic deaths to pedestrians and make this a safer neighborhood for seniors to walk in.

[I would] eliminate hazardous pedestrian crossing areas by having lights with a countdown, and varying them according to the crossing time needed, especially for seniors and people with disabilities.

Similar comments addressed pedestrian safety issues, including references to the dangers that bicyclists who don't follow traffic rules pose to pedestrians, sidewalk curb cuts that need to be improved for people in wheelchairs and scooters, and uneven pavements that cause pedestrians to trip and fall. The overall *instant read* was that older people and people with disabilities in these two neighborhoods are very much at risk when they leave their homes and try to navigate the streets.

Because this was a physical safety issue involving traffic flow and pedestrian crossings, the feedback the survey had generated was immediately taken to the city Department of Transportation. Interestingly, we learned that the department already had plans to install pedestrian countdown signals in neighborhoods throughout the city. These signals let pedestrians know how many seconds they have to cross the street before the light changes, and many survey respondents had urged their use. While a decision to install the signals was in the works, the department had not yet prioritized which neighborhoods would get the new signals first. The survey findings and the respondents' comments made a very compelling argument for beginning the installation process in the two neighborhoods surveyed.

...But It Also Reveals Community Assets

THROUGH OUR SURVEYS WE ALSO LEARNED some important things about how older residents feel about their role in community life. Several of the respondents pointed out the need for seniors to get involved in making their neighborhoods better places to live. One respondent wrote, "More outreach programs [are] needed to make citizens aware of how they can personally get involved in community affairs and problems existing on a particular block in the neighborhood..." Another said, "[We need to] make a real effort to get 90 percent turnout in every election and make the politicians take our neighborhoods' concerns seriously." Still another said, "[We need to] identify the seniors in the community and actively seek their participation in community affairs."

Survey findings and comments also strongly indicated that older individuals are seeking more personal involvement in *meaningful* activities. One respondent said, for example: "Programs for seniors should be more interesting and vibrant to keep them involved and growing, with many activities for them other than just games for the old! We need things that will keep us going."

While we found that most of the survey respondents are active in many different ways, they seem to crave even more engagement in community life. Nearly a quarter of the respondents said they are working either part or full time, and another 11 percent said they work occasionally. Nearly half of the respondents said that they volunteer — tutoring or mentoring young people, supporting programs that deliver services to older adults, advocating for political causes, and in many other ways. The vast majority of respondents — 60 percent or more — had gotten together with friends or neighbors or engaged in some other kind of social activity in the past week. Yet while nearly the same percentage (60 percent) of respondents said that they are happy with their level of work, volunteering, and social activity, nearly 40 percent said that they would like to be doing more. Again, some respondent comments are good illustrations:

> The senior center at [a local church] is wonderful. I hope the community leaders will give that program support and money. I should volunteer there… This survey made me realize that I don't do enough for others. Thanks for making me realize it.

Another respondent wrote:

> In my case, I am in good health and have a good business and financial background. If there was a [way to] put my services to some use for seniors, or for any other residents that might need them, I would consider that very productive for all parties concerned.

THE SURVEY AS A CALL TO ACTION

THE ADVANTAGE INITIATIVE SURVEY not only gave us the opportunity to learn a great deal about older people and conditions in the two neighborhoods — it was also an invitation to older adults to get involved in making their communities better places to live, not only for themselves but also for residents of all ages. Judging from the number of completed surveys and extensive comments we received, many older people in these two neighborhoods want to have a voice and meaningful roles in community life, and taking the survey seriously and sharing their thoughts was a first step toward potential ongoing involvement in community improvement. Just knowing that others are interested in their opinions prompted one respondent to comment, "I appreciate that there are those who care enough to want to know about us through this survey."

Older adults' willingness to get involved seems to be there; the challenge, of course, will be to keep older adults engaged over the long term. This means taking active steps to remain attentive to their voices and periodically take that *instant read* of their concerns; mobilizing older adults by providing meaningful roles for those who want to actively work on resolving community issues; finding ways for interested older adults to use their knowledge and skills to help others; and last but certainly not least, celebrating their contributions whenever the opportunities arise.

Mia Oberlink, MA, is a Senior Research Associate at the Center for Home Care Policy and Research (CHCPR) of the Visiting Nurse Service of New York. She manages the AdvantAge Initiative, a project that has collaborated with over 50 communities nationwide to measure their elder-friendliness and develop strategies to help older residents age in place. She is the Director of the technical assistance office that provides support to the grantees of the U.S. Administration on Community Living program, Community Innovations for Aging in Place (CIAIP). For more information about the AdvantAge Initiative, please visit their Web site: advantageinitiative.org.

Notes

[1] Tatiana Boncompagni, "Social media breathes life into shelved products," *The New York Times*, May 1, 2012. nytimes.com/2012/05/03/fashion/social-media-breathes-new-life-into-discontinued-beauty-products.html (accessed August 31, 2012).

Aging Better Together

by Anne P. Glass

I RECENTLY VISITED AN 82-year-old relative. I had been with her five months earlier when her husband died from pancreatic cancer. She says she is doing "all right." She continues to live in the same large house that has been her home for 54 years. It is on a busy road with no sidewalks. She has not missed a Sunday at church since her husband died, and she attends a "senior group" there once a month. Her son and his family are nearby, and she goes out for breakfast or lunch with her friends periodically. Despite these supports, there are weeks when she does not see anyone, other than at church. She showed me a book of word search puzzles that she had bought and said she used them to pass the time.

I could not help but reflect upon how different her life might be if she was living in an elder cohousing community. Elder or senior cohousing has flourished in northern Europe for decades but it is new in the United States. The first three elder-only cohousing communities opened during a two-year period between late 2005 and 2007, in Davis, California; Abingdon, Virginia; and Boulder, Colorado. The communities are small, with 12 resi-dents in the smallest to less than 40 in the larg-est. These self-directed intentional communi-ties represent an inno-vative type of living al-ternative in the United States. Older adults proactively choose how and where they want to live, and who they want to live with, in a close-knit com-munity where neigh-

Opting for old age on their own terms, the residents of Glacier Circle in Davis, CA, conceived and designed the community themselves, right down to its purple gutters

bors look after each other. It is a radical "do-it-yourself" approach that older people themselves envision and implement, with no administrator telling them what they can or cannot do.

I have been fortunate to have had the opportunity to visit each of these communities and interview the residents.[1] At one, I have a longitudinal study continuing in which I have collected data every year since the community opened in 2006. In these communities, I have observed neighbors helping each other and looking out for each other in a way that stands out in stark contrast to the neighborhoods in which many of us live — where we drive home at night, pull into our garages, and never even see our neighbors.

We know very little about the role of older friends and neighbors in helping and supporting each other. Our society has largely focused instead on assuming that old age is a time of dependence when people can only be on the receiving end of assistance. Both long-term-care policy and the vast body of caregiving studies assume that the family will be responsible for providing that care when it is required. There are at least two problems with these assumptions. First, this image of old age does not fit with the reality. Not all older people are dependent; most will have many years in which they are healthy and actively engaged in life. Simultaneously, they may have more unstructured time than they have had at any other point in their lives to spend as they choose. They want to have a sense of meaning and purpose in life. The second issue is that when the day comes that some help *is* needed, not all older adults can depend on family members to provide care — either because they are not close (whether physically or emotionally, or both), or they just do not have families. This gap will only increase with the aging of the baby boomers, as they are more likely to be single[2] and to have only one or no children,[3] compared to previous generations.

The concept of elders helping take care of each other has been little studied, but it offers a way to provide caregiving outside of institutional or traditional structures. It opens the possibility for provision of mutual support that encourages and allows independence at more advanced ages. Establishing the delicate balance between independence and accepting help when needed is one of the challenges that ultimately often comes with age.

These self-managed communities hold the potential to enrich residents' lives in many ways. Cohousing communities are physically designed with shared common spaces to facilitate social contact. When you move into a cohousing community, you can know all your neighbors within a matter of days. The design promotes a sense of community and mutual support. The concept and potential of mutual support assume even more significance for older adults, with many finding that giving assistance can be as rewarding as receiving it.

MUTUAL SUPPORT

LIVING IN SUCH A COMMUNITY is not without challenges, but a distinct sense of a close-knit neighborhood evolves over time, and mutual support occurs. The model of mutual support developed by the ElderSpirit Extension Team in Abingdon, Virginia, has three elements. Residents must be willing to (a) ask for help when needed, (b) accept help when needed, and (c) give help to others, to the extent that they are able. Additionally, residents also have the responsibility to take care of themselves. As part of their mutual support model, each resident in this community has named other residents to be their "care coordinators," who will step up when help is needed and organize the necessary assistance. These types of assistance have included grocery shopping, preparing meals, visiting, accompanying a neighbor on physician visits, dog walking, and even personal care. In addition, there is the invaluable knowledge that there is someone to call on, even in the middle of the night.

Dene Peterson, pictured above (right), was the burning soul" behind the establishment of ElderSpirit.

Beyond assistance when people are hospitalized or recuperating from illness or injury, there is another even more basic level of mutual support that is occurring: People are watching out for each other in this neighborhood, and this familiarity helps residents feel safe. They value the combination of having their own homes but not feeling alone, having the security of knowing that a neighbor would notice if something happened to them. One female resident stated that when she lived in her prior condominium, there was no sense of community or mutual support and that people just exchanged pleasantries. She then continued graphically:

One of the reasons I wanted to live in community, rather than isolated in my condominium [was]…just 'cause I thought, you know some morning I'm going to wake up dead and nobody will know for two weeks until they pass my door and say, "It really smells funny in here." And here, we're going to do like [others have] done, and check on one another.

Another expressed, "Here we are to some degree interdependent. That's the way it should be. That's the difference to me what a community is as opposed to just a bunch of neighbors."

BENEFITS OF AGING TOGETHER

THE "SOLIDARITY IN AGING" GAINED through living in an elder-only community helps individuals to accept their own aging and encourages a willingness among many residents to consider and discuss aging issues. They have purposefully chosen to live in an adult-only community. Most residents would agree with this statement: "It helps being with people who understand because the same things are happening to them." Some residents also mentioned that they found older neighbors to be excellent role

Silver Sage Village, a senior cohousing community in Boulder, Colorado, was developed by Wonderland Hill Development Company, the largest developer of cohousing communities in the United States.

models for aging. For example, a 70-year-old respondent expressed that she learned a lot about aging from observing residents in their 80s. The theme of role models was also expressed in another way: Some residents recognized that what they were pioneering was being viewed as a model by others in the larger community.

As residents age in the community, another significant benefit is support for the caregiver within the community. For example, there have already been cases of couples in which the husbands have been diagnosed with Parkinson's disease. Certainly it would be an enormous comfort to you as a caregiver whose spouse or partner is dealing with a life-threatening illness to know that you are not dealing with it alone, but have only to go out your front door to reach out for social support.

Respondents have exerted positive influences on each other in a variety of ways, such as encouraging exercise. Another theme many residents mentioned was the ability to have a sense of humor and laugh together about their limitations. Finally, living in this community was energizing to many respondents, simply from the sheer excitement of being part of pioneering a new model of how the later stage of life could be lived.

Thus, the mutual support is part of a larger phenomenon that is helping residents have a better experience with aging by going through the experience together. All the residents know each other, which facilitates convenient companionship and a sense of looking out for each other. This familiarity is important, as there is a strong connection between social networks and improved health outcomes,[4] and friends can play a significant role in well-being and mental health.[5]

A self-directed elder cohousing community is the ultimate example of residents being proactive and taking full responsibility for what happens in their retirement community. Pride in what they have accomplished in these elder cohousing communities is evident.

CREATING A "FAMILY OF FRIENDS"

MANY OLDER PEOPLE ARE HAPPILY ENSCONCED in a network of family and friends and meaningful activities and have all the support that they will need to help them deal with whatever the future holds. For others, however, especially those without close family, the aging process can be frightening if they see themselves walking that path alone. In fact, too many people face their older years solitary, isolated, and in denial about their own aging. We know now that isolation itself can increase health risks for individuals.[6] Some people, particularly the baby boomers, have witnessed with dismay the experiences of their aging parents and are hungry for a new approach. Building on a concept that has emerged from my work documenting the experience of these elder cohousing communities, my future research will explore an innovative approach for older adults and baby boomers to consider: forming a "family of friends" as an intentional way to build a sense of community and solidarity as a path toward resilient aging. People choose where and with whom they wish to share this journey.

The intentional "family of friends" community model is built upon the idea that older adults are capable of taking a proactive role to share the experience of aging together. Mutual support in this model is based on the concept developed at ElderSpirit Community. The fact that some individuals will eventually also need more formal services is recognized, but it provides an essential "social safety net." The "family of friends" idea would provide a supportive environment in which individuals grow old in solidarity, thereby enhancing their quality of life through this communal aging process.

The potential for older adults to experience this kind of arrangement is only beginning to emerge. Based on my research, if a group of individuals jointly commits to this idea, they will see each other regularly and often, and share a dedication to mutual support of each other. This mutual support could extend to each individual naming a "care coordinator" among the other members. This self-directed "intentional community" can exist in cohousing specifically designed for it, and some groups may follow the examples of the pioneers who have established the first elder cohousing communities in the United States. Indeed, a fourth elder cohousing community opened in 2010 in New Mexico, and others are opening in California and Oklahoma. However, I believe this "community" can also be created in a variety of existing sites, such as people organizing in an apartment building, a condominium association, or even a traditional neighborhood. Another possibility would be to explore the use of the new concept of a "pocket neighborhood," as described by Ross Chapin in this book (see page 49), within a standard subdivision or even within a retirement community.

Conclusion

Increasing the likelihood of older people helping each other and sharing information to improve their levels of knowledge about health and aging all lead to healthier older adults. Choosing to live with an enhanced sense of community cannot guarantee that an individual will completely avoid the need for nursing home admission, and it does not preclude receiving help from one's family, if available. With additional help, if necessary, however, the support provided by one's "family of friends" certainly increases the likelihood that one can remain longer in one's home. As one respondent in Colorado expressed:

I think it's less scary if you think you've got support, people are going to be dropping in or bringing you some soup or whatever, and it just makes you feel, I can get through anything better because I'm not frightened of being alone or isolated or ignored or something like that. So I think it definitely does help.

Individuals can remain *independent* in their housing and be part of the larger community, but still have the support and comfort provided by *interdependence* among a group of their peers, which can facilitate their ability to remain in the community longer. There are too many older adults who, like my relative, are spending too many days lonely and isolated. It is time to give thoughtful attention to innovative and creative ways that elders can build a sense of community in a way that will help them create solidarity and resilience in dealing with the aging process. Sharing the experience with a "family of friends" is a powerful way for elders to take back control of their own aging from the medicalized bureaucracy that sees aging as a disease and older adults as dependent.

Anne P. Glass, PhD, is internationally known as a leading researcher in the field of elder self-directed intentional communities. She is especially interested in the potential for older adults to provide mutual support and age better together, and how communities can facilitate this process. She is an Associate Professor and the Associate Director of the Institute of Gerontology in the College of Public Health at the University of Georgia. Visit her Web site at www.eldercohousing.info.

Notes

[1]   A.P. Glass. "Aging in a community of mutual support: The emergence of an elder intentional cohousing community in the United States." *Journal of Housing for the Elderly,* 23(4):283–303, 2009. Also see A.P. Glass, "Elder cohousing in the United States: Three case studies." *Built Environment,* 38(3):345–363, 2012.

[2]   I. Lin and S.L. Brown. "Unmarried boomers confront old age: A national portrait." *The Gerontologist,* 52(2):153–165, 2012.

[3] National Center for Health Statistics. (2005.) *Birth Rates and Fertility Rates.* Accessed December 29, 2012. http://www.cdc.gov/nchs/data/statab/t001x01.pdf.

[4] N.A. Christakis and J.H. Fowler. *Connectedness: The surprising power of our social networks and how they shape our lives.* New York: Little, Brown and Company, 2009.

[5] R.A. Blieszner. "A lifetime of caring: Dimensions and dynamics in late-life close relationships." *Personal Relationships,* 13(1):1–18, 2006.

[6] J. Tomaka, J., S. Thompson, and R. Palacios. "The relation of social isolation, loneliness, and social support to disease outcomes among the elderly." *J. of Aging and Health,* 18(3):359–384, 2006.

THE TIES THAT BIND

by Tobi A. Abramson

THE CURRENT COHORT of older adults is comprised of the generation who were at the forefront of developing and cultivating the growth of suburbia. Suburbia provided numerous, multifaceted opportunities for social connection to one's neighbors and community. However, as this cohort ages and experiences age-related physical challenges, this suburban reality — once an innocuous choice for a good quality of life — may now be fraught with less than optimal consequences. Buffers to these consequences, paired simultaneously with opportunities for vitality in one's later years, may be found in one's social networks and in the social capital within one's community.

What are social networks and social capital? Since both are key components to successful aging in community, an explanation of the two concepts is in order. The fundamental difference between the two relates to *how* and *to whom* we are connected. Our social networks tend to be composed of those individuals with whom we have social ties and from whom we receive social support *on a personal level.* They are dynamic, and our affiliations within these networks can — and usually do — change over time. On the other hand, our social capital refers to our deep social connections and resources *within our larger communities.* Social capital is more of a collective dimension focusing on the social relationships between groups of people, whereas social networks reflect an individual dimension. According to Robert Putnam, noted author of *Bowling Alone: The Collapse and Revival of American Community,* "'Social capital' refers to features of social organization such as networks, norms, and social trust that facilitate coordination and cooperation for mutual benefit."

Although these two concepts are intertwined, it is possible to have few individual social ties or little personal social support while at the same time having rich social community connections within one's environment. Communities with high social capital typically respond best to external physical and health threats (e.g., natural disasters), and this is true even for older adults who may be socially isolated.

THE VALUE OF SOCIAL NETWORKS

THROUGHOUT ONE'S LIFE, INDIVIDUALS ARE EMBEDDED in a variety of different interpersonal relationships that include family, friends, and neighbors. The value of these social networks increases as one ages. How extensively one engages with one's networks has a lot to do with availability, frequency of contact, and proximity to other people.

Those with the largest social networks tend to be married people with higher levels of education and income. Additionally, those in the early

years of later life — the "young–old" (65–74 years of age) — are more likely to be part of larger social networks than their "old–old" counterparts (75+ years of age). For these younger individuals, social networks include more non-family members. Not surprisingly, unmarried older men living alone are typically part of the most circumscribed social networks. In addition, one's functional status influences one's social connections: physical impairments lower the amounts of family and friend support.

The *type* of social network one belongs to — friend focused, neighbor focused, family focused, faith based, or restricted in focus and composition — is also a key indicator of social capital. Different types of networks have different outcomes for older adults. Those who are part of a diverse or friend-focused social network are apt to have the widest range of social connections and, consequently, the best outcomes — regardless of physical health status or other demographic characteristics. Interestingly, having family connections available (independent of the *quality* of these relationships) either lowers or has no impact on one's morale. Thus, just having family around is not enough to affect older adults' sense of well-being (which includes such subjective measures as morale, happiness, and life satisfaction).

Our physical and mental health is also impacted by our connection to others. In times of stress, social networks help to minimize the psychological distress. Those integrated into social networks experience less anxiety. This is significant, because anxiety has been linked to older adults' suffering from and experience of medical illnesses, cognitive decline, sleep disturbances, and even hospitalization. Being *lonely* — not being connected to or part of a social network — has also been shown to be a reliable predictor of cognitive decline, mortality, depression, self-harm or suicide, as well as problems with alcohol and drug use. In general, those with few social connections tend to have higher rates of major mental disorders.

The Role of Social Capital

Social capital is a critical component of successful aging. With age, the experience of loss increases at the same time one's social network is shrinking. As a consequence, older adults may become less dependent on their *individual social networks* and more dependent on the *social capital within their communities*. Similar to social networks, social capital positively impacts both physical and mental health, increasing life expectancy and decreasing rates of diseases such as cancer, cardiovascular disease, obesity, and diabetes.

Social involvement has been likened to the happiness of increasing one's income. Joining a group can reduce — by half — the risk of dying within the next year. Rates of depression and substance abuse problems decrease. Having a sense of purpose, feeling needed and useful — these add meaning to one's life and combat depression. Being able to depend on one's neighbors, the availability of neighborhood or community services, and social cohesion (interdependency among neighbors) all serve as buffers to life's stressors and lessen the adverse effect of the losses and declines older adults, especially those who are poor and single, experience.

As its population ages, social capital within a community naturally declines. It therefore becomes critical for adults of all ages to build their social capital throughout their lives, so that they can reap the benefits of their investment during their later years.

Thriving Where We Live

Where to live one's later years is not an easy decision for older adults. The decision is often presented as a false dichotomy — the choice to remain in one's current home (for many, the home they raised their families in) or to relocate (to retirement communities, assisted living facilities, or other long-term-care settings). Though numerous technical advances have made *aging in place* a more viable option than in the past, many of these same advances can actually create a more asocial environment for many older adults. Aging in one's own home has to be more than the ability to age in place; it must include the ability to continue to function and, yes, *thrive* in one's community.

Communities must be able to provide opportunities for older adults to engage in and leverage the community's social capital with appropriate social, cultural, educational, and religious opportunities. An *efficacious community* is one that provides these avenues of support. Examples can range from neighborhood-based volunteer programs or projects (like mentoring), to social clubs, to creative engagement. Libraries are becoming centers of activity, and research increasingly indicates that involvement in the arts has a wide range of mutual benefits for the individual and the community. This need to participate in lifelong learning, civic engagement, and cultural enrichment and religious activities will only continue to grow.

We would be remiss not to anchor this discussion in its important historical context. The generation now entering later life is the boomer generation noted for its high levels of civic participation, community involvement, and social capital. As a generation, they have long been accustomed to entertaining and socializing with friends, family, and neighbors at home. We know that volunteering has increased over the last 10 years, due mainly to the retiree workforce. Consequently, this generation is often referred to as the civic generation. They are used to giving back to and staying involved with their community. The challenge, then, is how to maintain this lifelong civic participation with rich social capital and social networks so that, when faced with the demands of aging and less-than-ideal housing alternatives, they can continue to thrive.

As the range of living arrangements has evolved — moving from institutional options to assisted living, to aging in place, to *livable communities* — the focus, both of the environments and the professionals serving within those environments, is also evolving. Transportation; safety; ADA compliance; affordable, accessible, and appropriate housing; adjusting the physical environment for accessibility; and creating walkable communities — these were the issues that livable communities initiatives usually focused on. What was often lacking in such initiatives was how to move beyond physical needs and be more inclusive of the social and psychological components of living.

It is only now that we are beginning to detect yet another shift — a further evolution beyond livable communities to a new focus on *aging in community*. The robustness of this new option depends upon our ability to strengthen and leverage the social capital for older adults. This means encouraging participation in a wide range of civic, cultural, social, and recreational activities. The organizations that exist within communities are a starting point for such an effort. Families, and even long-time friends, may be too spread out to fulfill some of the social network needs; consequently, the social capital within the community becomes critical for older adults wanting to maintain their independence and autonomy within their homes and communities.

Keep in mind that this is not one directional. Not only do older adults benefit from the social capital of their communities, they too give back in myriad ways and are a vital component of the community fabric. Many older adults are looking for ways to make meaningful contributions to their communities. For those that do, the benefits are not only physical, but also psychological.

Conclusion

INCREASING LONGEVITY AND THE ENORMOUS GROWTH of the aging population require a reappraisal of how we engage older adults to help them thrive in their later years. The need to belong is a fundamental human need which directs thoughts, emotions, and interpersonal interactions. Older adults face many barriers that prevent them from remaining part of their community, and there is a strong need to develop strategies to allow them to not only continue to reside in their communities, but to stay engaged and thrive within these milieus. Joining new groups and being involved in organized groups with some consistency greatly impacts both physical and mental health. Community connectedness can make a tremendous difference in the lives of older adults. Greater access to social capital and connections to one's community not only will enhance the well-being of older adults, but allow them to successfully age in community.

Tobi Abramson, PhD, is Director of the Center for Gerontology and Geriatrics, an Assistant Professor of Mental Health Counseling at New York Institute of Technology, and an Adjunct Assistant Professor of Family Medicine at New York College of Osteopathic Medicine. For over 25 years, Dr. Abramson has served in leadership roles on numerous national boards and professional associations in the fields of gerontology, geriatric medicine, and mental health. Dr. Abramson can be reached at tabramso@nyit.edu.

It was 1990. No one talked

much about aging issues then, as no one talked much about cancer then either. My wife Vicky and I were long-time residents of very livable Princeton, New Jersey, and active at leadership levels in community affairs. Our children were grown, with

lives of their own in other parts of the country. We had a lovely, large circle of friends and acquaintances. Career-wise we jointly owned and operated two small businesses serving clients in the environmental, safety, health care, and regulatory areas. We'd had significant experience working in larger organizations in both the private and public sectors where we had developed technical, entrepreneurial, administrative, and community organizing skills.

There had been a dark cloud over us, and then in April the storm hit. My father was retired from a career as a GS-15 civilian executive with an agency

Getting Older Then and Now

by Richard I. Bergman

of the U.S. Department of Defense in New Jersey. He had been coping well for some years with a lingering illness, then declined and

passed away. My mother, an outgoing person who had worked since she was a teenager and who was by then a retired school teacher and active community volunteer, had been my father's caregiver. That continuing effort had left her somewhat debilitated, and, of course, saddened. When we came back to their home from the burial service she told me that she just couldn't stay there any longer. She came home with Vicky and me that very night, lived with us for six months or so, and then moved into one of the first CCRCs, about a 40-minute drive from our home. We visited her regularly, usually three times a week, took her to our home often, and took her for drives and to visit family, all while running our businesses and continuing our community and social activities. But she never really adjusted to the loss of her husband of 60 years, or to living in her new home.

Conscious Aging

By 1992 Vicky and I had started to think about our own aging, and to wonder if there might be a way to plan ahead to age differently, hopefully better, than we thought my mother had been able to. Then unexpectedly, a flyer from the Omega Institute arrived in the mail. It announced a conference titled "Conscious Aging" to be held in New York City, just 50 miles away. Wow! That sounded like it could be just what we'd been thinking about. We went. What a mind-opening experience it was. We attended sessions on seniors' needs for housing and transportation; for appropriate physical, mental, and emotional activities and health care; and for spiritual connections and community involvement. We heard Ram Dass exhort us to live in the moment, and then tell us about his experience swimming with a dolphin. We heard Rabbi Zalman Schachter-Shalomi talk about sage-ing. Maggie Kuhn taught us the Grey Panther yell.

At the conference we encountered another attendee whom we recognized, Harriet Bogdonoff, a Princeton-based geriatric social worker. We started talking about the helpful conference sessions we'd attended, also agreeing that there didn't seem to be any sessions tying it all together — what might be done differently to address the interrelated and complex issues of growing older in America. We agreed to talk some more back in Princeton.

We got together again after the summer for further discussion, joined by Roz Denard. Roz had cared for her mother, was recently retired from the *Princeton Packet* newspaper, and was much involved in community affairs. Harriet told us about the three stages of aging which she called "Go-go, slow-go, and no-go," and about differing needs in those stages. She'd first heard that description at a builders' conference where age-restricted housing was a major topic among builders, older Americans, and community planners. Harriet pointed out that the overwhelming need she saw as a geriatric social worker, independent of the stage of aging, was for better social connections and support.

We agreed that if the four of us were interested in exploring a better way to age in our homes and community, and in how to provide better social support for seniors, others might be too. Roz then wrote what came to be known as the "falling leaves letter," an invitation to coffee and to talk about the possibility of creating a nurturing community of support. The letter was sent to 80 or so friends on our pre-e-mail Rolodexes. The opening sentence read, "With the start of the fall season many people think of a year coming to an end, and as we get older, there is frequently a bit of unease along with the falling leaves." The letter went on to ask, in part, "What lies ahead? Will I be well enough to live as I do now, and, if so, for how long? Do I have friends younger than I? Will I be able to stay in my own home?"

To our pleasant surprise, Vicky's and my house was filled to overflowing by over 60 people who animatedly discussed and questioned how they wanted to age, how best to provide support for aging relatives, what support they might want or expect from their children, what resources existed, and how aging was perceived in the community. We began meeting monthly in different attendees' homes to discuss issues of aging. At some of those meetings we had expert speakers on topics including housing, transportation, health care, and volunteering with community organizations. At other meetings attendees talked about their personal histories and current activities. Other meetings were purely social in nature. All meetings included member-brought food, ranging from snacks to potluck dinners.

These monthly meetings were informative in themselves, while also helping to enhance a feeling of community among attendees. Over time, the meeting attendees began to think of themselves as "members" of a new community within the larger community of Princeton and surrounding towns. As several social worker members told us, it takes time to build a new community, and building relationships with other similarly minded people is important if they are to provide social support to each other. So some of our meetings included specific community-building activities.

NEXT

The four of us had become founders of an organization which came to be called the Community Without Walls, to contrast it with the existing senior living options of nursing homes and retirement communities with walls. Soon almost 100 members were more than the monthly meetings in members' homes could accommodate. There was a waiting list. We wondered how large our group could be and still be small enough so that its members could know and develop relationships with each other. We found some research suggesting that number was 125 people. It became clear that more CWW groups needed to be formed. The original group incorporated in New Jersey and applied for and received nonprofit status from the IRS as a membership organization. New chapters, which we called "Houses," formed as membership increased.

NOW

CWW, Inc. now has some 450 members in six Houses. The Corporate "Steering Committee" (Board) is comprised of two members from each House plus the four founders. It sets policy, provides oversight, and arranges for common needs such as insurance and rental of space for the annual corporate meeting. We are a bottom-up organization, run by our members without any paid staff. Each House has its own Steering Committee, its own special character, and conducts its own programs within the scope of CWW Inc.'s Mission Statement and policies. Each House sets its own membership dues to pay for its programs, adding an amount for the common expenses which CWW, Inc. incurs. We are a low-cost operation. Yearly dues are currently just $25–$35 per member.

Most Houses have a monthly meeting with a speaker or activity. In contrast to our early days, information and resources pertinent to aging issues are more readily available, so these House programs now tend to be more social in nature. Every House also has interest groups: ethnic eating, moviegoing, memoir and poetry writing, walking, opera, gardening, books, daytrips, potluck suppers, end-of-life planning. These small groups have proved to be popular, interesting, and informative, while at the same time enhancing the sense of community among members.

Houses' members continue to support each other in times of need, doing the sorts of things friends do for friends. For example, members have driven others to appointments, changed high light bulbs, and the technologically savvy have helped out when others were flummoxed by their electronics. When members have been recovering from surgery at home, other members have provided and shared meals at their homes. More sadly, members have stayed at the homes of deceased members during their funerals so the house would not be empty and possibly an inviting target for crime.

CWW recognizes an obligation to the greater communities in which its members live. A recent survey showed that two-thirds of our members currently volunteer with organizations such as the public library, the medical center, the Trenton Area Soup Kitchen, and SAVE. CWW was a catalyst in the formation of secure@home, a nonsectarian program of the Jewish Family and Children's Service. For a fee, secure@home provides professional care management and other services primarily of interest to older members of CWW and in the greater community who choose to join it. CWW was also a catalyst in the formation of RideProvide, a county-run program enhancing transportation options for seniors.

Periodically, CWW holds a major conference on issues of aging, open to the general public. These conferences are organized and implemented by CWW members, with the participation of expert guest speakers. The past two conferences have been generously hosted by the Department of Community and Regional Affairs of Princeton University.

Another CWW project, started by members of several Houses, is CWW On Stage. Now including non-CWW members as well, this theatrical troupe documents and dramatizes aspects of the lives of seniors. They've interviewed community residents and, under the guidance of a professional director, have written and performed pieces such as "Learning Something New" (with high school student participants), "The Best Of …," "About Family," and "First Jobs." Performances have been held at libraries, senior centers, and other venues in New Jersey.

Seniors continue to join CWW for many reasons. With generations now often widely scattered across the nation and even around the globe, some new members are more concerned about growing older on their own. Some want to learn as much as they can about the manifestations natural to growing older. Others primarily seek congenial new friends who share their interests and concerns.

Much has changed since CWW was started in 1992, though many of the concerns and issues remain the same. Early CWW members are all 20 years older, and while younger and newer members — and some octo- and nonagenarians — are still go-gos, many of those in the vanguard are moving into the slow-go and no-go phases of elderness. Now it is even more reassuring to know that when there is a health crisis and our family members are far away, we have others available to support us, and someone who knows whom to contact in an emergency and how we'd like the crisis to be managed. Some of our older members have moved into retirement communities with walls, while still maintaining their CWW membership and participation, but perhaps not being as involved.

What does the future hold? Will the boomers change aging? Will organizations such as CWW remain relevant in a changing society? What might be down the pike which we can't yet even imagine? Well, as a physician once told me when asked about a prognosis, "I'm not very good about the future." Nor am I. So, we'll see.

Richard I. Bergman, SB, SM in engineering, is an entrepreneur, executive, and a community volunteer. He is a co-founder, Past President, and continuing Board member of Community Without Walls, Inc. of Princeton, NJ. (More information about CWW can be found at www.princtoncww.org; a recent feature retrospective by the accessed by going to www.princetoninfo.com, and then to the October 3, 2012 issue in the U.S. 1 Print Archives section.)

This concluding section offers two essays meant to spark reflection and conversation among colleagues and friends about aging in community.

Cultural anthropologist, **Philip Stafford**, the author of *Elderburbia:Aging with a Sense of Place in America*, takes us along on his own "Trip to Bountiful" as he reflects on "Irony and Remembering in Late Life" (page 225).

Finally, my soul sister **Janet Stambolian** and I bring the book to a close with our essay, "Back to the Garden" (page 235), whose seed was planted several years ago, when our paths first crossed at a Second Journey Visioning Council held at Bill and Jude Thomas' farm in upstate New York. For the generation that came of age in the '60s, Woodstock was a seminal experience. Now, over 40 years later, we can trace a striking congruity between the values of Woodstock Nation and the values that underpin Aging in Community.

Part 5
Reflections

Isn't This Where We Started?
Irony and Remembering in Late Life

by Philip B. Stafford

A couple of years ago, after a long absence, we made a sentimental journey to the old neighborhood and realized the truth of the saying, "You can never go back." Gone was the casual and tolerant informality in lifestyles, along with the former graciousness displayed in area neighborhoods. Victorian houses had been razed and replaced by imposing new mansions, creating an atmosphere of wealth and even arrogance. New stores

had ushered out the old familiar ones. New York merchants, with high-priced offerings, had moved into a huge, elaborate shopping mall a few miles distant. The lovely little village we cherished had vanished — like Brigadoon — and been replaced by ostentatious wealth and class distinction attesting to moneyed success.[1]

NOT TOO LONG AGO, I made a similar "Trip to Bountiful" — back home to explore my old neighborhood in Hobart, Indiana.

This essay is adapted from a paper read at the 2005 meetings of the American Anthropological Association, Washington, DC, entitled "Talking about Memory: Zero Signs, Irony and the Cultural Construction of Truth."

My parents moved to Hobart in 1948, seeking a small town alternative to life in the city. They purchased an 1850s farmhouse on the edge of town, initiating a 20-year remodeling project that engaged all five members of the family. We moved the kitchen so many times we came to call it the "whichen."

The acreage behind the house was mostly undeveloped woods and field, leading down to "Duck Crick," where we spent hours and hours, in every season, wading, swinging, exploring, building forts, sledding, and occasionally smoking. Across the creek lay *danger*, as the area bordered the "hoody" part of town, and kids from that neighborhood would shoot their BB guns at us as we played. It was a classic idyllic childhood, I have to say.

I left that neighborhood for college in 1967, my parents moved soon after and, in subsequent years, it rapidly developed into a suburban zone with ranch houses, cul-de-sacs, and neatly trimmed lawns. No wonder I was totally disoriented on my return to that neighborhood about 40 years later. It was difficult to imagine myself in the woods while looking around at asphalt and grass. As I was sitting at a street corner in my car, trying to orient myself to the area of the creek, I looked up at the street sign. It read "Memory Lane."

That is irony. The (street) sign, in semiotics, would be called a zero-sign, where a presence derives its significance, for me, from an absence. How ironic that the sign is meant to evoke the value of memory (or, rather, nostalgia) when, in fact, the memory of the place has been radically erased.

As we reach advanced old age, much of our reality is defined by absences rather than presences. The scales begin to tip in favor of things gone, over things remaining. Positively and meaningfully engaging with absences becomes another of those existential challenges facing us in old age, akin to Erikson's notion of integrity versus despair. Irony is perhaps the singular dramatic trope that defines our condition at this stage of life,[2] as we are surrounded by signs that signify absence — a landscape of trees and buildings razed, a house full of photographs of people no longer alive, a newspaper replete with wars that have been fought before.

To return to a landscape we inhabited in the past is to experience the dialectic tension between who we are and who we think we were. Irony occurs when there is a dissonance between the two identities and, as Vesperi has noted, citing Kenneth Burke, the irony can be tragic or comic. Erikson appears to have dwelt on the tragic, without considering the healthy function that the comic can play in sustaining our sense of psychological health (ego integrity). I can laugh at the Memory Lane sign. I can hold the cherished landscape in my heart even though it no longer exists.

RALPH REMEMBERING

Some time ago I became interested in the process of individual remembering while listening to and working with an audio-recorded life history of an old friend, now deceased, whom I came to know initially through a counseling relationship during my days as a geriatric mental health worker. (I will call him Ralph to protect his anonymity.)

I recall with fondness how much of my so-called therapy with my older client (and others) centered around a process of reminiscence. I wouldn't be so presumptuous as to call this "reminiscence therapy," however, for that lends an overly professional label to something that felt much more like good company. What was remarkable about my old friend was his depth of attention to his past and his serious obsession with life review. Perhaps most notable about the six hours of audiotape is that they were produced by a man completely alone in his room, door closed, speaking into a microphone, like Samuel Beckett's figure, Krapp,[3] and unprovoked by the interviewer, so ubiquitous in most life history studies as an external condition of remembering.

To borrow these tapes, I phoned Ralph's widow, with whom I had intermittent contact since his funeral several years ago, and inquired as to the availability of his tapes for my research. Graciously, she invited me to visit and took me to his room, which I found completely unchanged since his death — not a thing moved from the closet nor bureau, though clean and tidy as a pin, as is always the case with her entire house. Atop the bureau, among numerous family pictures, sat his wooden, slotted case, holding perhaps 100 or more audio cassettes, carefully labeled with dates and themes. Most of the tapes were "mixes" he created from country music stations on the radio. But, sure enough, there were five tapes labeled *Golden Memories*, and I suspected these contained his personal memories. With her permission, I borrowed the tapes to duplicate, including a couple of music mixes on the theme he called "Old Age Ain't So Bad."

Listening to the tapes has been an emotional experience for me. Hearing his gentle and articulate voice lent a renewed presence to our friendship. Discovering them five years after his death was like finding a secret gift, left by a friend too unassuming to demand instant recognition and gratitude.

It would be my wish to identify my friend and provide the recognition he never received during his life. But my friend is dead. He cannot provide his informed consent. My interpretation of his life cannot be confirmed nor co-authored. There is textual evidence, however, that he presumed an audience. Frequently, throughout the tapes, he makes comments such as: "Listen to this," or "On this tape, we'll talk about..." Moreover, he explicitly deletes major areas of his life story that he doesn't want to talk about because they are too painful. While I am personally familiar with those events, I cannot make reference to them, out of respect for his wishes.

There are, in other words, things that are to be forgotten, but, as I reflect on the meaning of the story, the things forgotten lend meaning to the things remembered. The vividness and animation of his childhood memories stand in stark contrast to the brief and reportorial character of his summary of later life. Whole decades of his adult life are essentially elided. Yet, in his last tape, he brings his life full circle and, while sparing the details, makes reference to the role that failure has played in his life. He authors his own obituary and waxes philosophical as he reflects on his life as he has lived it, standing outside of the remembering itself.

In constructing a retrospective of his life, my friend relied on several tools. The primary tool was his own introspection, and I use the term consciously as a "looking in." Frequently, he employs visual imagination, "his mind's eye," to revisit and describe the landscape of his childhood, experienced on foot. He employs self-drawn maps to recreate the expanding automobile-supported geography of his adolescent and adult years. He uses old photos to recollect his schools, teachers, and fellow students. Old-time songs taped from the radio support his sense of what things "were like" during the Depression. Occasionally, he makes reference to conversations with his brother and phone calls with school mates that helped to confirm memories.

For the most part, he did not, however, use the physical return to origins — the proverbial Trip to Bountiful — as a technique to jog his memory. The closer he came to the end of his life, the more painful did his visits back home become, as the landscape changed and the buildings disappeared. Increasingly, his comfort was derived from dwelling among things absent, not things present. It might be said that his childhood identity was no longer supported by the physical environment. Yet, alternatively, insofar as emotional pain was part of his adult identity, it *was* supported by the physical environment — an environment of zero signs, where the meaning (as a world lost) is derived from absences and not presences.

I don't think it is paradoxical to suggest that my friend's identity as a child and his identity as an adult were maintained concomitantly. In the privacy of his room, he was a time traveler, moving back and forth from the comfort zone of his past as reconstructed through remembering to the painful zone of his present, characterized, ironically, by absences — things he might have done. Some have argued that the work of autobiography in old age seeks continuity of self.[4]

My friend, like Krapp, experienced discontinuity, moving to his childhood through the embodied tool of visualization, but continuingly reencountering his adult self upon reentrance into and reflection upon the present. I think he felt trapped by this paradox. Though I occasionally saw Ralph exhibit the comic, for him the irony was, sadly, too often tragic.

> And finally, this could well be my obituary, if they would use it, heh, I don't know if they would or not… born June the 21st, 1920, in a house long ago torn down, to John and Eunice Deckard, in Monroe County, at the foot of what is known as the Handy Hill. Of five children of John and Eunice, two lived beyond the first few months, John Jr., born on the 16th of August, 1917, and myself. I spent my childhood days on Handy Ridge from 1924, when they moved into the house there. I attended the first through eighth grade at the Red Hill School and four years at Unionville High School, graduating April the 21st, 19 and 39. [Dates and names are fictionalized.] The only accomplishment worth mentioning in my life is that I surpassed the allotted time that the Bible allows man, three score years and ten. And time will not permit to tell of all the blunders and mistakes in those years but I can always look back and think of what might have been.

In Wendell Berry's short novel *Remembering*,[5] Andy Catlett, a figure quite reminiscent of my friend, struggles with the pain of self-hatred, focused on the literal loss of a member — his hand — to a corn-picking machine and the figurative loss of his attachment to his own past. In his role as a farm agent, Andy is attending an agri-business conference in San Francisco and lapses into a deep depression as he ruminates obsessively about days gone by. When experienced as something which is absent, his past brings pain, as he thinks about the good old farmer and mentor Elton Penn:

> To Andy, Elton's absence became a commanding presence. He was haunted by things he might have said to Elton that would not be sayable again in this world. That absence is with him now, but only as a weary fact, known but no longer felt, as if by some displacement of mind or heart he is growing absent from it. It is the absence of everything he knows, and is known by, that surrounds him now.

He is absent himself, perfectly absent. Only he knows where he is, and he is no place that he knows. His flesh feels its removal from other flesh that would recognize it or respond to its touch; it is numb with exile. He is present in his body, but his body is absent.

For Andy, recovery and redemption require remembering — *re-mem-bering*[6] the long chain of personal relationships over time and centered around a place, Port William, Kentucky. In a reverie near the end of the novel, Andy revisits Port William and discovers it occupied by the shades of his ancestors, not absent but present; and it is the world of the dead that leads him to the world of the living. The paradox is resolved, and his depression lifts as absence and presence are revealed as a unity.

While my friend's obituary might suggest that he could not find the redemption that Andy Catlett found, perhaps at times he did. On his last tape he spoke something that he had composed and written down on the previous New Year's Day, 1991. He wrote:

> Let me do what I can, be it ever so small each day, and if the dark days of despair and depression overtake me, let me not fail to recall the strength that comforted me in the desolation of other dark days. Let me remember the bright days and hours that found me in the days gone by as I wandered in the woods behind my home on Handy Ridge and as I fished in Griffy Creek with my Dad. Let me recall the comfort that would quiet my puzzled mind as I sat beside a little stream and listened to the crows in the trees overhead. Let my memory relive the enjoyment I shared with others at Unionville High School and the fellowship of the church…
>
> Though many of my former friends may seem to have forgotten me, let me not forget myself in despair. Though all the world may seem unfriendly, please do not let me become unfriendly with myself. Lift my downcast eyes upward as I jog my memory of the worth of friends, loved ones, and the sunshine and the moonbeams that flow in my bedroom window as I sit here and write here today…
>
> Let not my disappointments of the past overcome my appreciation of all the good things that have befallen me in those seventy years plus. Give me a few friends who still love me just for what I am, and let me not condemn others lest in so doing I condemn myself. No, don't let me get lost in the clamor of this world and all its effects, but let me just walk calmly down the path that is chosen for me in my latter days.
>
> Though my sicknesses and my inabilities of these past few years tend

to overtake me and I realize I have fallen so very short of the goals that I once had for myself and for my family, in days gone by, then Lord, teach me to be thankful for life and for time's golden memories that are so good and sweet and will continue to the grave. Then, may I, as dust begins to settle on my life, be thankful for living, and for the privilege of family and friends, and the companionship of those who may, if they didn't understand me... but, who kinda liked old Ralph, anyway, and were my friends.

Remembering and forgetting constitute a dialectic of presences and absences, each of which cannot exist without the other. What is said always leaves something else unsaid. Voice cannot exist without silence. As for my friend's personal memory and autobiography, it is not my place to describe things he wants forgotten to an audience he didn't create. Indeed, I suspect that, for most of us, our obituaries will recount things we did and not things "we didn't." Yet, as anthropologists who engage in cultural critique, an important role is to reveal and even resist the forces at work in the forgetting. Chief among those forces are the bulldozers of modern development, scraping the soil of its memory, creating new environments that bear no relationship to a past. When the bulldozers can't be stopped, it becomes ever so important to employ story to sustain that connection to our past. Old people, as the *rememberers*, represent a treasure we must protect. They re-member our communities.

Philip B. Stafford, PhD, is a cultural anthropologist and Director of the Center on Aging and Community, Indiana Institute on Disability and Community at Indiana University in Bloomington, Indiana. He is a founding board member of the Memory Bridge Foundation and the author of numerous articles on culture and dementia, participatory research and planning, and the meaning of home for older people. His recent book, *Elderburbia: Aging with a Sense of Place in America*, was published by Praeger Press.

Notes

[1]   Francis Sanden, in E. Peterson-Veatch, ed., *Experiencing Place*. Bloomington, IN: Bloomington Hospital Evergreen Project, 1995.

[2]   Maria Vesperi. "A use of irony in contemporary ethnographic narrative," in Philip B. Stafford, ed., *Gray Areas: Ethnographic Encounters with Nursing Home Culture*. Santa Fe: SAR Press, 2003.

[3]   Samuel Beckett. *Krapp's Last Tape and Other Dramatic Pieces*. New York: Grove, 1960.

[4]   Sharon R. Kaufman. *The Ageless Self: Sources of Meaning in Late Life*. Madison: University of Wisconsin Press, 1986. Also in *Medical Anthropology Quarterly* 2(2):189–90, June 1988.

[5]   Wendell Berry. "Remembering," in *Three Short Novels*. New York: Counterpoint, 1992.

[6]   Barbara Myerhoff uses the hyphenated term re-membering in an essay entitled "Life history among the elderly: Performance, visibility, and re-membering." Kaminsky notes in his Introduction to that volume that Myerhoff claimed that the term originated with Victor Turner. See Barbara Myerhoff, *Remembered Lives: The Work of Ritual, Storytelling, and Growing Older*. Ann Arbor: University of Michigan, 1992.

Friends — In and Out of Aging

A Poem by John Clarke

The story is now, the story was then.
The story will be, or perhaps will never.
Beyond all the tales, one story is ever.

Friends are like coffee, everything bagels,
surprising schmears of cream cheese
(lox of luck with them).

Friends are like bread —
broken with others, body's new life.

Friends are like water, like wine —
a toast where blood may cool and flare as one.

Friends are like breath — in and out of our times.
Who knows how it comes, goes, upholds our lives?

Friends are like dreams, like morning dew.
Who knows where they vanish, returning so fresh?

Friends are like poems —
just when you think you've grasped them,
they carry you where you never knew you'd go.

Friends are like koans — there is no answer.
Be with them, accept their gift.

Friends are like stories — ours and theirs.
They see beyond our little tales of failure.
Remember us at our fleeting best,
and maybe at our dogged worst.
See us now and how we dream to be.
Accept us entirely, even our nightmares.
They see our shadows long before we do.

Sharing of stories mellows and flows —
each one becomes another.
Ballplayers, philosophers, favorite writers,
gather with children, seekers, lovers —
all sorts of strangers, lost and found.

Sometimes a gift comes to us through them.
Takes us in and out of all our stories,
to a longer, shorter one that endures.
Who says it? Now I call you friend.
Now you call me to the feast of love.

Poet **John Clarke**, a regular contributor to *Itineraries*, lives in Chevy Chase, MD.

Back to the Garden:
Woodstock Nation Values Re-emerge

by Janet Stambolian and Janice M. Blanchard

> *By the time we got to Woodstock, we were half a million strong.*
> *and everywhere there was song and celebration...*
> *We are stardust, we are golden*
> *and we've got to get ourselves back to the garden.*
> — Joni Mitchell, "Woodstock," 1969

Were You There?

IN THE INTEREST OF FULL DISCLOSURE, Janet wishes to preface this essay with the following true confession: "I didn't actually go to Woodstock. In August of 1969, I was working in the inner city in New Jersey at Upward Bound. My sister attempted to defy our mother and go, but when our mother threatened to kill herself, my sister changed her mind."

Janice, likewise, did not go to Woodstock. Although technically a boomer, she was only nine-years-old. Although her oldest brother wanted to go, their mother wouldn't hear of it either!

235

Whether or not you were there, if you were a certain age or older — and had a pulse — you knew that something really big had happened on Yasgur's Farm. All these years later, the event still has power as a cultural watershed moment for many baby boomers.

PERHAPS WE WERE JUST LOOKING FOR A BIT OF GOOD NEWS

WE BOOMERS ENDURED SERIOUS, WRENCHING political turmoil and trauma during our youth, and in those days no grief counselors or school psychologists were on hand to help out. Kids essentially dealt with it on their own and within their families, already grappling with grief of their own: four assassinations (including Malcolm X), a war that tore the country apart, the infamous chaos at the 1968 Democratic convention in Chicago, and the election of Richard Nixon. Boomers were lurching to the end of the decade crushed, anxious, and yearning for evidence that goodness could still be realized somehow, somewhere.

What happened at Woodstock presented that evidence.

The Woodstock Music and Art Festival occurred during the height of the counterculture movement of the 1960s. From August 15–17, 1969, the place to "be-in" was Max Yasgur's farm, in Bethel, New York. Nearly half a million young free spirits gathered for "three days of peace and love" to hear stellar music and, in the process, became a spontaneous community that would come to be known as Woodstock Nation.

Despite the rain, mud, shortage of water and food, and an over-abundance of mind-altering drugs, there were no riots, fights, nor acts of violence. Instead, the hallmark experience for many who attended was the sense of community fostered through people sharing what they had, helping one another cope with adversity while grooving to the music and each other. For the generation that had become best known for what we stood *against*, Woodstock showed the world what we stood *for* — freedom to be our truest selves, acceptance of one another, and living together in peaceful harmony, even in adversity.

Inspired by the possibility of a different way of living, millions of young people joined others in communes, ashrams, and kibbutzim, or banded together in old houses, farms, and school buses to intentionally create community and live out the values that many felt epitomized Woodstock Nation — communitarianism, egalitarianism, environmentalism, social activism, and a general rejection of traditional values and conventional institutions such as marriage, gender roles, and mainstream religion. In sharing the rhythms of daily life, we created bonds between us in ways unheard of by our parents — sharing personally, intimately, deeply with unrelated people outside of our families. While most eventually rejoined mainstream society, many of us recall this period of living in community with other like-minded individuals as one of the most remarkable, growth-oriented, and satisfying times of our lives.

At the Crossroads Again

Boomers once again stand at a crossroads as we leave middle-aged adulthood and begin the journey into elderhood. As was true when we left adolescence and entered adulthood, the customary path that our parents and grandparents traveled is not one that many are willing and/or able to take into the "sunset years of retirement." For better or worse, the mid-twentieth-century paradigm of life past age 65 as a time to withdraw from work, collect a pension, and enjoy a life of leisure — in a Sunbelt retirement community or in one's home — has become a mirage.

While many boomers, especially leading-edge boomers born between 1946 and 1955, tend to be healthier, wealthier, and better educated than their parents, this is a broad generalization for an enormous and diverse generation. For example, unlike our parents and grandparents, a significant number of boomers have never married or are divorced; nearly 20 percent do not have children, and the majority live a great distance from relatives. Furthermore, a significant number of our generation do not have adequate savings or retirement income, especially since the economic downturn of 2008. Chuck Durrett, of McCamant & Durrett, a pioneering architectural firm that specializes in ecologically sensitive cohousing projects for seniors and others, says: "Cooperation is the watershed in grappling with this economic downturn. It doesn't make any sense — economically, emotionally, and environmentally — for retired people to be living in these isolated homes, making thousands of individual trips to the grocery store and pharmacy."

For many boomers, this life-stage transition evokes that earlier period in our lives when we rejected the well-worn path ahead and sought out like-minded others to forge a new trail. The values inspired at Woodstock and kept alive in our hearts and minds all these years might once again provide a road map into the future. As the country has changed and become in many ways a strange and foreign land, economic, social, and environmental trends suggest a scenario where it is not only appealing, but increasingly necessary, to "get back to the garden."

WOODSTOCK AND AGING IN COMMUNITY — TENDING THE SAME GARDEN

THE TWO AUTHORS OF THIS ESSAY MET in the spring of 2005 at Dr. Bill Thomas's farm in central New York. An emerging nonprofit organization, Second Journey, had convened a group of thought leaders to re-think the meaning and purpose of growing older including *where* we grow older. Janet recalls feeling the same elation and anticipation she had felt 36 summers earlier when that "other" event was happening at another New York farm. She remembers singing along with Joni Mitchell, replaying the song "Woodstock" over and over again, as she made the long drive from Burlington, Vermont. She was two years shy of 60. "Sixty is the new forty," as our peers are so fond of saying. Though Janet recognized the implicit ageism in that adage, she also recognized that hers was not going to be her mother's 60! Indeed, boomers have redefined every other life stage; undoubtedly we will change old age as well.

Every now and again, a group comes together that just clicks — the sum of their combined energy is much greater than the individuals themselves. The group gathered in upstate New York was such a group. And for nine years now, many of us have continued to work together on various projects, including this book. At the end of a powerful weekend, we crafted a phrase to reflect our values and our approach to elderhood: *aging in community*. Below you will find two tables which suggest some striking similarities between the values that epitomize Woodstock Nation (Table 1) and the principles of Aging in Community (Table 2).

While these parallels are not intentional, they do not surprise us. The majority of those who gathered at Thomas's farm were boomers; most had experienced living in community and (likely) felt strong affinities to the values of "Woodstock Nation." More broadly, many who currently live or who are considering living in housing arrangements that support "aging in community" are boomers. Like our core group, most tasted the experience of community earlier in their lives and are also likely to strive to live the values and principles outlined in the two tables below. This is not to say that all people who embrace the values of Woodstock are necessarily interested in an aging-in-community living arrangement — but they are likely to agree with the core principles. Alternatively, if the values of Woodstock Nation do not resonate for a person, it's unlikely that the aging-in-community model would be an appealing lifestyle choice.

"As a generation, boomers have a unique relationship to the idea of community," notes Tony Sirna of The Fellowship of Intentional Communities.

"Partly because of the Counterculture, many retirees are choosing to create non-corporate senior cohousing, as opposed to traditional senior communities in which they feel institutionalized."

Economics, demographics, and politics may once again rally boomers to rebel against the current prescribed social norms for old age. Already, we are seeing signs across the cultural landscape that many boomers — particularly in their choice of living arrangements — are coming full circle back to their Woodstock-era values. Whether they live in a group house with services brought in as needed, a shared apartment, a full-on hippie-style commune, or an aging-in-community neighborhood, they will likely live longer and more fulfilling later lives if they choose to grow old together. "The results here are truly amazing," declares Kirby Dunn, of Homeshare in Burlington, Vermont. Referencing a number of studies that gauge the effects of shared housing, Dunn concludes, "Across all programs and age-brackets, people say they feel safer, are less lonely, happier, and sleep better."

TABLE 1: WOODSTOCK NATION VALUES

- **COMMUNITARIANISM** is based on a belief that "we are all in this together," that people are interdependent, need one another, and mutually benefit from loving one another. This philosophy led to the flowering of communes, ashrams, intentional communities, and other collaborative economic and social arrangements that centered on living more interdependently. The back-to-the-land movement embraced sustainability, self-sufficiency, living simply, raising children consciously, and caring for the land and all living beings.
- **EGALITARIANISM** is a commitment to treating everyone equally regardless of sex, gender, race, ethnicity, or age. This value was the basis of the social movements in the 1960s and 1970s (Civil Rights, Women's Movement, and Gay/Lesbian Rights).
- **ENVIRONMENTALISM** is grounded in a belief that the earth is a fragile and interdependent ecosystem that has finite resources, and humans have a moral obligation to be good stewards of these resources. Environmental activism led to the creation of the E.P.A., Earth Day, the Greenpeace movement, and numerous nonprofit organizations dedicated to protecting animals, plants, air, ocean, and land.
- **INTEGRATION OF MIND, BODY, AND SPIRIT** is based on the holistic belief that the body, mind, and spirit are interconnected. In their

youth, boomers began exploring other religions, philosophies, and spiritual practices as well as adopting a more holistic view of health, which led to interest in organic foods; alternative medicine, such as acupuncture, homeopathy, and natural childbirth; and physical and mental fitness practices such as tai chi, yoga, and meditation.

- **SOCIAL ACTIVISM** grew out of the belief that the status quo or "Establishment" of the time was unfair, corrupt, based on greed and authoritarianism, and headed in the wrong direction for the health of the people and the planet. Further, this value implied direct action such as protests, marches, boycotts, and sit-ins to promote social, economic, political, and environmental change.

TABLE 2: AGING IN COMMUNITY PRINCIPLES

- **INCLUSIVE** — People of all ages, races/ethnicities, and abilities, especially elders, are welcome.
- **SUSTAINABLE** — Residents are committed to a lifestyle that is sustainable environmentally, economically, and socially. Size matters. People need to know each other, and scale determines the nature of human interaction. Small is better.
- **HEALTHY** — The community encourages and supports wellness of the mind, body, and spirit and, to the same degree, plans and prepares programs and systems that support those dealing with disease, disability, and death.
- **ACCESSIBLE** — The setting provides easy access to the home and community. For example, all homes, businesses, and public spaces are wheelchair-friendly and incorporate Universal Design features. Multiple modes of transportation are encouraged.
- **INTERDEPENDENT** — The community fosters reciprocity and mutual support among family, friends, and neighbors and across generations.
- **ENGAGED** — The community promotes opportunities for community participation, social engagement, education, and creative expression.

In comparing these two tables, it is easy to see how the values of Woodstock Nation and the principles of aging in community harmonize in a number of ways when building community. Combining them together, they can be implemented in the design, structure, and interaction of a community in the following ways:

EMBRACE INTERDEPENDENCE

No person is an island — by our human nature, we need one another. Like other primates, we do best in small groups such as villages or neighborhoods, even when located in urban settings. By acknowledging this human condition, we can better design and build homes and neighborhoods to maximize human interaction and interdependence, particularly in later life. By sharing common space, pooling and sharing resources, and fostering reciprocity and mutual support, we give up some privacy and the illusion of "independence" in exchange for deeper human connections and potentially a more meaningful quality of life.

PLAN FOR EVERYONE

Diversity is the spice of life, and inclusiveness builds the most cohesive and welcoming community. Planning and building for all ages, abilities, income levels, and backgrounds includes incorporating accessible design features (such as Universal Design principles), housing for all income levels, and community spaces that can be used by all age groups and ability levels.

INCORPORATE SUSTAINABILITY

At every level we should strive to reduce an individual's or the community's use of natural resources. For example, at the planning and building levels, we can draw on the criteria established for L.E.E.D. (Leadership in Energy and Environmental Design) certification; build smaller living units/dwellings and more densely designed neighborhoods; aim for net zero or very low carbon footprint buildings; and plan site orientation to maximize daylight, views, and solar gain. Within the day-to-day operations, we should maximize ease for residents to recycle, compost, reuse, reclaim, or redirect resources; use alternative or public transportation; support the local economy; and incorporate other measures that increase sustainability.

ENCOURAGE WELLNESS OF MIND, BODY, AND SPIRIT

Whether in the home or in the community, there should be thought given to creating spaces for spiritual and physical practices that encourage wellness. A meditation garden, labyrinth, community garden, or an area in which to practice yoga or tai chi are just a few examples of places where individuals or small groups can practice wellness. In larger communities, paths that can accommodate walking, skating, or biking; sports areas; or an exercise facility not only encourage personal fitness and health — they also provide opportunities to form social connections and friendships that build community.

Promote social activism

Ideally, aging in community not only promotes activism within the community through self-governance, volunteerism, and other social contributions — it also reaches out to the larger community in similar ways. Creating a good place to live requires consciousness and action on issues inside and outside the neighborhood, whether it is creating a community "time bank," lobbying for access to public transportation, or protesting a new development on environmental grounds.

Aging in Community:
A 21st-Century Approach to Community Development

The aforementioned strategies are more than theoretical ideas of how to build great communities. Comprehensive design — master site planning, architecture, landscape — plays a critical role in furthering the social values and principles that inspire the aging-in-community model. Ideally, the model anticipates from the beginning the integration of what might be thought of as *dual axes*: (1) the *built environment* and (2) the *social architecture*.

The built environment refers to *tangible aspects* of community development — site plan, layout and relationships of formal to informal interaction, unit design, building orientation, and the incorporation of green and Universal Design principles, with a special focus on design elements that create a sense of place. Examples of the built environment could include new neighborhoods or master-planned communities, retrofitted apartment or condominium buildings, cohousing neighborhoods, housing cooperatives, shared housing, affinity housing, or other housing and neighborhood configurations including ones for those in need of more intensive medical or supportive environments.

Social architecture refers to those aspects of a community that feed social, spiritual, physical, emotional, educational, creative, and civic life that help establish a sense of community connectedness among neighbors and residents. The social architecture includes programs and activities that enhance the quality of life of all community members but which, ultimately, maximize the ability of elders to remain in their own homes (or residences of choice) and remain connected to their communities. Examples of social architecture include community-based health services such as Eden at Home; the Nurse Block Program and Share the Care; cultural enrichment programs like the Circle of Care Project and Elders Share the Arts; civic engagement programs such as the Experience Corp and Environmental Alliance of Senior Involvement; and community-building programs such as community gardens and farmers' markets.

The degree to which both the built environment and the social architecture are brought into alignment from conception exponentially increases the probability of creating the hoped-for outcome — a supportive neighborhood that enhances an individual's well-being and quality of life at home and as an integral part of the community across the age continuum.

The aging-in-community model draws on the expertise of developers and builders to expedite the design and construction of new projects; however, it also invites future residents to become involved and consulted in decisions affecting their eventual community.

CONCLUSION

AGING IN COMMUNITY REPRESENTS a proactive model that intentionally creates supportive neighborhoods to enhance the well-being and quality of life for residents of all ages and abilities, particularly elders. The model promotes a deliberate consciousness about being a good neighbor and a good steward of our fragile planet.

It encourages a sense of social trust and interdependence which is strengthened through positive interactions and collaboration in shared interests and pursuits. The model recognizes elders' wisdom and experience and creates opportunities to share these qualities with others in the community and in the community-at-large.

For the past 40 years, through life's changes and against formidable odds, many idealistic boomers have retained their commitment to the values that inspired them during the amazing period of transformation and expansion in their youth. The time *is now* for planners, architects, developers, and builders to work diligently and help those who want to "get back to the garden" do so with a strong sense of community, meaning, and full engagement.

Coauthor **Janet Stambolian**, MEd, is Director of Business Development for Mackenzie Architects. She has devoted her 35-year career in construction, project management, marketing, and business development to creating environments that enhance the quality of life, promote meaningful intergenerational connection, and tread lightly on the environment. A lifelong community builder, Janet connects and engages people in a common

goal through a team-centered, holistic approach. She works to expedite the design, development, and construction of new models of communities nationally. Contact Janet at 802-578-6255 or jstambolian@mackenziearchitects.com.

Janice M. Blanchard, MSPH, is a gerontologist and nationally recognized writer, speaker, and consultant on aging issues. See her full biography on page 246.

About the Editor

Janice with her daughter Hannah.
Photo was taken at Red Rocks Amphitheatre near Denver, Colorado, by Meg Watson.

Janice M. Blanchard, MSPH, is a gerontologist and nationally recognized writer, speaker, and consultant on aging issues. For 20 years she has worked on the cutting edge of public policy and programs promoting a new vision of elders as valuable members of our communities and of elderhood as a distinct phase of the human life cycle. Renowned for her seminal work on "aging in community," Janice consults with government, nonprofit, and private organizations to develop innovative housing and community-based solutions that strengthen the fabric of our communities, for all ages and all abilities — especially our elders. You may contact her at 720-934-7985 or denverjanice@gmail.com.

Acknowledgments

This anthology grew out of an issue of *Itineraries*, Second Journey's online journal, which was published on the Web in October, 2012, then reprinted in a limited distribution. When we decided to expand the issue into a book, we cast a wide net among colleagues, inviting their contributions. We were thrilled that all but two were able to contribute — given that we were on a very tight editorial calendar which was made even tighter by the intervening winter holidays. What time did *not* allow is a second, wider casting of the net. So, later in these acknowledgments, when I thank all those whose work *does appear* in these pages, my "slighted" colleagues should consider themselves forewarned and anticipate my next call for contributions as we work on plans for a follow-up volume.

Now — to begin where it started — I start closest to home with my own family, for it is they who cajoled and then later inspired me to leave my first career working with young adults and shift my focus to the other end of the age spectrum. I owe much of my passion about how and where we grow older to my father, Wesley Blanchard, whose fierce determination and steadfast love persuaded me to join him and my sister, Alice Holmes, in bringing my grandmother home from the nursing home so many years ago. Truly it was Alice who sealed the deal for me by promising me it would be an adventure — and as usual, she was right. Alice's adorable baby daughter, Sadie, was the sunshine of our days and gifted us with the perspective of how a multigenerational family from ages 18 months to 88 years navigates daily life better, together.

Words fall short in recognizing the influence and gratitude I have for my mother, Betty Blanchard, who taught me so much about love and family, and that in old age, true north on the compass of decision-making can often be found by the direction of what is easiest for those who will care for us. I am grateful to my brothers Guy, Wayne, Bill, and Bob and my youngest sister, Amy, for teaching me that everyone brings a different perspective and their own unique skills for navigating the uneven terrain of the Caregivers Road. None of my work would be possible without the stalwart support and unwavering love of my husband Lenny, and my two beautiful, loving, and supportive children, Hannah and Ben. They give up so much for me to be able to write and travel for work, in addition to now traveling to care for my dad. They are the anchor to my world and remind me daily what is really important in life.

For providing excellent guidance, support, and learning opportunities in becoming a midlife gerontologist, I am deeply indebted to Eric Pfeifer and Helen Susik Moore, at University of South Florida's Suncoast Gerontology Center; Larry Polvika at the Florida Policy Exchange Center on Aging; and Neil Henderson, Jeannine Coreil, and Terri Albrecht in the Community and Family Health Department at the University of South Florida's College of Public Health. At a time when there wasn't a track for aging in public health, they provided the support for me to trailblaze my own.

In Australia, I learned the importance of community in the lives of elders. More specifically, I learned that the love of family and friends serves different roles in defining and affirming who we are in the world — we need them both. I am ever grateful for the generous hospitality and unwavering support of two daring women in purple, Professors Jenny Onyx at University of Technology, Sydney, and Rosemary Leonard at University of Western Sydney. After meeting me but once, they arranged a job teaching at University of Western Sydney Nepean, settled me into their beautiful old cottage in the Blue Mountains, and provided wise counsel and encouragement as I worked on my post-graduate research. They also introduced me to a dear friend and mentor, Liz Reedy, who provided friendship and the important life lesson that sometimes less is more! Special thanks to all the women of the Older Women's Network and the Older Women's Wellness Center. During my research with these amazing women the seed was planted that aging in place is a hollow victory if one is not meaningfully connected to their community.

In October 2003 I had the good fortune to attend Second Journey's inaugural Visioning Council at a mountain retreat outside Asheville, North Carolina. There I met many kindred spirits who were also searching for a better place and a better way to live in later life. I am especially grateful to have met several new friends and colleagues there — Lynne Iser, Connie Goldman, Jan Hively, and Second Journey founder Bolton Anthony, among them. A couple years later, they were among a visionary group of thought leaders who met at Bill and Jude Thomas' retreat center in upstate New York, where for the first time we began to define the paradigm shift we saw underway and articulate the model for aging in community. I am deeply indebted to all those who attended that weekend, but especially to Bill and Jude Thomas, and Janet Stambolian, who became close colleagues and friends. Bill and Jude's nonprofit, the Center for Growing and Becoming, provided the initial grant for the Aging in Community Network, an incubator for articles and conference presentations that helped further articulate the concepts and practices for aging in community. Morning, noon, and night, and from coast to coast, Janet has been in the forefront of the aging in community movement and by my side, presenting at conferences, writing papers, and educating builders, architects, and developers. I am especially grateful for her willingness to spend countless hours over the phone discussing "the good work."

I am deeply indebted to the leadership at the American Society on Aging (ASA), especially Founder and Former CEO, Gloria Cavanaugh, who was willing to support us early on by providing us prominent platforms at the annual ASA conference via Critical Issues sessions and Special Program days to share our ideas and work about aging in community. My most sincere thanks to all my colleagues and friends that early on answered our call for putting together presentations for ASA and other national aging conferences, including Bill Thomas, Elinor Ginzler, Sandy Markwood, Nancy Henkin, Paula Dressel, Janice Jackson, Gordon Walker, Fredda Vladeck, Stephen Golant, Phil Stafford, Mia Oberlink, Dace Kramer, Jan Hively, Steve Mackenzie, Chuck Durrett, Jim Leach, Laura Fitch, Michael Kephart, Emi Kiyota, Gerald Weisman, Mark Profitt, Brenda Krause Eheart, Marvin Nisly, Susan Brecht, Sharon Nielson, Janet Stambolian, Dene Peterson, Joy Silver, Neshama Abraham, Zev Paiss, Ruven Liebhaber, Joe Angelelli, Sue Bozinovski, Tim Carpenter, Ken Pyburn, Bolton Anthony, Lynne Iser, Judy Willet, Raines Cohen, Anne Zabaldo, and the many others I am likely forgetting but who have been so valuable in launching and continuing this important work.

At home in Colorado I have been blessed with so very many colleagues within the City of Denver and State of Colorado government, as well as nonprofit organizations and businesses, that have been supportive of making our communities great places for people of all ages in which to live, work, and play. A special thanks to Sarah McCarthy, Mike Green, and Ronica Rooks for including me in grant and research opportunities to expand our understanding and work on aging in community in the Denver area. Much of the good work would not get done if not for the generous support of foundations like the Rose Community Foundation, Daniel's Fund, Colorado Health Foundation, AARP, and the many other funders in Colorado that support creating healthy, livable communities.

Notably, this collection of writings would have never come to fruition without the encouragement, nudging, prodding, and fine attention to detail provided by Second Journey Founder, Publisher, and General Editor, Bolton Anthony. Much sincere appreciation is also due to Bolton's partner in all things, Lisa Anthony, whose eagle eye for editing details and occasional diplomatic communications smoothed the way to completion. Second Journey Board members have also been incredibly supportive and helpful through navigating this process, especially Alex Mawhinney, who helped with connecting me to contributing authors, as well as providing sound advice and leadership in moving things along in general. I am especially grateful to all the visionaries, architects, poets, artists, community builders, policy makers, and academics who have contributed to this volume, and more importantly, who have given so much of themselves and their work to aging in community. It has been my great pleasure and honor to work with some of the most innovative leaders in aging in community in assembling this book. All gave freely of their time, despite their own personal hectic schedules and a very tight editorial calendar, to share their knowledge and passion.

My deep appreciation and thanks to my two coauthors, Bill Thomas and Janet Stambolian, and to the other colleagues who contributed the essays that make up this volume: Tobi Abramson; Candace Baldwin, **Natalie Galucia, Rita Kostiuk, and** Judy Willett; Carol Barbour; Bill Benson and Nancy Aldrich; Dick ; Kristin Bodiford; Ben Brown; Tim Carpenter; Ross Chapin; Chuck Durrett; Joan Englander; Gaya Erlandson; Ann Glass; Marianne Kilkenny; Susan McWhinney-Morse; Mia Oberlink; Dene Peterson; Susan Poor; Joan Raderman; Teddi Shattuck; Philip B. Stafford; Sarah Susanka; and Ann Zabaldo. I also want to thank the poets and painters whose imaginative renderings enliven the pages: Dolly Brittan, Jack Clarke, Craig DeBussey, Kit Harper, Walter Hurlburt, Suzanne Knode, and Karolyn Merson.

I reserve my last note of thanks and deepest appreciation for those to whom this work is dedicated — my elders. I thank you for sharing your wisdom, your laughter, your struggles, sorrows, and joys, and for your insights, personal stories, and the life lessons you have shared. The world is a better place for you being a part of it, and I am a wiser person for having spent time with you. Thank you.

— Janice M. Blanchard
January 24, 2013

Also from Second Journey Publications

Anthologized from our 2011 series on THE SPIRITUALITY OF LATER LIFE published in *Itineraries*, Second Journey's online magazine.

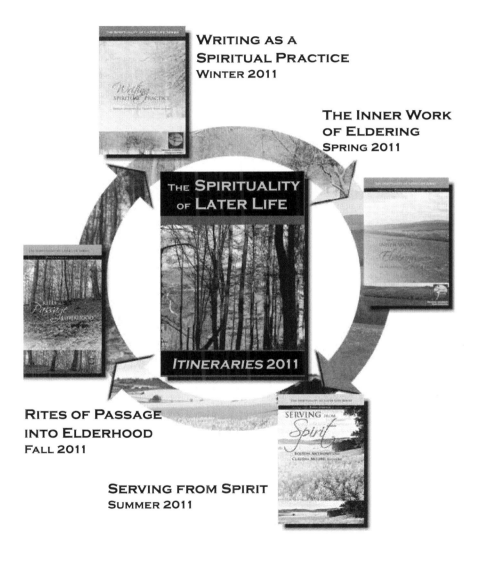

WRITING AS A
SPIRITUAL PRACTICE
WINTER 2011

THE INNER WORK
OF ELDERING
SPRING 2011

RITES OF PASSAGE
INTO ELDERHOOD
FALL 2011

SERVING FROM SPIRIT
SUMMER 2011

SecondJourney.org/bookstore.htm

Also from Second Journey Publications

exploring **community** in our later years **& interdependence**

Friday Center • Chapel Hill (NC)
April 11-14, 2013

a Second Journey visioning council

Mercy Center • Burlingame (CA)
Oct. 31-Nov. 3, 2013

The Visioning Council was a truly memorable experience. I met some great people, with whom I established warm, ongoing relationships.

— Alidra Solday
Director of "Granny D Goes to Washington"

New! from Second Journey

Baby boomers are assets for building our communities. We bring energy, experience, and passion to service. We combine reflection with action. Second Journey connected me with other older adults who share similar (or these) values, and affirmed that we are leaders for the future. — Jim Scheibel
Former mayor of St. Paul (MN)

Like they did with ice cream...
...boomers are creating a
thousand new options in
where we grow old.

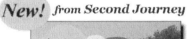

SecondJourney.org/VC.htm

About Second Journey

Second Journey is among a small number of emerging social-change organizations helping birth a new vision of the rich possibilities of later life...

- to open new avenues for individual growth and spiritual deepening
- to birth a renewed ethic of service and mentoring in later life
- to create new model communities—and new models OF community—for later life, and
- to marshal the distilled wisdom and experience of elders to address the converging crises of our time

Captured in the shorthand of our logo... Mindfulness, Service and Community in the Second Half of Life.

We pursue this mission through publications, including our online magazine, *Itineraries*, and occasional book releases; through workshops and Visioning Councils with their focus on the challenges of Creating Community in Later Life; and through the rich resources on our Web site.

WWW.SECONDJOURNEY.ORG

Made in the USA
Charleston, SC
01 March 2013